Neoliberalism, Gender and Education Work

How does neoliberalism in the education field shape who teachers are and what they can be? What are the effects of neoliberal logic on students? How is gender at the core of what it means to teach and learn in neoliberal educational institutions? *Neoliberalism, Gender and Education Work* examines the everyday labour of educating in a variety of contexts in order to answer these questions in new and productive ways. Neoliberal ideals of standardisation, accountability and entrepreneurialism are having undeniable effects on how we define teaching and learning. Gender is central to these definitions, with care work and other forms of affective labour simultaneously implicated in standards of teacher quality and undervalued in metrics of assessment. Gathering research from across four continents and education settings ranging from elementary school to higher education, to popular social movements, the methodologically diverse case studies in this book offer insight into how teachers and students negotiate the intertwined logics of neoliberalism and gender. Beyond an indictment of contemporary institutions, *Neoliberalism, Gender and Education Work* provides inspiration with its documentation of the creative practices and selfhoods emerging in the 'cracks' of the neoliberal ideological apparatus.

This book was originally published as a special issue of *Gender and Education*.

Sarah A. Robert is Associate Professor at the University at Buffalo (SUNY), USA. Her research and teaching focuses on how to harness the power of teachers' knowledge and education reform for education equity. Her ultimate goal is to mediate the often diverging interpretations of what 'problems' a policy should address and forge a more inclusive policy making process.

Heidi K. Pitzer is an interdisciplinary scholar and teacher with expertise in the Sociology of Education. Her interests include social justice education, race and class inequality, critical and media literacies, and teacher labour. She currently teaches at Syracuse University, USA.

Ana Luisa Muñoz García is currently an Assistant Professor in the School of Education at the Pontificia Universidad Católica de Chile, Chile. She also is a History and Geography teacher. Her investigations have focused on educational research and practice in poverty areas and the construction of knowledge in academia within the framework of internationalisation policies.

Neoliberalism, Gender and Education Work

Edited by
Sarah A. Robert, Heidi K. Pitzer and
Ana Luisa Muñoz García

LONDON AND NEW YORK

First published 2018
by Routledge
2 Park Square, Milton Park, Abingdon, Oxon, OX14 4RN, UK

and by Routledge
711 Third Avenue, New York, NY 10017, USA

Routledge is an imprint of the Taylor & Francis Group, an informa business

© 2018 Taylor & Francis

All rights reserved. No part of this book may be reprinted or reproduced
or utilised in any form or by any electronic, mechanical, or other means,
now known or hereafter invented, including photocopying and recording,
or in any information storage or retrieval system, without permission in
writing from the publishers.

Trademark notice: Product or corporate names may be trademarks or
registered trademarks, and are used only for identification and
explanation without intent to infringe.

British Library Cataloguing in Publication Data
A catalogue record for this book is available from the British Library

ISBN 13: 978-0-8153-8266-9

Typeset in Myriad Pro
by RefineCatch Limited, Bungay, Suffolk

Publisher's Note
The publisher accepts responsibility for any inconsistencies that may have
arisen during the conversion of this book from journal articles to book chapters,
namely the possible inclusion of journal terminology.

Disclaimer
Every effort has been made to contact copyright holders for their permission to
reprint material in this book. The publishers would be grateful to hear from any
copyright holder who is not here acknowledged and will undertake to rectify
any errors or omissions in future editions of this book.

Contents

Citation Information	vii
Notes on Contributors	ix

Introduction
Sarah A. Robert, Heidi K. Pitzer and Ana Luisa Muñoz García — 1

1. When solidarity doesn't quite strike: the 1974 Hortonville, Wisconsin teachers' strike and the rise of neoliberalism
Eleni Brelis Schirmer — 8

2. Gettin' a little crafty: Teachers Pay Teachers©, Pinterest© and neo-liberalism in new materialist feminist research
Elizabeth A. Wurzburg — 28

3. Neoliberalism and higher education: a collective autoethnography of Brown Women Teaching Assistants
Ileana Cortes Santiago, Nastaran Karimi and Zaira R. Arvelo Alicea — 48

4. Encountering gender: resisting a neo-liberal political rationality for sexuality education as an HIV prevention strategy
Andrée E. Gacoin — 66

5. Contesting silence, claiming space: gender and sexuality in the neo-liberal public high school
Susan W. Woolley — 84

6. An education in gender and agroecology in Brazil's Landless Rural Workers' Movement
Sônia Fátima Schwendler and Lucia Amaranta Thompson — 100

7. Aligning the market and affective self: care and student resistance to entrepreneurial subjectivities
Luciana Lolich and Kathleen Lynch — 115

Index — 133

Citation Information

The chapters in this book were originally published in *Gender and Education*, volume 29, issue 1 (January 2017). When citing this material, please use the original page numbering for each article, as follows:

Introduction
Introduction
Sarah A. Robert, Heidi K. Pitzer and Ana Luisa Muñoz García
Gender and Education, volume 29, issue 1 (January 2017), pp. 1–7

Chapter 1
When solidarity doesn't quite strike: the 1974 Hortonville, Wisconsin teachers' strike and the rise of neoliberalism
Eleni Brelis Schirmer
Gender and Education, volume 29, issue 1 (January 2017), pp. 8–27

Chapter 2
Gettin' a little crafty: Teachers Pay Teachers©, Pinterest© and neo-liberalism in new materialist feminist research
Elizabeth A. Wurzburg
Gender and Education, volume 29, issue 1 (January 2017), pp. 28–47

Chapter 3
Neoliberalism and higher education: a collective autoethnography of Brown Women Teaching Assistants
Ileana Cortes Santiago, Nastaran Karimi and Zaira R. Arvelo Alicea
Gender and Education, volume 29, issue 1 (January 2017), pp. 48–65

Chapter 4
Encountering gender: resisting a neo-liberal political rationality for sexuality education as an HIV prevention strategy
Andrée E. Gacoin
Gender and Education, volume 29, issue 1 (January 2017), pp. 66–83

CITATION INFORMATION

Chapter 5
Contesting silence, claiming space: gender and sexuality in the neo-liberal public high school
Susan W. Woolley
Gender and Education, volume 29, issue 1 (January 2017), pp. 84–99

Chapter 6
An education in gender and agroecology in Brazil's Landless Rural Workers' Movement
Sônia Fátima Schwendler and Lucia Amaranta Thompson
Gender and Education, volume 29, issue 1 (January 2017), pp. 100–114

Chapter 7
Aligning the market and affective self: care and student resistance to entrepreneurial subjectivities
Luciana Lolich and Kathleen Lynch
Gender and Education, volume 29, issue 1 (January 2017), pp. 115–131

For any permission-related enquiries please visit:
http://www.tandfonline.com/page/help/permissions

Notes on Contributors

Zaira R. Arvelo Alicea gained her PhD from Purdue University, USA. She was an educator at the Department of Education, University of Puerto Rico.

Andrée E. Gacoin is a Senior Researcher at British Columbia Teachers' Federation, Canada. She completed her PhD in Educational Studies at the University of British Columbia, Canada.

Nastaran Karimi is a Graduate Teaching Assistant at Purdue University, USA.

Luciana Lolich is a Postdoctoral Fellow at the Equality Studies Centre at University College Dublin, Ireland. Her work centres on critically examining consumer choice in palliative care and identifying potential inequalities in the access and delivery of care for patients at the end of life.

Kathleen Lynch is Professor of Equality Studies at University College Dublin, Ireland. She has a lifelong interest in equality and social justice both at the level of theory and practice.

Ana Luisa Muñoz García is currently an Assistant Professor in the School of Education at the Pontificia Universidad Católica de Chile, Chile. She also is a History and Geography teacher. Her investigations have focused on educational research and practice in poverty areas and the construction of knowledge in academia within the framework of internationalisation policies.

Heidi K. Pitzer is an interdisciplinary scholar and teacher with expertise in the Sociology of Education. Her interests include social justice education, race and class inequality, critical and media literacies, and teacher labour. She currently teaches at Syracuse University, USA.

Sarah A. Robert is Associate Professor at the University at Buffalo (SUNY), USA. Her research and teaching focuses on how to harness the power of teachers' knowledge and education reform for education equity. Her ultimate goal is to mediate the often diverging interpretations of what 'problems' a policy should address and forge a more inclusive policy making process. She has published across disciplines, languages and geographies on teachers' work, policy, school food and textbooks.

Ileana Cortes Santiago is a PhD student at the College of Education, Purdue University, USA.

Eleni Brelis Schirmer is a Project Assistant at the School of Education, University of Wisconsin–Madison, USA.

NOTES ON CONTRIBUTORS

Sônia Fátima Schwendler is a Lecturer and Researcher at the Federal University of Paraná, Brazil. She has developed research projects and published on gender issues, rural education, adult literacy and the Movement of the Landless Rural Workers of Brazil (MST).

Lucia Amaranta Thompson was a SI Leader at the Graduate School, Lund University, USA.

Susan W. Woolley is Assistant Professor of Educational Studies at Colgate University, USA.

Elizabeth A. Wurzburg is a Clinical Assistant Professor at the College of Education and Human Development, Georgia State University, USA.

INTRODUCTION

Sarah A. Robert, Heidi K. Pitzer and Ana Luisa Muñoz García

This special issue explores the intersections of gender and education work in the global context of neoliberalism. When the call for papers was designed, we purposefully left the interpretation of neoliberalism and of work/worker open in order to encourage submissions that examined deep and broad global dynamics of the relationship in a variety of educational settings. We read Robertson's (2008) definition of neoliberalism, which traced out the term's historical roots in classical philosophical and economic theories, to then illustrate the ideology's movement into education. 'Neoliberalism has transformed, albeit in both predictable and unpredictable ways, *how* we think and *what we do* as teachers and learners' (original author's emphasis, 12). In our own work, we have continued 'to make these things evident' (Robertson 2008, 12), expanding on theorisations of how neoliberalism has shaped and is shaped by education workers in the Southern Hemisphere (Robert 2013, 2015) and the Northern Hemisphere (Pitzer 2010; 2015), and by their movement between these hemispheres (Muñoz García 2014). Our past work and this present endeavour aim to 'confront face on what has happened [to the work of educating and earning an education] and why' (Robertson 2008, 25). Unlike Robertson's focus on class, however, we have been drawn intellectually, physically, and viscerally to understanding the ways that gender and sexuality are involved in the everyday negotiations of neoliberal assemblages of governance, which, with few exceptions, have not been well attended to in the literature (e.g. Lynch, Grummell, and Devine 2012; Robert 2014).

Policies as texts, discourse, and practices (Ball 1994) were starting points from which the authors represented in the special issue analysed local manifestations of global processes in/through education work. This reflects well-established theorisations of femininities and masculinities as *involved* in education policy (Stambach and David 2005) and as embedded in the historical conceptualisations of school actors (David 1980; Smith & Griffith, 2004), and their work (Acker 1999; Apple 1986; Biklen 1995; Cortina and San Román 2006; Fischman 2007; Morgade 1992; Morgade and Bellucci 1997). The gendered implications of new logics for work, for the worker, and the new forms through which both are controlled by an ever-morphing labour process (Reid 2003) are brought into view in the following pages to address the *absent presence* (Apple 1983; Lather 1994; Robert 2012; 2015) of the gendered work of educating long overlooked in policy and public discourse.

We also hope that the special issue contributes to much-needed views of the gendered negotiations of boundaries of new assemblages of governance, the economy, and education (Ball and Junemann 2012). Contingent neoliberal concepts of standardisation, accountability, and entrepreneurialism are given form through policies and programmes such as merit pay, high-stakes testing, knowledge standardisation, hyper-credentialing, the publishing of ratings/rankings and other so-called performance indicators. Thus, to overlook femininities' and masculinities' powerful role in producing the new manager, the new global teacher-technician, and the new student-entrepreneur also means potentially to misunderstand (and under theorise) the very processes through which neoliberalism reshapes education subjects, communities, and the nature of education/to be educated. How are policies and the work of enacting them gendered and re-gendered in these new assemblages of control and governance?

Scholars have recognised how neoliberalism reshapes 'the good teacher' (Connell 2009) and redefines 'teacher quality' (Cochran-Smith and Lytle 2006) in harmful, constricting manners. Still questions remain as to who is the emergent 'global teacher' and what they do in which context (Maguire 2010; Robert 2014). The rational economic subject whose choices and ability to make decisions are ostensibly constrained in the absence of a free-market educational system is to be freed by neoliberal projects. Unleashed to engage in rational economic decision-making emerges a natural, heterosexual, economic animal and westernised liberal man to carry on the labour of educating (Dillabough 1999). The imagined form of the individualised education worker embedded in the new education arena needs to be illustrated and critiqued in light of all the new forms that have been introduced to control the education worker.

Not only is 'the teacher' in need of contours, individuals engaged in decision-making need to be situated within contexts where presumed rational and economic-oriented decisions may be made. Decision-making is complex, constrained by a multitude of factors that bind persons to multiple communities and the roles fulfilled within those communities. Decisions entail affective work and identity work; both valued less by the capitalist market that is presumed to float free from historical and sociocultural constraints and power differentials. While neoliberalism frames the values by which decisions are to be made, that value frame is not absolute and the cracks in the ideological apparatus can be and are scrutinised by participants in the studies contained here. Ironically, and perhaps a bit perversely, accountability policies and discourses require that education workers be made *visible* – sometimes as technicians, other times as professionals. Work and workers must be measureable and accountable. The nature of visibility becomes a way to probe how education work/workers are transformed. What subjectivities emerge from the cracks in neoliberalism? What subjectivities form from the continued resistance to oppressive and care-less expectations?

Entrepreneurial policies and discourses also call for erasure of the gendered, classed, and aced nature of the labour of educating and the targeted 'outcomes' of educational projects in nations. Powerful discourses of choice and self-actualisation contained in the entrepreneurial-friendly labour market again unleash workers with new-to-acquire 'freedom' and the ability to 'become' in an unlimited realm of possibility. That same sense of entrepreneurialism is to be woven into learning, such that future entrepreneurs – or contrived future citizens of the global market – are produced. In fact, individuals excluded from education institutions and opportunities, as well as those enveloped by them, are accountable to the forces of the market and to the need to self-govern and thus take the blame for their very exclusion. Current and future education workers negotiate global ideals of entrepreneurialism and individualism within the local contexts of their full, complicated lived experiences.

Schwendler and Thompson (2016) remind us that neoliberalism demands *dehumanisation* (Freire, 2000), a distortion of the vocation of becoming more fully human. Research must 'perceive social, political, and economic contradictions, and take action against the oppressive elements of reality' (this issue). Neoliberalism does not resolve the tensions between economic productivity and social reproduction. Both are masked in discourses of freedom and presumed choice in decision-making that extend from market logics into the most intimate of social relations and constructions of being/becoming. Attention must be paid to the everyday labour – affective and productive – of humans in a variety of formal and informal educational settings around the world. The ways that masculinities and femininities within a normative and binary framework of heterosexuality are waged by and for the workers is a part of a struggle against new techniques of governance that distort and inhibit one from becoming more fully human.

Neoliberalism not only affects the occupation and worker, but also affects teaching, and what 'counts as good teaching' (Wurzburg, 2016) in gendered ways as it seeps into local contexts. While some teachers' knowledge becomes an economically profitable product, one must question at what cost. Some teachers may realise profits in this 'impossible subject position' (Walkerdine 2003), many may never measure up, and still others may never wish to measure up to such positions from within their classrooms or beyond it in the expanded profit-making education marketplace.

Discussions of the work of educating also bring forth discussions of pedagogy. As Gacoin (2016) writes, 'a pedagogical approach can [set] the conditions for *what* is said in terms of *who* speaks, *what* is expected to be spoken about, and *how* that speaking occurs'. In curating this special issue, we aimed to avoid a *pedagogy of definition* (see Gacoin, 2016), understanding such acts as constraining the potential learning endeavour that might emerge when researchers from around the world construct meaning from field data and the lived experiences of their participants. Our view is that education (and education research) should set the conditions for critical inquiry of experiences and structures. The articles variously highlight the ways educators and students negotiate neoliberalism and gender in and through their work. How do these forces collude to mould education policy, conceptualisations of education workers, the work of educating, working conditions, professional preparation, and the possibilities for educating in and of itself?

Synthesis of selected articles

The articles in this special issue are situated in a number of places, with studies carried out in South Africa, Brazil, the United States, and Ireland. Issues taken up in these articles include a focus on the history of teacher unions, the contemporary working lives of women teachers, a sexuality and HIV programme, undergraduate and high school students' negotiations of neoliberal education systems, and gender negotiations in an education programme within a rural social movement. Methodologically diverse, these papers utilise, for example, historical case study, surveys, and collective ethnography.

The first paper is a historical case study in a rural Wisconsin town (USA) of how teacher unions organised their political power during a period of rising militancy in the mid-1970s. Schirmer draws on an oral history of teachers, union activists, townspeople, and school board members to explore the ways that made teachers subsequently more vulnerable to public resentment towards public sector workers' rights as a result of the 1974 Hortonville teachers' union strike. According to Schirmer, the diminished political power of public sector unions is a decidedly gendered issue: most public sector employees are women; their work sustains public institutions; and this work constitutes public care labour. The strike made teacher unions more vulnerable to future neoliberal offensives of public education and its workers. Attending to this history suggests that teachers must defend their rights as workers amidst a rising tide of neoliberal regulations. Although the Hortonville teacher strike exemplifies the burgeoning militancy of unionised teachers and public sector workers broadly, the subsequent strikes failed to gain state-wide sympathy, signifying a shift towards an opportunistic labour movement in which workers pursued their interests through legal provisions and institutional security rather than by developing a broader community of teachers and labour solidarities. The main issue in the 1974 strike was not simply that the Hortonville teachers decided to strike, but that the other Wisconsin teachers did not participate in a state-wide sympathy strike, revealing fractured solidarity across the state. This lack of solidarity translated to teacher vulnerability to the growing rise of anti-union conservatism from the late 1970s onwards. Embodied by growing arguments for local control, the repression of teachers' autonomy and democratic school governance, as well as attacks on public sector unionisation in general, characterises the assent of neoliberalism.

The next two papers focus on issues concerning the work of teachers. In 'Getting a Little Crafty', Wurzburg shares data from a year-long study investigating the socio-political, embodied, discursive, and material manifestations of neoliberalism in the working lives of five women elementary school teachers in the Southeastern United States. Through the analysis of the participation of these teachers in Pinterest© and Teachers Pay Teachers©, which are online markets to display, buy, and sell 'goods' generally (Pintrest) and to display, buy, and sell curriculum and other classroom materials specifically (Teachers Pay Teachers), the author theorises how gendered and neoliberal discourses contribute to what counts as good enough in teaching while simultaneously producing and upholding the pervasive yet impossible subject position of the good enough (woman) teacher. In her analysis, the concept of the good enough teacher serves as an analytical tool for deconstructing and problematising the impossible situations and constraints – at times contested and still other times embraced in order to fulfil new work norms – in which teachers find themselves in current socio-political context.

Cortés Santiago, Karini, and Arvelo Alicea's paper analyses the systematic 'Othering' of Brown women teaching assistants pursuing doctoral degrees in a large, research-intensive US institution. The term Brown women teaching assistants, which the authors also refer to as the Brown elephant in the classroom, is adopted by the authors to bring attention to the racial, ethnic, gendered, sexualised, and sexuality profiling of the 'Other' worker in the hierarchical neoliberal work space. In order to disrupt the rigidity of dominant structures, the ones that call for predetermined and valid forms of research and beings in academia, collective auto-ethnographies and an arts-based lens were used as a methodology. Auto-ethnography provides an opportunity for reflection on researchers' practice and how they, as Brown women in the neoliberal academy, were positioned in relation to others in a highly competitive environment. Through this study, the authors reflected on their constant negotiation for status as teaching assistants with limited bargaining power in the higher education institution where they studied and worked. The research findings invite a deep reflection on the ways our identities and subjectivities are created, enacted, and debated in this neoliberal context. The authors argue that in neoliberal academic spaces where the quest for knowledge and investigation translate as currency aiding the corporatisation of higher education, the individuals working in and within this system must engage in conscious reflection of how the self can be an entryway to understand larger systemic conditions affecting underserved communities. According to them, the current rhetoric of competition and corporatisation is used to reiterate power and nationhood; they also inform us of how students, faculty, and administrators conceptualise academia, in general, and Brown women teaching assistants, in particular, as subjects in higher education. Their creative methodology also suggests that countering neoliberal norms may require opening the self to vulnerability and searching for and constructing collective voice.

The fourth paper, by Gacoin, focuses on neoliberal political rationality for and within sexuality education of an HIV prevention programme. Gacoin conducted a two-year ethnography with educators and youth as they teach and learn about gender, gender relations, and empowerment in the context of sexuality education in the South African non-governmental organisation Love Life. From the results of this study, the author argues that making the political claims of sexuality education explicit is crucial for problematising how a definition of gender has been adopted in HIV prevention with South African youth. According to Gacoin, the question is no longer what should be taught, or how effective that content is in terms of predefined outcomes, but rather how sexuality education is already entangled in relations of power and knowledge that settle into and have lived effects for the conceptions of the self, the other, and their relationships. This article invites a deep reflection of the ways sexuality education either reproduces normative ideas of sexual identities and behaviours or provides a space for youth to challenge those constructions and engage in conversations about who they are and who they desire to become.

Woolley offers a similar and timely piece for readers following the current polemic over transgender bathroom use in public schools and other institutions in the United States. The article, similar to the ongoing legal battle, is concerned with the reinforcement and preservation in institutions, everyday practices, identity, and talk of an ideology of heteronormative binary gender. Based on three years of fieldwork in a Northern California high school, she examines the social semiotic project through which heterosexuality is maintained in and through 'safe spaces' for questioning/queer/other sexualities and genders. Using the theoretical imagery of the panopticon, she articulates how isolated and isolating safe spaces can be within the dominant and not-to-be-contested heterosexual space of the school. Of import to this special issue is the way she situates her study as revealing a hidden agenda of the neoliberal project, one that requires intensified self-surveillance of individual future workers, capable not only of disciplining her/himself at work but also of relegating her/his identities to designated spaces.

Schwendler and Thompson's paper focuses on education within the Landless Workers Movement (MST), which is one of Latin America's largest social movements. The MST proposes an alternative model of agriculture based on a food sovereignty paradigm, in which food and farming are more than just the production of commodities to be traded. This stands in stark contrast to the neoliberal model of agricultural and food production, which prioritises market efficiency, mass production, and cost cutting, resulting in the reduction of wages for the poorest sectors of society, as well as the destruction of the environment as a result of unsustainable practices. The food sovereignty model translated to MST's education programmes has had a particularly great impact on young women, providing them with access to knowledge in the agricultural field and empowering them within their settlement communities. Drawing on oral history, this article analyses interviews taken with students and staff from the Educar Institute, a technical school for secondary and continuing education focused on agro-ecology. The paper specifically analyses the MST's gender-oriented pedagogy, in which dominant, local gender ideologies and roles have been intentionally contested through the restructuring of gender relations. The authors argue that women's leadership within the MST has been crucial to placing gender inequity on the land struggle agenda and in a promoting gender-oriented pedagogy within the Educar Institute. The implications of both for a more gender equitable future are echoed in the next generation of landless activists' experiences.

Finally, Lolich and Lynch's article examines the impact of neoliberal reform of higher education on *affective labour*. They examine the ways in which students in Ireland negotiate contemporary global transitions premised on improving competitiveness and opportunity for all citizens in a knowledge-based economy. Using survey data from a large cohort of students (4265) drawn from three different types of higher education institutions (public university, public institute of technology, and a private for-profit college) analysed against a backdrop of policy developments in recent years, this paper shows how there is an explicit requirement to create entrepreneurial students in Irish higher education. However, this study also shows how the students mediate this narrative that contradicts their desires to be better cared for in the colleges that they are currently attending; and it highlights the importance of care (affective relations) in the work lives of students outside of and after college. These results challenge the idealised myth of the self-sufficient independent adult learner and care-less and detached future entrepreneurial worker.

In closing, neoliberal and gendered logics intertwine to shape the *boundary work* of educators in early childhood, primary, secondary, higher education, and informal settings (Seddon, Ozga, and Levin 2013). We see this special issue as initiating further critical discussions on the situated, diverse ways in which neoliberalism and gender intersect in national education projects as part of the challenging work of educating to become human in and for complex contexts around the world.

Disclosure statement

No potential conflict of interest was reported by the authors.

References

Acker, S. 1999. *The Realities of Teachers' Work*. New York: Bloomsbury.
Apple, M. 1983. "Work, Gender, and Teaching." *The Teachers College Record* 84 (3): 611–628.
Apple, M. W. 1986. *Teachers and Texts: A Political Economy of Class and Gender Relations in Education*. New York: Routledge & Kegan Paul.
Ball, S. J. 1994. *Education Reform: A Critical and Post-Structural Approach*. Buckingham: Open University Press.
Ball, S. J., and C. Junemann. 2012. *Networks, New Governance and Education*. Bristol: Policy Press.
Biklen, S. K. 1995. *School Work: Gender and the Cultural Construction of Teaching*. New York: Teachers College Press.
Cochran-Smith, M., and S. L. Lytle. 2006. "Troubling Images of Teaching in No Child Left Behind." *Harvard Educational Review* 76 (4): 668–697.
Connell, R. 2009. "Good Teachers on Dangerous Ground: Towards a New View of Teacher Quality and Professionalism." *Critical Studies in Education* 50 (3): 213–229.
Cortina, R., and S. San Román. 2006. *Women and Teaching: Global Perspectives on the Feminization of a Profession*. New York: Palgrave Macmillan.
David, M. E. 1980. *The State, the Family, and Education*. London: Routledge & Kegan Paul.

Dillabough, J.-A. 1999. "Gender Politics and Conceptions of the Modern Teacher: Women, Identity and Professionalism." *British Journal of Sociology of Education* 20 (3): 373–395.

Fischman, G. 2007. "Persistence and Ruptures: The Feminisation of Teaching and Teacher Education in Argentina." *Gender and Education* 19 (3): 353–368.

Freire, P. 2000. *Pedagogy of the Oppressed*. New York: Continuum.

Gacoin, A. E. 2016. "Encountering Gender: Resisting a Neo-liberal Political Rationality for Sexuality Education as an HIV Prevention Strategy." *Gender and Education*. doi:http://dx.doi.org/10.1080/09540253.2016.1197378

Griffith, A. I., and D. E. Smith. 2005. *Mothering for Schooling*. New York: Routledge Falmer.

Lather, P. 1994. "The Absent Presence: Patriarchy, Capitalism and the Nature of Teacher Work." In *The Education Feminism Reader*, edited by L. Stone, and G. M. Boldt, 242–251. New York: Routledge.

Lynch, K., B. Grummell, and D. Devine. 2012. *New Managerialism in Education*. Hampshire: Palgrave Macmillan.

Maguire, M. 2010. "Towards a Sociology of the Global Teacher." *The Routledge International Handbook of the Sociology of Education*, 58–68.

Morgade, G. (1992). *El determinante de género en el trabajo docente de la escuela primaria* [The gender determinant in primary school teachers' work]. Unpublished manuscript, Buenos Aires.

Morgade, G., and M. Bellucci. 1997. *Mujeres en la educación: Género y docencia en Argentina, 1870–1930 (Women in Education: Gender and Teaching in Argentina, 1870–1930)*. Buenos Aires: Miño y Dávila.

Muñoz García, A. L. 2014. "Academic Mobility: The Intellectual in Chilean Academia in a Global Economic Context." Unpublished diss., Buffalo, NY: University at Buffalo.

Pitzer, H. 2010. ""What's Best for Kids" vs. Teacher Unions: How Teach For America Blames Teacher Unions for the Problems of Urban Schools." *Workplace* 17: 61–74.

Pitzer, H. 2015. "Urban Teachers Engaging in Critical Talk: Navigating Deficit Discourse and Neoliberal Logics." *Journal of Educational Controversy* 9 (1): 8.

Reid, A. 2003. "Understanding Teachers' Work: Is There Still a Place for Labour Process Theory?" *British Journal of Sociology of Education* 24 (5): 559–573.

Robert, S. A. 2012. "(En)gendering Responsibility. A Critical News Analysis of Argentina's Education Reform, 2001–02." *DISCOURSE: Studies in the Cultural Politics of Education* 33 (4): 485–498.

Robert, S. A. 2013. "Incentives, Teachers, and Gender at Work." *Education Policy Analysis Archives* 21 (31): 1–25.

Robert, S. A. 2014. "Extending Theorisations of the Global Teacher: Care Work, Gender, and Street-Level Policies." *British Journal of Sociology of Education*.

Robert, S. A. 2015. *Neoliberal Education Reform: Gendered Notions in Global and Local Contexts*. New York, NY: Routledge.

Robert, S. A., and H. K. McEntarfer. 2014. "Teachers' Work, Food Policies, and Gender in Argentina." *Anthropology & Education Quarterly* 45 (3): 260–275.

Robertson, S. 2008. ""Remaking the World": Neoliberalism and the Transformation of Education and Teachers' Labor." In *The Global Assault on Teaching, Teachers, and their Unions*, edited by M. Compton, and L. Weiner. New York: Palgrave Macmillan.

Seddon, T., J. Ozga, and S. Levin. 2013. "Global Transitions and Teacher Professionalism." In *Educators, Professionalism and Politics: Global Transitions, National Spaces and Professional Projects*, edited by T. Seddon, and S. Levin, 3–24. London: Routledge.

Schwendler, S. F., and Thompson, L. A. 2016. "Gender Education and Agroecology within the Landless Workers Movement in Brazil." *Gender and Education*. doi:http://dx.doi.org/10.1080/09540253.2016.1197382

Stambach, A., and M. David. 2005. "Feminist Theory and Educational Policy: How Gender has been "Involved" in Family School Choice Debates." *Signs* 30 (2): 1633–1658.

Walkerdine, V. 2003. "Reclassifying Upward Mobility: Femininity and the Neo-Liberal Subject." *Gender and Education*, 237–248.

Wurzburg, E. 2016. "Gettin' a Little Crafty: Teachers Pay Teachers, Pintrest, and Neoliberalism in New Materialist Feminist Research." *Gender and Education*. doi:http://dx.doi.org/10.1080/09540253.2016.1197380

When solidarity doesn't quite strike: the 1974 Hortonville, Wisconsin teachers' strike and the rise of neoliberalism

Eleni Brelis Schirmer

ABSTRACT

As public-sector unions such as teachers' unions used the boon of post-war liberalism to form their political power, they imported many of liberalism's key contradictions: its formation of racial contracts, its misappraisal of affective labour, and its opportunistic collective action logics. This article suggests cracks within liberalism weakened the political power of teachers' unions, disempowering a feminised workforce. Using a historical case study of teachers' strike in rural Wisconsin in 1974, this article shows how the tenuous solidarity afforded by liberal accords made teachers' unions more vulnerable to future neoliberal offensives on public education and its workers. The aftermath of the strike generated an opportunistic labour movement in which workers pursued their interests through legal provisions rather than by developing teachers' broader community and labour solidarities, subverting feminist possibilities of teachers' unions. This history suggests *how* teachers defend their rights as workers amidst a rising tide of neoliberalism matters.

Introduction

Critical scholars increasingly expose the effects of 'neoliberalism' on public education, documenting how such policy regimes divest from public institutions such as schools, relax state regulations, weaken workers' rights and open new educational arenas for private ventures (e.g. Burch 2006; Ball 2007; Scott 2009; Anderson and Donchik 2014). A body of literature describes the deleterious impacts of these programmes, such as their exacerbation of social inequalities and loss of democratic processes (e.g. Bartlett et al. 2002; Cucchiara, Gold, and Simon 2011; Lipman 2011). Increasingly, teachers' unions are hailed as leaders of resistance to these policies, and for good reason (Compton and Weiner 2008; Hagopian and Green 2012; Weiner 2012): mobilised teachers' unions have a powerful voice to speak against market-based education reforms, highlight racial and economic disparities, and revalorise teaching work, depreciated by its feminisation (Weiner 1996; Rousmaniere 2005; Gutstein and Lipman 2013; Uetricht 2014). Yet, despite notable recent examples, teachers' unions typically do not mobilise for gender, racial or economic justice within and beyond schools, instead tending to short-term, economistic interests of individual members. This economism has spurred political whiplash against teachers' unions, who are critiqued for acting against the interests of students and communities (e.g. Lieberman 2000; Moe 2011). Yet critics and defenders alike treat teachers' unions as monolithic and predetermined characters, rather than polyvalent creations of a contingent history. Furthermore, this perspective assumes political economic changes affecting teachers' unions originate entirely outside of schools, obscuring the relative autonomy of schools and teachers.

This article aims to add historical nuance to this conversation by exploring the residual pathways from which neoliberal policies – specifically the weakening of workers' rights – have emerged. Through a historical case study, the article suggests that how teachers' unions configured their political power during a period of rising militancy in the mid-1970s made them subsequently more vulnerable in the burgeoning resentment towards the public sector and workers' rights of the late 1970s. The diminished political power of public-sector unions is a decidedly gendered issue: most public-sector employees are women, their work sustains public institutions and thus constitutes public care labour. Weakened labour rights for public-sector worker politically disempowers women and care labour. Diminishing teachers' unions' rights evident today, I aim to suggest, is best understood not simply as the rise of neoliberalism, but the failures of liberalism, the political and economic programme of individual rights that hailed in the United States between 1940 and 1970 (Mills 1997; Rodger 2011; Cowie 2016). As public-sector unions, including teachers' unions, used the boon of post-war liberalism to form their political power, they imported its key contradictions: its formation of racial contracts, its misappraisal of affective labour and its opportunistic collective action logics. This article shows how cracks within liberalism weakened the political power of teachers' unions, disempowering a feminised workforce.

To do so, this article takes a historical detour through a small town in rural Wisconsin in 1974, during a violent teachers' strike in which all 88 striking teachers were fired. The town of Hortonville's violent response to the striking teachers triggered calls for a statewide sympathy strike, and ultimately sparked successful arbitration legislation in Wisconsin for public-sector workers. Therefore, the Hortonville strike is often interpreted as something of a victory for labour because of its role in yielding arbitration legislation (Saltzman 1986; Mertz 2015). However, the following analysis suggests the Hortonville teachers strike and its aftermath is better understood as the advent of labour's weakening, an emblematic fulcrum between public-sector union's vigorous assent in the early 1970s and its swift decline in the late 1970s (McCartin 2008a). Drawing from oral histories of teachers, union activists, townspeople and school board members, collected in 1974 by a Wisconsin Historical Society field researcher, as well as archives from the Wisconsin Education Association Council archive collection, housed in the Wisconsin Historical society and the Milwaukee Teachers Education Association (MTEA), I show how the state teachers' unions assumed a pragmatic form of action post-Hortonville, which ultimately undermined teachers' solidarity and contributed to the advance of market liberalism. After a brief note on the strike's significance for the present, this article assumes the following trajectory. First, I will provide a narrative of the 1974 Hortonville teachers' strike and the actions leading up to it, and the significance of the strike and its blowback for a feminised workforce. Then, I will review the decision of the statewide teachers' union federation decision not to strike, and the racial contract embedded and urban–rural divide embedded within that decisions. Finally, I will assess the shifting collective action logics resultant from

Hortonville, turning to sociologists Offe and Wiesenthal's (1980) to explore the theoretical and practical implications of this strategy shift.

I suggest that the strategy shift post-1974 Hortonville teachers' strike had fundamentally gendered effects, depreciating not only a workforce that was predominantly female but also the rights of care workers and affective labour. One of the chief impacts of the Hortonville teachers' strike was a decisive turn against public-sector unions' rights to strike, a resulting in a long-term weakness of US labour power, a position taken up by both labour and its opponents (e.g. Burns 2014). In the early 1970s, public-sector workers were predominantly female and workers of colour (Bell 1985; McCartin 2006). Therefore, the shift away from striking and other legal rights represented a fundamental loss of power for a significant number of female workers. What's more, the popular blowback teachers received from striking revealed a basal antipathy towards the rights and remuneration of affective labourers (Shelton 2013). Because a central element of teachers' work is to care for dependent (students), many viewed their pursuit of independent rights as inapt, even offensive. This negative reaction revealed deep-seeded fault lines in the economy's growing reliance on immaterial labour – labour that provides service, information and communication (Hardt 1999). As the Hortonville strike foreshadowed, the economic misrecognition of immaterial labour – despite the economy's increasing reliance on such labour – would come characterise the political economy of neoliberalism, creating gendered inequalities in educational work and beyond (McRobbie 2010; Kostogriz 2012). Therefore, the Hortonville strike reveals not only the growing conservatism outside of teachers' unions, but also the problematic organisation within teachers' unions that failed to offer a strong alternative to external threatens. The weakening of teachers' unions characteristic of neoliberal programmes not only disempowers a predominantly female workforce, also it devalues affective labour.

Ultimately, I wish to communicate that in order to understand the potential of teachers' unions to act as transformative agents of education justice and effectively lead resistance against the neoliberal order, we must understand the – perhaps unstable – forms of collective action with which teachers unions built their power. If teachers' unions are to be a means of defence against the neoliberal devaluing of public education, they must be prepared to chart new political ground to redefine solidarity and its requirements.

Why does the 1974 Hortonville strike matter for today?

Mounting conservative pressures from the changing political economy put teachers' unions like those in Hortonville, Wisconsin in a defensive position in the 1970s as the economy collapsed, and conservative ideology took root, transforming citizens from public beneficiaries to private taxpayers (Apple and Oliver 1996; Apple 2006; Cowie 2010). Between 1940 and 1970, Wisconsin led the nation's labour movement. In 1959, after nearly a decade of organising and lobbying for legal protection, Wisconsin's council of municipal employees won the right to bargain collectively with their employers, becoming the first state in the country to provide public-sector collective bargaining rights. Over the next two decades, Wisconsin's public-sector employees continued to push for legal expansion of their union rights, establishing key legal victories of compulsory bargaining and setting pace for the rest of the nation. Across the nation, teachers' unions witnessed a growth in power and militancy in the early 1970s. Yet by the late

1970s, growing rural conservatism shifted popular support away from public institutions and unionised workers (Slater 2004; Cowie 2010; Scribner 2013).

My intention in this essay is not to condemn teachers' actions. Indeed, I view the teachers' opportunistic tactics post-Hortonville as rational given the political balance of public opinion at that time, which generally favoured public-sector unions in the 1960s and 1970s. The legal victory embodied in interest arbitration was made possible by a sympathetic state legislature, a progressive governor and energised labour lobbyists. However, when this leadership and these political forces were no longer in power, an important question surfaced: was labour strong enough to hold itself up on its own? This question is especially pertinent today, given the radically different political forces in power today. In the past five years, Wisconsin has heralded a nation-wide evisceration of public-sector employees' rights, with historic anti-labour legislation passing in 2011 in Wisconsin, again in 2015 when Wisconsin became the nation's 25th 'right-to-work' state, and the pending current Supreme Court decision that would nationally dismantle public-sector unions (Antonucci 2015). In addition to highlighting both the rational and unstable tendencies of political opportunism, the Hortonville case offers important resources for labour's next horizons. The nation-wide changes to public-sector union rights which erupted in 2011 in Wisconsin begs the question, on what basis did these rights form? What cracks may have been present in the initial formation of these rights that contributed to their subsequent political vulnerability?

1974: Hortonville, Wisconsin

Hortonville, Wisconsin is a small rural town located near the Fox River Valley. In the mid-1970s, the town mostly comprised of small-scale farmers and small industrial owners of a local paper mill, who had maintained long-time influence over the school system. The school board was controlled by the small-town power elite, described by a local organiser as 'a country-club circle [with] a whole mystique wrapped up around them ... and one-hundred years of traditional subservience to that power.'[1] Yet, in the 1970s, as the nearby city of Appleton's economy shifted to more white-collar employment, Hortonville experienced suburbanisation pressures, particularly as the population grew in the adjacent town of Greenville. This put increasing pressure on the Hortonville's school district, which covered a large geographic area that was fifteen miles wide. The town of 1500 people now served 1900 students in its schools (Hensel 1974). Between 1970 and 1973, a referendum to build new schools to deal with overcrowding was proposed three different times. Each time, the referendum was voted down, in high-turn out votes; the majority of local voters were rural, conservative and resistant to increases in property-taxes, despite a documented need for expanded facilities (Lee 1973).

The lack of public investment in education bore heavily on Hortonville's teachers. Rising growth in student population and lack of sufficient space and resources made the work of teaching more difficult. For one thing, overcrowding meant that classrooms took on multiple purposes; teachers and students crisscrossed through buildings, holding art classes in the gym and cramming high-school courses in the elementary school classrooms. Second, overcrowding constrained the student-centered pedagogy implemented by Hortonville teachers, such as individually guided education. This alternative teaching model involved a coordinated system of planned, individualised instruction in which students progressed at their own rate through personalised curricular materials, with one-on-one support from teacher (Holzman 1972). This programme had become an important component of the Hortonville school district. It received positive attention and enthusiasm from parents, educators and statewide administrators and was used as a model for other districts in the state (*Appleton Post-Crescent* 1973). Without public money to expand the facilities, administrators proposed lengthening the school day by two hours in order to have multiple shifts of instruction (Scribner 2013, 114). The failed referendum also eliminated the individually guided instruction programmes (Lee 1975).[2]

In addition to increasing work pressures and a loss of professional autonomy, teachers started the 1973–1974 school year without a contract, and had not had a pay raise in three years, putting their wages $1000 lower than those of teachers working in nearby Appleton (Sherman 1974). In the fall of 1973, the Hortonville Education Association (HEA), the local teachers' union affiliated with the National Education Association (NEA), began bargaining for higher wages, hoping to get a contract in place for the reminder of the year. Their initial bargaining proposal asked for a salary raise from $7900 to $8100 for teachers with a bachelor's degree. For the HEA, not only was this raise fairly modest on its own terms, but it was also well within the school's allocated budget for teachers' salaries, which reported a $100,000+ surplus in 1973–1974 ("Hortonville Fact Sheet" 1974). The school board did not agree to the union's offer, but upon the union's request it agreed to a non-binding fact-finding procedure in December of 1973, in which a neutral third-party mediator would review the case and recommend a solution.

Despite their best attempts to improve their working conditions, teachers ended the fall semester of 1973 sourly. The fact-finding mediator did not support a raise for teachers, and instead offered a recommendation nearly identical to the board's own proposal. The union refused to accept the offer and returned to negotiation once more. Meanwhile, the town of Hortonville voted for the third time not to allocate funds for school expansion, making it obvious that teachers would have even fewer resources and face more job pressures in the coming months. When the new semester started after winter break, patience among the teachers was wearing thin. Though they continued to pursue bargaining, teachers unanimously authorised a strike vote in January ("Hortonville Education Association Strike Timeline" 1974).

More than their pay increase, teachers were most concerned about securing a contract with specific language protecting minimum standards of working conditions and an agreed-upon definition of their workday. The HEA asked for the present working conditions to be treated as minimum standards, which the board rejected, claiming it wanted the flexibility to assign teachers to duties and tasks as it needed. Furthermore, the board wanted to change the school day from 8 a.m.–4 p.m. to 7 a.m.–5 p.m., in order to accommodate extra shifts. The union was willing to agree to a longer day, as long as teachers would be able to have eight-hour shifts during the day rather than split shifts, and they asked that the understanding could be renegotiated the next year. The board did not agree. Desperate to get a contract in place, the union dropped all other bargaining issues – such as pay for substitute duty during prep time, release time, dental insurance and car insurance for transporting students (Sherman 1974). The board still did not agree.

The union grew increasingly frustrated with the board's paltry attempts at bargaining, which were interpreted by union members as a refusal to engage in the bargaining process, or as a refusal to offer any concessions. As Mike Wisnoski, the president of

HEA, said, 'It was the board's adamant refusal to sit down and negotiate. They'd just stall and stall and frustrate everything. They don't know what negotiations are. They'd just say take it as it is. They counter-proposed us down to nothing' (Sherman 1974). By February, the HEA had offered to split the difference once again between the board's last non-offer, and the union's last concessions.

Throughout the negotiations, Hortonville teachers conducted a slow build of actions – they stopped their extracurricular commitments, such as advising and coaching, and instead spent their after-school hours informally picketing the high school and handing out leaflets to update the community about the stalled negotiations. In mid-February, the board promised a counter-offer by 15 March, and the teachers stopped picketing in anticipation of a settlement (Barrington 1979). However, when the deadline came and went, teachers decided they had reached their limit. The HEA went on strike on 18 March 1974. As one teacher said,

> If I were asked six months ago, or before the Hortonville situation, I would have said, no I wouldn't go on strike … But I think at this point, I would answer that if situations become such that no bargaining can go on, and that none of my needs will be met and that the children will suffer because of these things, the other alternative is that I would go on strike.[3]

The strike

Over the next two weeks, schools remained closed in Hortonville while the board and the HEA engaged in unsuccessful negotiations. After a week, parents joined the striking teachers on the picket line and opened an alternative school for children ("1974 Hortonville Strike" 1974). Even when the union attempted to renegotiate to the board's last offer, the board now refused to accept its own offer. This uncompromising action led many teachers to believe the board was engaging in intentional union-busting rather than good-faith negotiations. Indeed, instead of re-opening the contract negotiations, the board offered to review each teacher's case individually. The union refused to participate, declaring its members would have all of their cases reviewed together or none at all (*The Racine Journal Times* 1974c). The board chose to review none of the teachers' cases, and fired all 88 of the striking teachers on 2 April 1974.

This bold manoeuver hit a nerve with teachers and other public-sector workers around the state. Though state law prohibited public-sector employees from striking, a number of teacher unions around the state and nation engaged in increase job actions and strikes between 1971 and 1974 (McCartin 2008b). Most of these strikes were settled within two weeks, often in accordance with the unions' demands. Though in some places workers were threatened with being fired, as in Wild Rose, Wisconsin, usually the school board did not follow through. Occasionally, teachers' unionists were issued fines for striking (Holter 1999). Rarely were teachers actually fired for conducting an illegal strike. However, in Hortonville, the board's actions – both its unwillingness to bargain in good faith and its decision to fire the teachers – shifted the debate away from the substantive issues at stake, such as the pay and protections bestowed to teachers, to a broader question about teachers' right to strike.

Within a week of firing the striking teachers, the board hired replacement teachers and re-opened Hortonville's schools (Barrington 1979). The board's decision to fire the striking teachers and to hire replacements escalated the struggles between the teachers and the board and galvanised all sides. The teachers hired to replace the striking teachers became a focal point for HEA's struggle. Many of the scab teachers were students from nearby colleges and universities without teaching credentials or certifications. The fact that the Board was willing to hire illegal teachers provoked the ire of HEA, prompting a lawsuit against the board, and triggering a series of resolutions and campaigns pressuring university education programmes to educate their students about the legality of teaching without certification as well as the ethics of strike-breaking ("WEAC Staff Updates" 1974).

The split between strike-supporters and strike-opponents literally divided the town. At one end of the city block that constituted downtown Hortonville, strike-opponents gathered at a local bar, McHugh's Tap, where they formed a small gang, self-dubbed the Vigilante Association. Mostly conservative farmers, the Vigilantes painted their gang name on their pick-up trucks and drove throughout town bantering the striking teachers. Down the block was the striking teachers' headquarters. The town's bakery, tavern, electrical shop and sandwich shop lay in between. Caught in the middle of the struggle, these small business owners wrung their hands. 'It's hell on earth,' said Glen Lathrop, the owner of the town's electrical shop. And at Glenn's Restaurant, just a few doors from the Vigilante Association's stakeout, the dining room buzzed with debates about the controversy. School board supporters ate their sandwiches huddled around the lunch counter. Striking teachers and their supporters filed into booths on the other side of the room (Hensel 1974).

Discourse was no more civil or deliberative on the picket lines. While the school board continued to deny the striking teachers' calls to renegotiate, they also issued calls for students not to talk to their striking teachers on the picket line (Hensel 1974). Furthermore, the newly formed Vigilante Association took it upon itself to reprimand the striking teachers and protect the replacement teachers on behalf of the broader community. A few days after replacement teachers entered the school, the Vigilantes issued a call to action to area farmers. Early the next morning, retired farmers came into town armed with canes, broomsticks, and even firearms. Initially, the vigilantes patrolled only the downtown, but as the crowds of picketers around the high school continued to grow, they expanded their targets to those picketing the school.

In turn, the picketers expanded their targets from the high school to area businesses connected to school board members. Teachers received threats and in several cases picketers were struck by moving vehicles. The president of the statewide teachers union, Laurie Wynn, an African-American woman from Milwaukee, became a special target. In addition to hurling racial slurs at her, Vigilantes struck her with a car and dragged her behind the vehicle for nearly an entire city block. Rocks hurtled through the windows of the striking teachers' headquarters. Vigilantes accused teachers of hanging two dogs. Derogatory slogans covered houses in town. The Outagamie County Sherriff called in supporting deputy officers from surrounding counties in an attempt to maintain public safety, costing taxpayers $100,000. In one day, police arrested 34 people (Barrington 1979). Local newspapers announced they would no longer print letters to the editor about the strike.

If the townspeople and school board was not on the side of the striking teachers, the academic calendar was. Spring break fell only a few weeks away from the teachers' firing, making it easier for sympathetic teachers in other parts of the state to join the strike. Roughly 500 teachers vacationed in Hortonville that spring, using their days off to picket alongside the fired teachers, particularly targeting replacement teachers; cries of 'scab' and 'strikebreakers' filled the air. Protestors from Madison passed around song sheets with the lyrics to 'Solidarity Forever,' 'We Shall Not Be Moved,' and a 1974 original, 'Hortonville Has a Bad Case of Scabs' ("Hortonville Picket Line Song-Sheet" 1974). Yet many in Hortonville, a conservative town unfamiliar with unions and labour struggles, reacted strongly to the influx of strike-supporters, decreeing strike-supporters as 'consciousness thugs,' and meddling outsiders. As one Vigilante declared,

> We started to get involved when all these outsiders started to come in, and started raising all this chaos. We decided we had to do something in Hortonville to protect the merchants. People in Hortonville weren't even coming downtown to buy groceries. It was like a ghost town down here during the strike.[4]

Notably, teachers were the only unionised workers in town (Rafferty 1974).

Despite the chaos and unrest, solidarity continued to grow for the striking teachers across the state. The NEA organised an 'Adopt-A-Teacher' programme to fundraise for the striking teachers, and a 'Save the Children' fund was organised by Wisconsin teachers' union locals to send supplies to the alternative school ("National Hortonville-Timberlane Adopt-A-Teacher Program" 1974). Hortonville parents sent their testimonies of support for the striking teachers and the individual-guided education programme to local papers; a group of parents filed a motion in the HEA's lawsuit against the board, claiming their children did not receive the same quality of instruction from the replacement teachers ("Hortonville – Summary of Litigation" 1974). One parent poignantly summarised the tension between teachers, parents and a more rural, conservative community in an unpublished letter to the editor. She wrote:

> Due to the fact that we live in a rural community that cares little about education, we are in the minority and our children will suffer. We were also the minority who served anytime with all school activities, including P.T.O., room mothers, open house, school bond referendums, field trips, disciplinary committees, etc. We were the minority that cared! Now, the majority who never bothered to attend any of these school functions are the ones backing the board, manning the school halls so that the interested parents cannot enter the locked and guarded public school building. It's sad, because they will never know what we've lost, simply because they never really knew what we had! This same majority helped considerably in defeating the three school bond referendums, simply because they did not care about education. (Milliren 1974)

As this parent noted, a key issue that came to light in Hortonville was the lack of contact between the townspeople and the teachers, much less public employees or unionised public employees. Ed Gollnick, WEAC Human Relations Direct also noted many in the community had very little awareness of what occurred inside the classroom, much less the details about teachers' work. As he stated, 'One of the problems teachers face is that … the communications that come out about schools are put out by the school board and the administration … because the teachers are teaching.'[5] As a result, Gollnick noted, much of the caring work done by teachers on the behalf of the children of the community was invisible to many outside of the communities. This misunderstanding, Gollnick surmised, fuelled some of the antagonism in Hortonville. And indeed, many community members found the strike 'rude, impolite and abusive.'[6]

Teachers around the state showed their solidarity with the striking teachers, joining rallies and pickets over their spring break and during weekends. The act of participating in the protests significantly affected their outlook on the strike, transforming many teachers who were previously adverse to 'militant' actions taken by teachers, such as striking. One teacher reflected on her experience in Hortonville picket lines. She said,

> I think it's hard to explain [the impacts of being on the picket lines in Hortonville] because like you said, it affects you personally. Because once you've been through something like that – and we didn't even see the worst of it – you know, you don't forget it. And it's hard to impart that kind of feeling.[7]

Solidarity for the striking Hortonville teachers grew beyond just teachers and local parents. Other labour unions around the state joined the picket lines, and leadership in these unions declared their support. For example, Ray Majerus, the state president of the United Autoworkers, gave a speech at an April rally and Ed Durkin, the president of the state's fire-fighters union, was arrested in a protest ("It Happened in Hortonville" 1974). The Wisconsin Democratic Party supported the striking teachers, as did a women's political caucus (*Appleton Post-Crescent* 1974). The Federation of State, County and Municipal Employees and the AFL-CIO also showed their support for protests. On 18 April 1974 when a judge ordered an injunction not on the teachers' strike activity, but on their picketing, Ed Muelver, president of the Federation State, County and Municipal Employees, urged widespread demonstrations, and called for a labour day teach-in for Hortonvillers. 'In lieu of a settlement,' he said 'I am requesting a labor-day in Hortonville to teach the town that they can't shove teachers around' (*The Racine Journal Times* 1974a).

Muelver's comment reflected more than just a quip – it suggested bigger questions about labour's strategy going forward. The growing energy on the picket lines at Hortonville – both among strike-supporters and opposition – posed strategic calculations about the statewide teachers' union, the Wisconsin Educational Association Council (WEAC), next moves. In order to legitimise the teachers' union's rights and defeat the school board, would WEAC elevate the strike tactics, calling for greater militancy, wider-solidarity and pedagogic strategies associated with direct action? Or would it channel its fight towards legal strategies – such as seeking relief from the injunction against the teachers' picketing, suing the board for hiring replacement teachers without appropriate teaching credentials or legalising strikes – to defend the affective requirements of education and teachers' rights?

Militant care workers: a liberal contradiction
By striking, the Hortonville teachers made public the need for increased resources for education work. The strike constitutes what Fraser calls 'politicising run-away needs,' in which social needs unmet by the existing political conditions get brought into public discourse (Fraser 1989, 300; Fraser and Honneth 2003). The striking Hortonville teachers brought their unmet need for more pay and protection into public discourse. In addition, the striking teachers aimed to redress the undervaluation of their skills and jobs coded as feminine and care labour. Even when teachers dropped all demands for their own pay increases and simply requested basic protections of their working condition, the Board still refused to negotiate. Nonetheless, the teachers understood that their collective voice was strengthened by threatening a possible exit (Hirschman 1970). By striking, teachers entered their

concerns over working conditions and care duties into matters of public and political discourse.

Yet such claims met friction from the surrounding community, many of whom disapproved of teachers' use of economic arguments for care labour, revealing liberalism's limited evaluation of affective labour, and therefore, predominantly women's work (Fraser 1997; Lynch, Baker, and Lyons 2009). First, liberal accords relegated affective needs to the private sphere, offering neither measure nor metric of care work. Instead, mostly women care workers, such as teachers, were seen as compelled by 'natural instinct' for tending to the needs of others, such as students. The belief of a presumed 'naturalised calling' not only ignored the intellectual and emotional skills required of care work, it justified low wages for women. Tending to the complex needs of students was in fact beyond material value, went the argument and therefore could not possibly be captured by pay (Lynch, Baker, and Lyons 2009). Furthermore, in the late 1970s, striking teachers' demands for increased value of their 'immaterial labour' ran counter to the loss of 'material' industrial labour experienced by white, working-class men at this time. Therefore, teachers' attempt to exercise both exit and voice – by way of a strike – met an onslaught of non-support, first and foremost from the surrounding community, and more subtly, from supporting teachers across the state, as we shall soon see.

Finally, Hortonville's community members' response to the teachers' union strikes highlights a fundamental contradiction of teachers' unions as organised care workers: teachers were granted the legal right to unionise but *not* to strike (Shelton 2013). Popular belief held that by striking, teachers reneged their social obligation to care and educate students. Yet this contradiction illuminates a core dilemma collective in conditions of care workers under liberalism. If care workers, such as teachers, are defined by their relationship to dependents, what *independent* rights does the worker have? And, importantly, how do these rights operate on an individual *and* collective levels (Abel and Nelson 1990; Lynch, Baker, and Lyons 2009)?

The not-strike: social justice unionism, racial contracts and rural-urban divides

The reaction of Hortonville's external community – townspeople, parents and other unionists – was not the only significant response; the statewide teachers' union reaction also revealed important cracks in liberalism's foundation. Whereas the state AFL-CIO unequivocally called for a statewide strike, WEAC presented members with a range of options and ultimately left the final decision to union locals (*Stevens Point Daily Journal* 1974). In a pamphlet to membership calling for support, WEAC asked its members to support the striking teachers, but did not mandate any form of action.

> Our organization wishes to convey to you our willingness and eagerness to help you in whatever way we can in joining your actions and your fights because we feel that what happens to one of us happens to all of us. ("It Happened in Hortonville" 1974)

Furthermore, WEAC implored its statewide members to frame their collective identities as workers, rather than as an association of professionals. They explicitly acknowledged this shift and called members to action accordingly. They wrote:

> The help and support of unions is critical … We recognize the criticism that occasionally comes to us from some unions that we are not well-established in the labor movement. It is true that in the past we viewed ourselves as an association. We had no bargaining laws

or any regulation governing public employee laws. With the advent of collective bargaining, we have moved into the labor movement very deeply and we believe effectively. As a state organization, we see ourselves as very much a union of workers. ("It Happened in Hortonville" 1974)

After the court ordered an injunction against the picketing teachers, WEAC decided to put forward a vote to ratify a call for a one-day statewide sympathy strike, but again required that locals determine such a decision. Affirming a commitment to democratic decision-making from locals to guide the state's decision-making, WEAC spokesman Leonard Jacobs stated, 'There is no way the state or regional units can mandate this. This is going to be a grass-roots effort' (Stevens Point Daily Journal 1974). It was a fateful strategic choice.

Despite widespread support for the striking Hortonville teachers, the vote for a state-wide sympathy strike failed by a four to one margin. The statewide solidarity vote failed in large part due to insufficient support from the state's largest locals. Milwaukee, Kenosha and Racine did not vote in favour of the action, echoing the calls from the state superintendent that teachers should not violate their own contracts by participating in a solidarity walk-out. As the president of the MTEA said, 'The executive committee feels that it would be very unproductive for Milwaukee to strike. It would be a violation of our contract, and we are working to make good relations with the school board' (*The Racine Journal Times* 1974a).

Though large unions were willing to provide statements of support and monetary donations for the Hortonville teachers, they were not willing to support sympathetic job actions. MTEA's decision to not participate in the statewide sympathy strike was particularly curious, since the relative strength of the union and the labour-friendly environment of Milwaukee minimised potential risks for Milwaukee teachers. Furthermore, Lauri Wynn, the president of WEAC and proponent of a statewide direct action campaign, was herself a former Milwaukee school teacher and MTEA member. Given MTEA's internal strength, its political sympathies with the striking Hortonville teachers, and its direct connection to the statewide leadership group, why did its members vote overwhelmingly against partici-pating in the strike? This decision reveals several important tendencies forming in the union at the time.

First, it displayed tensions within the Milwaukee teacher union between a conservative executive body and progressive factions of the membership. The executive board of the union voted against the solidarity strike before members took a vote, setting the tone for the rest of the union. On Monday 22 April 1974, the board voted 13-2 against the proposed strike (MTEA Executive Board Minutes, April 22 1974). When MTEA membership voted on the issue two days later, the vote also failed. Though the board recommended that MTEA members send money to HEA and support HEA through its pickets and actions, it would not conduct a solidarity strike. However, not all teachers agreed. As one teacher scribbled on a note clipped to her check to the HEA Donation Fund: 'From a Milwaukee teacher who voted to support your cause. Thoroughly disgusted with the position of the MTEA's executive committee on your strike. Good luck. More money to come.'[8]

Second, it revealed growing antagonism between local unions and the statewide fed-eration. During the spring 1974, members of MTEA's Executive Board had begun question-ing the nature of their relationship with WEAC more generally, and had begun formally discussing disaffiliation. MTEA president Don Feilbach argued his local spent too much money on dues to WEAC for too little in return, and questioned what the additional $40 in dues to WEAC provided to MTEA. Feilbach contended WEAC needed MTEA for its large membership and dues revenue more than MTEA needed WEAC as an organisational, legal or political resource. As he said, 'We are not paying for what we are getting. We are paying five times for it … What Milwaukee has always done is help the state association provide services for the rest of the state' (*Milwaukee Journal Sentinel* 1974).

In addition to an objection based on sheer cost for MTEA members, Feilbach and others in MTEA disagreed with the social justice programme WEAC had begun to develop. Perhaps most significantly WEAC executive secretary Morris Andrews and Wynn had begun to re-consider teacher seniority – a union stronghold issue – in order to prioritise racial integration of teaching staff. This signalled a major pivot in teacher union priorities, from the protection of individual rights to advocating for collective justice. In addition, WEAC had begun to actively engage with a broad range of social issues and educational improvements beyond the struggle for teachers' wages and benefits, organising campaigns for additional state aid for schools, migrant workers' rights, racial integration, neighbourhood action groups and women's rights. Andrews described the reasons for the union's turn towards a social justice mission beyond teachers' material interests. He stated, 'I think we have a responsibility to do this. We have to make sure the teacher fulfils the role of making the democratic process work' (Bednarek 1974).

The political vision of the leadership of the statewide union marked a significant reworking of the racial contract embedded within education and unionism alike (Mills 1997; Glenn 2002; Fletcher 2008; Leonardo 2013). Teachers' employing contracts, a staple of liberal accords, was often used not only to advance teachers' professional rights, but also to provide legal structure for white supremacy, a dynamic made vivid by the Ocean-Hills Brownsville strikes of 1968 (Podair 2002; Perlstein 2004; Perillo 2012): white teachers increasingly turned to professionalism's platform of 'transfer' rights to a more specific version: the right to 'transfer-out-of-poor-black-schools.' Even more alarmingly, teachers formed unions as a means to secure legal protection to administer corporal punishment to black students (Dougherty 2004). By the 1950s and 1960s, 'teachers increasingly framed their struggles as one about freedom *from* the influence of black parents and activists' (Perillo 2012, 8). This dynamic was especially true in Milwaukee, which was on its way to becoming the nation's most racially segregated city (Miner 2013).

Don Feilbach, president of MTEA, did not view WEAC's burgeoning social justice mission as the way towards a stronger political environment, but rather a violation of MTEA's 'local control.' MTEA wanted to be able to retain control over all decisions, rather than having the statewide federation set conditions and policies for teachers' units. As MTEA's executive director James Colter claimed, 'At present WEAC wants complete control, whereas Milwaukee and other urban affiliates want to make decisions within their local jurisdiction' (Rosario 1974). Milwaukee in particular felt it had sufficient power on its own, deeming the benefits of joining the statewide federation irrelevant. Echoing eerily similar arguments to those deployed by the Hortonville school board, who wanted local control over education in order to protect the town from outsiders such as teachers and unionists, the Milwaukee teachers' unions used the idea of 'local control' as a way to justify the protection of MTEA's autonomy from the state federation's political project (*Milwaukee Journal* 1974).[9]

Yet, MTEA's desire for 'local control' was coded with a growing sense of 'freedom from' – that is, freedom from anti-white supremacy and legal forms of redistribution and recognition – echoing a mounting conservatism (Foner 1999; Mohan and Stokke 2000; Apple 2006; Anderson 2015). In Hortonville, rural conservative forces argued for local control of school districts to guard against outsiders and calls for higher taxes. In Milwaukee, local control was used to protect political conservatism of those who were not willing to adhere to the social justice oriented political programme of the statewide federation. In both rural and urban cases, calls for 'local control' excluded possibilities for broader, widespread solidarity, or, the willingness to surrender immediate short-term advantages for the sake of a longer-term, more egalitarian advantage. Therefore, the union's turn to a rights bestowed by 'local control' created a number of problems on its own, exacerbating – not correcting – the errors of liberalism (Lichtenstein 2002). In the case of the Hortonville strike, it exacerbated internal contradictions within teachers' unions, specifically along race, the value of affective labour and unions' power to strike.

Competing understandings of the statewide teachers' union strategy was evident in a public discussion between WEAC leadership and MTEA members in May 1974 about the impacts of statewide affiliation impacted MTEA. Although MTEA members were concerned that WEAC affiliation would mean that 'the state will come in and tell [MTEA] what to do,' Wynn and Andrews corrected this position, reassuring members that WEAC wanted Milwaukee to be a powerful local and for teachers to have power over their working conditions. However, they disagreed with the MTEA's understanding of local control, particularly given MTEA's commitment to use local control as a means to avoid school integration. Frustrated with MTEA's resistance towards enacting socially progressive policies, Andrews bemoaned: 'Milwaukee should be a powerful local. Things should have been done in social issues. Power is only what you chose to do with it. MTEA evidently doesn't want to use theirs' ("Riverside Meeting Minutes, May 7" 1974).

The decision of large locals like MTEA to not to support the strike changed the calculation for teachers from smaller locals. For teachers in small-school districts who empathised with Hortonville teachers, the contractual illegality of striking was secondary to the need to stand up for their collective rights. As one teacher bluntly put it, 'I think when you're down, you got nothing to lose.'[10] Madison attorney John Lawton, whose firm represented the Wisconsin Council of Country and Municipal Employees, the State Employees Union, as well as police officers, fire-fighters and teachers, commented on the particular vulnerability of small-school districts to take job actions. He said,

> In an urban area which is somewhat labor oriented, it's very unlikely a municipal employer would attempt such a thing. The size of the work force, the skills involved, and community attitudes – all are important. I think it does put the small union in a small town and rural area at a terrible disadvantage. (Hinant 1976)

A teacher from Germantown, Wisconsin described the impacts of the large-district's vote against the sympathy strike on small-school districts, noting that the loss of solidarity from the larger school districts weakened the impact of small schools' actions:

> See, I come from an association of about 70 people, less than what Hortonville has. And there's a lot of insecurity when you only have got seventy people … But at least what you people have is, you're working with numbers. And I think looking from the small schools stand point, when we saw that, well, Milwaukee isn't going to go out and a couple of the other

larger schools aren't going to go out, you're kind of sticking your neck out, because you don't know how many other people are going to go out.[11]

In response to this failed vote, WEAC announced a major strategy shift: away from direct action strategies, and towards legal advancements. As HEA President Mike Wisnoski stated, 'We will lobby to get legislation which will assure that the Hortonville situation will never happen again, and seek financial support for upcoming litigation' (*The Racine Journal Times* 1974b). WEAC president reflected upon the failed solidarity strike vote and announced that the teachers union would redirect its strategy towards legal advocacy rather than direct action.

> We would hope that the public would understand that our concern for the Hortonville teachers have not died, but rather has turned in another direction. We have been in the courts and we will be in the courts. We will be at the Legislature so that they can understand that the law under which we find ourselves working is a deformed law and needs to be changed. (Holter 1999)

After Hortonville: the rise of opportunism

Over the next months, WEAC mobilised members and lobbyists to advance legislation to resolve bargaining impasses without striking, primarily through provisions of compulsory interest arbitration.[12] As a public radio broadcaster, Ed Hinshaw, announced the weekend after the failed solidarity strike,

> The Hortonville school strike leaves us with one – and only one – solid, positive development. It is the clear demonstration of the uselessness of the state law on collective bargaining for public employees. The law simply does not work … The problem with the law is that it has no method of forcing agreements between the unions and public boards and councils. The solution is painful, but obvious. The state must create a system of compulsory mediation and arbitration to resolve those disputes which cannot be settled at the local level. (Hinshaw 1974)

Under these provisions, a neutral third-party sets the terms of a new contract, rather than disputing the existing contract, a procedure known as grievance arbitration. Interest arbitration is generally considered to be a legal alternative to a strike (Anderson and Krause 1987). In Wisconsin, this legal provision was first granted to police officers in 1972. In 1975, when it was proposed to extend to teachers and other municipal employees, urban and rural teachers in Wisconsin showed divided support.[13]

Labour scholars frequently credit the event in Hortonville as a decisive factor in securing interest arbitration for public-sector employees. However, Hortonville also constitutes a concrete pivot in the strategy of teachers' unions towards legislative channels as the best means to recognise their rights, rather than building the solidarity and militancy of teachers. Indeed, Wisconsin's unique political and legislative support of public-sector unionism provided a strategic context for public-sector unions to secure their legal survival, without having to risk more Hortonvilles. While this calculation may have granted short-term legal safety for the labour movement, it failed to develop stronger forms of labour organising – workers' power to dialogically determine their interests and develop widespread solidarity with other workers and community members to transcend the narrow and economic interests of employers, be they businessmen or administrators.

It represented a shift from understanding the important labour mechanisms of striking and bargaining as rights enjoyed by workers, to privileges granted by politicians and judges (Burns 2014). It also abandoned the formation of the collective identity of teachers as workers capable of exercising a political voice that is publicly recognised and valued. It side-stepped the question of teachers' right to strike, and therefore de-centered both the solidarity and collective identity necessary for effective job actions, and importantly, for the issues that are central to teachers' lives as workers, such as the need for just compensation for their affective labour and for programmes of racial solidarity. Finally, it minimised the legitimacy of teachers' independent rights as care workers,

The neoliberal logics of collective action

WEAC's shift in strategy represents what political sociologists Claus Offe and Helmut Wiesenthal (1980) call an opportunistic logic of collective action. For Offe and Wiesenthal, opportunism is the tendency for working-class organisation to move along parliamentary and electoral channels to gain power, strategically self-limiting the means and forms of struggles. They characterise opportunism in three mains ways. First, it typically inverts means and ends, pursuing institutional and readily available mechanisms, over the organisational priorities. Second, opportunism prioritises short-term gains over long-term struggles and consequences. Finally, opportunism focuses on quantitative factors, such as number of supportive votes, recruits or financial contributions, rather than qualitative factors, such as the formation and expression of collective identities (Somers 1994; Melucci 1995).

Put briefly, Offe and Wiesenthal suggest opportunism is both a rational and unstable system for working-class organisations. Working-class organisations, Offe and Wiesenthal remind us, derive their primary power from: (1) their ability to democratically and deliberatively determine their interests and priorities; and (2) their ability to withhold their labour, through systematically organised job actions such as strikes. Yet in order to successfully bargain demands, such organisations must often concede this broader power to actualise the specific demands. This creates a contradictory moment for working-class organisations. They must simultaneously develop democratic strengths and militancy amongst its members – what Offe and Wiesenthal calls its 'dialogic power' – to suggest a sufficient threat to the employer at the bargaining table. But they must simultaneously concede this power in order to maintain the organisational legitimacy and achieve bargaining successes.

As Offe and Wiesenthal suggest, organisations must make their survival 'as independent as possible of the motivation, the solidarity, and the "willingness to act" of the members,' making a transition to opportunism necessary, as it is 'neither threatens the survival of the organisation, nor interferes with its chance of success' (Offe and Wiesenthal 1980). To conduct the opportunist transformation, unions must substitute external survival guarantees for the internal sources of power and dialogic logics. Notably, these guarantees are typically accorded when social democratic parties are in power, especially when these parties are both willing and able to provide institutional support and sanctions. This, Offe and Wiesenthal point out, is a very rational solution to the problems of working-class collective action. Yet, it is also unstable, for it moves the provision of working-class power to an external source, rather than an internal one. Put simply, the organisation is no longer able to 'guarantee the guarantees,' but instead relies up on the state to do so. When political conditions shift, as they nearly always will, the organisation is significantly weakened, posing long-term instability in the opportunistic strategy. In order to overcome this instability, organisations must re-orient their strategy to their key power elements – the willingness of members to act – in a wider terrain of political, legal and institutional arrangements.

Conclusion

Wisconsin's statewide teachers' union's, WEAC, shift towards legal and electoral channels after the failed solidarity strike post-Hortonville exemplifies Offe and Wiesenthal's notion of opportunism. First, WEAC inverted means and ends. It decided to pursue the swelling tide of legal support for public-sector unions by advancing interest arbitration lobbying, instead of advancing the underlying struggle: whether or not teachers have a right to strike, and how to build solidarity for such a struggle. Second, it prioritised the short-term gains of legislative action, rather than the long-term struggle to secure democratic and collective voice of teachers in their workplace. Finally, it abandoned the deeper dynamics developing in Hortonville: teachers' understanding of themselves as workers standing in solidarity with each other, amidst a broader social context. As Joseph McCartin highlights, advancing claims for justice through appeals to rights alone can easily be countered by counter rights claims (McCartin 2012). For example, the right to unions has been successfully countered by a call for a right to freedom from unions (e.g. 'right to work'). Or in the case of Hortonville, potential allies in the Milwaukee teachers' union can also adopt the claim to 'local control' used by the conservative school board.

The central issue raised by the Hortonville strike was what form of voice and action are legitimately available to teachers, or more bluntly, whether or not teachers should strike. This issue is grounded in a larger set of questions about the need for a strong public education system, as well as the type of public voice legitimately available to care workers. In the face of violent repression, hostile administrators and weak solidarity among rural and urban unions, the statewide teachers' organisation consolidated their energy and tactics, and turned towards external provisions to secure the rights of teachers. This adoption of opportunism rationally looked to the sympathetic state to preserve teachers rights, by mandating interest arbitration as a bargaining impasse technique when it became evident that local school boards and administrators may not actually respond to teachers' attempts to bargain.

However, as the recent political climate suggests, turning to the state alone to recognise the rights of public-sector employees, much less the central issues of public education, can be an unstable solution, as it depends on the nature of the reigning political power. This article shows that teachers' union attempts to *maximise* their political power vacated the potential to *reconfigure* their political power in the face of rising conservatism. As a result, the union was not able to create a new political discourse that: valorised teaching work as a form of public care labour; bolstered the rights of teachers' unions to strike; developed solidarity with other teachers around the state; and reformed the educational racial contract. To this day, the costs of not having such a political vocabulary remains high.

Re-examining the 1974 Hortonville teachers' strike suggests that in order for teachers' unions to resist the inequalities imposed by neoliberalism, they must overcome the limitations of liberalism. They must reckon with the liberalism's rights-based discourse and its imposed contradictions, specifically along race, care work and unions' power to strike. Teachers' unions will need to reconfigure their power in ways that value the affective components of teachers' work, rather than bending to the contours of neoliberal pressures.

Notes

1. Oral History Interview with Ed Golnick, Tape 4/Side 1, WEAC Records, WHS.
2. Also, see 'Oral interview with Hortonville teachers, Tape 38/Side 1, WEAC Records, WHS' for a longer discussion of Hortonville's alternative and experimental pedagogies.
3. Oral interview with Hortonville teachers, Tape 38/Side 1, WEAC Records, WHS.
4. Oral interview with self-identified vigilantes. Tape 56/Side 1, WEAC Records, WHS.
5. Golnick, Tape 4/Side 1, WEAC Records, WHS.
6. Oral interview with Hortonville mill-owner, Tape 54/Side 1, WEAC Records, WHS.
7. Oral interview with Hortonville teachers, Tape 38/Side 1, WEAC Records, WHS.
8. Un-authored letter, Disaffiliation folder, MTEA Archives.
9. Interestingly, despite MTEA's calls for devolved democratic control, internally they operated using representational system. Only building representatives, for example, were allowed to vote to in disaffiliation debate, leaving the majority of the 5800 teachers in the district without 'local control.'
10. Oral interview with Hortonville teachers, Tape 38/Side 1, WEAC Records, WHS.
11. Oral interview with unidentified teachers from Chippewa Falls, Germantown, and Stanley, Tape 45/Side 2, WEAC Records, WHS.
12. Notably, an assembly bill (AB 758) proposed in 1974 would have legalised strikes for public-sector employees, provided they notify the employer ahead of time they intended to strike. The bill, however, did not pass.
13. The provision of interest arbitration remained contested for other reasons beyond its alternative to a strike – many school teachers felt it gave employers and school boards the upper hand in bargaining. For more details on this debate, see (*Stevens Point Daily Journal* 1977).

Disclosure statement

No potential conflict of interest was reported by the author.

References

"1974 Hortonville Strike". 1974. Wisconsin Educational Associational Council Records, Wisconsin Historical Society.

Abel, Emily K., and Margaret Nelson, eds. 1990. *Circles of Care: Work and Identity in Women's Lives*. Albany: State University of New York Press.

Anderson, Elizabeth. 2015. "Equality and Freedom in the Workplace: Recovering Republican Insights." *Social Philosophy and Policy* 31 (2): 48–69.

Anderson, Gary, and L. M. Donchik. 2014. "Privatizing Schooling and Policy Making: The American Legislative Exchange Council and New Political and Discursive Strategies of Education Governance." *Educational Policy*: 1–43. doi:10.1177/0895904804270777.

Anderson, Arvid, and L. A. Krause. 1987. "Interest Arbitration: The Alternative to the Strike." *Fordham Law Review* 56 (2): 153–179.

Antonucci, Mike. 2015. "Teachers Unions at Risk of Losing 'Agency Fees': Friedrichs V. California Teachers Association Could Fundamentally Alter the Education Labor Landscape." *Education Next* 16 (1): 22–29.

Apple, Michael W. 2006. *Educating the 'Right' Way: Markets, Standards, God and Inequality*. 2nd ed. New York: Routledge.

Apple, Michael W., and Anita Oliver. 1996. "Becoming Right: Education and the Formation of Conservative Movements." *Teachers College Record* 97 (3): 419–445.

Appleton Post-Crescent. 1973. "'Yes' Vote Campaign Mapped on Hortonville School Referendum," October 11.

Appleton Post-Crescent. 1974. "Democrats Back Teachers," May 5.

Ball, S. J. 2007. "Education Plc: Understanding Private Sector Participation in Public Sector Education." http://www.tandfebooks.com/doi/pdf/10.4324/9780203863701?isOnline=false#page=444.

Barrington, Ray. 1979. "Hortonville Teachers' Strike: The Memory Lingers On." *Oshkosh Advance-Titan*, March 15.

Bartlett, Lesley, Marla Frederick, Thaddeus Gulbrandsen, and Enrique Murillo. 2002. "The Marketization of Education: Public Schools for Private Ends." *Anthropology & Education Quarterly* 33 (1): 5–29.

Bednarek, David. 1974. "WEAC Tackling Wider Issues." *Milwaukee Journal*, May 7.

Bell, Deborah E. 1985. "Unionized Women in State and Local Government." In *Women, Work, and Protest: A Century of US Women's Labor History*, edited by Ruth Milkman, 280–299. Boston, MA: Routledge & Kegan Paul.

Burch, P. 2006. "The New Educational Privatization: Educational Contracting and High Stakes Accountability." *Teachers College Record* 108 (12): 2582–2610.

Burns, Joe. 2014. *Strike Back: Using the Militant Tactics of Labor's Past to Reignite Public Sector Unionism Today*. Brooklyn, NY: Ig Publishing.

Compton, Mary, and Lois Weiner, eds. 2008. *The Global Assault on Teaching, Teachers and Their Unions*. New York: Palgrave Macmilliman.

Cowie, Jefferson. 2010. *Stayin' Alive: The 1970s and the Last Days of the Working Class*. New York: The New Press.

Cowie, Jefferson. 2016. *The Great Exception: The New Deal and the Limit of American Politics*. Princeton, NJ: Princeton University Press.

Cucchiara, Maia, E. Gold, and E. Simon. 2011. "Contracts, Choice, and Customer Service: Marketization and Public Engagement in Education." *Teachers College Record* 113 (11): 2460–2502.

Dougherty, Jack. 2004. *More Than One Struggle: The Evolution of Black School Reform in Milwaukee*. Chapel Hill: University of North Carolina Press.

Fletcher, Bill, Jr. 2008. *Solidarity Divided: The Crisis in Organized Labor and a New Path toward Social Justice*. Berkeley: University of California Press.

Foner, Eric. 1999. *The Story of American Freedom*. New York: W.W. Norton.

Fraser, Nancy. 1989. "Talking about Needs: Interpretive Contests as Political Conflicts in Welfare-state Societies." *Ethics* 99 (2): 291–313. http://www.jstor.org/stable/2381436.

Fraser, Nancy. 1997. *Justice Interruptus: Critical Reflections on the "Postsocialist" Condition*. New York: Routledge.

Fraser, Nancy, and Axel Honneth. 2003. *Redistribution or Recognition? A Political-philosophical Exchange*. London: Verso.

Glenn, Evelyn Nakano. 2002. *Unequal Freedom: How Race and Gender Shaped American Citizenship and Labor*. Cambridge, MA: Harvard University Press.

Gutstein, E., & Lipman, P. 2013. "The Rebirth of the Chicago Teachers Union and Possibilities for a Counterhegemonic Education Movement." *Monthly Review* 65 (2): 1–12.

Hagopian, Jesse, and John T. Green. 2012. "Teachers' Unions and Social Justice." In *Education and Capitalism: Struggles for Learning and Liberation*, edited by Jeff Bale and Sarah Knopp, 141–175. Chicago, IL: Haymarket Books.

Hardt, Michael. 1999. "Affective Labor." *Boundary 2* 26 (2): 89–100.

Hensel, Patricia. 1974. "Strike at Hortonville: Clashes Continue." *The Milwaukee Journal*, April 14.

Hinant, Mike. 1976. "Hortonville Case Opinions Are 'Cautious.'" *Appleton Post-Crescent*, June 20.

Hinshaw, Ed. 1974. "Public Broadcast Comments." Hortonville Files, Milwaukee Teachers Education Association Archives, May 1.

Hirschman, Albert O. 1970. *Exit, Voice, and Loyalty; Responses to Decline in Firms, Organizations, and States*. Cambridge, MA: Harvard University Press.

Holter, Darryl, ed. 1999. "The Hortonville Teachers' Strike of 1974." In *Workers and Unions in Wisconsin: A Labor History Anthology*, 240–243. Madison: State Historical Society of Wisconsin.

Holzman, Seymour. 1972. *IGE: Individually Guided Education and the Multiunit School*. Washington, DC: National School Public Relations Association.

"Hortonville – Summary of Litigation." 1974. Hortonville Files, Milwaukee Teachers Educational Association Archives.

"Hortonville Education Association Strike Timeline." 1974. Folder 5, Box 29. Wisconsin Educational Council records, Wisconsin Historical Society.

"Hortonville Fact Sheet." 1974. "Hortonville Strike" Folder 5, Box 29, Wisconsin Educational Associational Council records Part 1, Wisconsin Historical Society.

"Hortonville Picket Line Song-Sheet." 1974. "Hortonville Strike" Folder 5, Box 29, Wisconsin Educational Associational Council records Part 1, Wisconsin Historical Society.

"It Happened in Hortonville." 1974. Wisconsin Educational Associational Council Records, Folder 5, Box 29 of the WEAC Collection, Wisconsin Historical Society.

Kostogriz, Alex. 2012. "Accountability and the Affective Labour of Teachers: A Marxist-Vygotskian Perspective." *Australian Educational Researcher* 39 (4): 397–412. doi:10.1007/s13384-012-0072-x.

Lee, John. 1973. "Close Vote Seen on Hortonville's $2.2 Million School Project Issue." *Appleton Post-Crescent*, October 16.

Lee, John. 1975. "HEA to Move Offices to Appleton." *Appleton Post-Crescent*, June 4.

Leonardo, Zeus. 2013. "The Story of Schooling: Critical Race Theory and the Educational Racial Contract." *Discourse: Studies in the Cultural Politics of Education* 34 (4): 599–610.

Lichtenstein, Nelson. 2002. *State of the Union: A Century of American Labor*. Princeton, NJ: Princeton University Press.

Lieberman, Myron. 2000. *The Teachers Unions: How They Sabotage Educational Reform and Why*. San Francisco, CA: Encounter Books.

Lipman, Pauline. 2011. *New Political Economy of Urban Education: Neoliberalism, Race and the Right to the City*. New York: Routledge.

Lynch, Kathleen, John Baker, and Maureen Lyons. 2009. *Affective Equality: Love, Care and Injustice*. New York: Palgrave Macmilliman.

McCartin, Joseph A. 2006. "Bringing the State's Workers in: Time to Rectify an Imbalanced Labor Historiography." *Labor History* 47 (1): 73–94. doi:10.1080/00236560600385934.

McCartin, Joseph. 2008a. "Turnabout Years: Public Sector Unionism and the Fiscal Crisis." In *Rightward Bound: Making American Conservative in the 1970s*, edited by Bruce J. Schulman and Julian E. Zelizer, 210–226. Cambridge, MA: Harvard University Press.

McCartin, Joseph. 2008b. "A Wagner Act for Public Employees: Labor's Deferred Dream and the Rise of Conservatism, 1970–1976." *The Journal of American History* 95: 123–148.

McCartin, Joseph. 2012. "Beyond Human Rights: Understanding and Addressing the Attack on Public Sector Unions." *Human Rights Review* 13: 399–403.

McRobbie, Angela. 2010. "Reflections on Feminism, Immaterial Labour and the Post-Fordist Regime." *New Formations* 70: 60–76.

Melucci, Alberto. 1995. "The Process of Collective Identity." In *Social Movements and Culture*, edited by Hank Johnston and Bert Klandermans, 41–63. Minneapolis: University of Minnesota Press.

Mertz, Adam. 2015. "The 1974 Hortonville Teachers' Strike and the Public Sector Labor Dilemma." *Wisconsin Magazine of History* 98: 1–13.

Milliren, Ann. 1974. "A Parent's View of Hortonville." Hortonville Files, Milwaukee Teacher Educational Association Archives.

Mills, Charles W. 1997. *The Racial Contract*. Ithaca, NY: Cornell University Press.

Milwaukee Journal. 1974. "City Teachers Votes on State Union Won't Count," May 9.

Milwaukee Journal Sentinel. 1974. "Teachers Break from WEA Seen," March 14.

Miner, Barbara. 2013. *Lessons from the Heartland: A Turbulent Half-century of Public Education in an Iconic American City*. New York: The New Press.

Moe, Terry. 2011. *Special Interest: Teachers Unions and America's Public Schools*. Washington, DC: Brookings Institution Press.

Mohan, Giles, and Kristian Stokke. 2000. "Participatory Development and Empowerment: The Dangers of Localism." *Third World Quarterly* 21 (2): 247–268.

MTEA Executive Board Minutes, April 22. 1974. Milwaukee Teachers Educational Association Archive Collection.

"National Hortonville-Timberlane Adopt-A-Teacher Program." 1974. Hortonville Files, Milwaukee Teacher Educational Association Archives.

Offe, Claus, and Helmut Wiesenthal. 1980. "Two Logics of Collective Action: Theoretical Notes on Social Class and Organizational Form." *Political Power and Social Theory* 1 (1): 67–115.

Perillo, Jonna. 2012. *Uncivil Rights: Teachers, Unions, and Race in the Battle for School Equity*. Chicago, IL: University of Chicago Press.

Perlstein, Daniel H. 2004. *Justice, Justice: School Politics and the Eclipse of Liberalism*. New York: Peter Lang.

Podair, Jerald E. 2002. *The Strike That Changed New York: Blacks, Whites and the Ocean Hill-Brownsville Crisis*. New Haven, CT: Yale University Press.

Rafferty, Max. 1974. "Strike Backlash." *Richardson Daily News*, August 18.

"Riverside Meeting Minutes, May 7". 1974. Building Representative Meeting Minutes, Milwaukee Teachers Educational Association Archives.

Rodger, Daniel T. 2011. *Age of Fracture*. Cambridge, MA: Harvard University Press.

Rosario, Aenone. 1974. "Local, State Teachers Association Split Seen." *Milwaukee Courier*, May 11.

Rousmaniere, Kate. 2005. *Citizen Teacher: The Life and Leadership of Margaret Haley*. Albany: State University of New York Press.

Saltzman, G. M. 1986. "A Progressive Experiment: The Evolution of Wisconsin's Collective Bargaining Legislation for Local Government Employees." *Journal of Collective Negotiations in the Public Sector* 15 (1): 1–25.

Scott, Janelle. 2009. "The Politics of Venture Philanthropy in Charter School Policy and Advocacy." *Educational Policy* 23 (1): 106–136. http://epx.sagepub.com/content/23/1/106.short.

Scribner, Campbell. 2013. *The Exurban Exchange: Local Control of Education on the Metropolitan Fringe, 1945–1980*. Madison: University of Wisconsin, Madison.

Shelton, Jon K. 2013. *'Against the Public': Teacher Strikes and the Decline of Liberalism, 1968–1981*. College Park: University of Maryland.

Sherman, Diane. 1974. "Emotions as Well as Issues Led to Hortonville Impasse." *The Capital Times*, April 29.

Slater, Joseph. 2004. *Public Workers: Government Unions, the Law and the State, 1900–1962*. Ithaca, NY: Cornell University Press.

Somers, Margaret R. 1994. "The Narrative Constitution of Identity: A Relational and Network Approach." *Theory and Society* 23: 605–649.

Stevens Point Daily Journal. 1974. "Teachers Urged Not to Join Sympathy Strike," April 23.

Stevens Point Daily Journal. 1977. "Passage Seen for Public Employee's Arbitration Bill," April 4.

The Racine Journal Times. 1974a. "Teacher Picketing Injunction Asked," April 18.

The Racine Journal Times. 1974b. "State Protest Canceled; Hortonville Focus Shifts," April 26.

The Racine Journal Times. 1974c. "Strike," April 28.

Uetricht, Michael. 2014. *Strike for America*. New York: Verso.

"WEAC Staff Updates". 1974. Hortonville Files, Milwaukee Teachers Educational Association archives.

Weiner, Lois. 1996. "Teachers, Unions, and School Reform: Examining Margaret Haley's Vision." *Educational Foundations* 10 (3): 85–96.

Weiner, Lois. 2012. *The Future of Our Schools: Teachers Unions and Social Justice*. Chicago, IL: Haymarket Books.

Gettin' a little crafty: Teachers Pay Teachers©, Pinterest© and neo-liberalism in new materialist feminist research

Elizabeth A. Wurzburg

ABSTRACT

In this paper, I share data from a year-long study investigating the manifestations of neo-liberalism in the working lives of five women elementary school teachers in the United States. I discuss how gendered discourses of neo-liberalism construct what is understood as possible in the material-discursive production of the women's subjectivities concerning a surprising market created by teachers for teachers that is largely promoted through the social media site, Pinterest©: Teachers Pay Teachers©. Utilising new materialist feminist theory [Braidotti, R. 2000. "Teratologies." In *Deleuze and Feminist Theory*, edited by I. Buchanan, and C. Colebrook, 156–172. Edinburgh: Edinburgh University Press; Dolphijn, R., and I. van der Tuin. 2012. *New Materialism: Interviews & Cartographies*. Ann Arbor, MI: Open Humanities Press], I analyse how the teachers intra-act [Barad, K. 2007. *Meeting the Universe Half Way: Quantum Physics and the Entanglement of Matter and Meaning*. Durham, NC: Duke University Press] with curricular material actants [Bennett, J. 2010. *Vibrant Matter: A Political Ecology of Things*. Durham, NC: Duke University Press] that have the capacity to alter the course of events in women's work and lives. I argue that these material actants further entangle the material-discursive, virtual-real production of subjectivity and influence women teachers in variegated but particularly gendered ways that ultimately reinforce emerging theories around the gendered nature of neo-liberal subjectivity [Gill, R. 2008. "Culture and Subjectivity in Neoliberal and Postfeminist Times." *Subjectivity* 25 (1): 432–445. doi:10.1057/sub.2008.28; Walkerdine, V. 2003. "Reclassifying Upward Mobility: Femininity and the Neo-liberal Subject." *Gender and Education* 15: 237–248. doi:10.1080/09540250303864].

Joplin and I sat in her fifth-grade classroom at Creekveiw Elementary School.[1] The students had left for the day, and she was giving me a tour of her classroom via her pointed finger while we remained seated at children's desks in the middle of the room. While this was only our second meeting for the purposes of this study, I'd been in this space many times before, as Joplin and I were colleagues during my five years teaching fifth grade at Creekview and remained friends after I no longer taught elementary school.

However, with each bulletin board she described, each buzzword she used and each resource she explained, I became increasingly aware that I no longer recognised this once-familiar space. It was not so much the aesthetics of her classroom that had changed, but it was instead the curricular materials and educational resources she described that were completely unfamiliar to me. She continued showing me around her classroom using new words such as *strategy groups* and *task cards*. This language confused me.

Thinking it must be the result of some new textbook or computer-based resource due to the recent implementation of the Common Core State Standards (CCSS),[2] I asked her to tell me more about the curriculum they were using. She immediately replied, 'The [Common Core] standards are the curriculum ... The only curriculum we've got is the standards.' She elaborated in telling me how the school district provided pacing guides detailing when each standard for each subject was to be taught but how the curricular materials she and her colleagues used to plan and implement instruction was increasingly *not* provided by the district. In other words, even though the standards driving the mandated content had changed over the past school year, the district had not purchased new textbook series to address the new standards. Teachers were instructed to retrofit the textbook series and curricular resources that were aligned with the former state standards to the new standards when possible and to supplement with other resources where it was necessary so that they could address content that was not required under the former set of standards.

Adequately creating materials for the content that was previously taught in other grade levels proved to be extremely time-consuming, and Joplin told me that she refused to work the extra and unpaid hours, as it required to produce materials for four reading groups on a daily basis in addition to the other four subject areas she was responsible for teaching. As a result, she had begun using more of her own money than she had in previous years to buy curricular materials to teach the required standards/curriculum. In describing the process of gathering materials to teach the new CCSS she said, 'So then I got a little crafty, and I was like screw it, I'm just going to start buying things on Teachers Pay Teachers' – which was a marketplace I had never heard of before. As Joplin got up to retrieve and subsequently discuss an at least three-inch thick binder full of Teachers Pay Teachers[©] (TpT[©]) lesson plans (each of which contain *task cards* that focus on a particular skill that is to be used in a *strategy group*), I realised that the work of teaching at Creekview had changed significantly since my departure just two short years before. As I continued discussions about their working lives with more teachers, I soon found out that the work of teaching had changed in other places too and that Joplin was not the only one getting 'a little crafty' in obtaining curricular materials.

Context of the study

Over the past several decades, neo-liberalism has significantly shifted sociopolitical landscapes on a global scale (Harvey 2005; Ong 2006; Klein 2007; Steger and Roy 2010; Peck 2013). The impacts of neo-liberalism specific to educational institutions, policies and discourses have been widely theorised in contexts outside of the United States (e.g. Davies 2005; Davies and Bansel 2007; Duncan 2007; Watkins 2007; Connell 2008; Ball 2012) as well as within the United States particularly around education policy (e.g. Bartlett et al.

2002; Taubman 2009; Baltodano 2012; Costigan 2013; Gabriel and Lester 2013). Relatedly, there is an emerging body of scholarship theorising the gendered nature of neo-liberalism and neo-liberal subjectivities (e.g. Walkerdine 2003; Walkerdine and Ringrose 2006; Gill 2008), and it is important for feminist educational researchers to further investigate how this gendered nature of neo-liberalism manifests itself within the subjectivities available to women broadly conceived as well as the overwhelmingly feminised teaching force in potentially problematic ways. Indeed, Gill (2008) speaking to the gendered subject of neo-liberalism posits, 'Further exploration of this intimate relationship is urgently needed to illuminate ... contemporary neoliberal social relations' (443).

This neo-liberal subjectification in addition to the pervasive and persistent 'bad teacher' narratives within media and popular discourses (Kumashiro 2012; Goldstein 2014) as well as the myth that 'since women can now do anything, only the least able become teachers' (Maher and Tretreault 2000, 199), it appears as though women teachers in neo-liberal times are up against seemingly impossible odds. Taking a nuanced look at the working lives of women teachers within localised contexts can tell us a great deal about how gender and neo-liberalism are operating within not only these localised contexts but also potentially more broadly as well.

The well-established bodies of scholarship around the history and impacts of the feminisation of the work of teaching (Grumet 1988; Nias 1989; Biken 1995; Munro 1998; Bartky 1990), the impacts of capitalism on teaching (Giroux and McLaren 1988; Apple 2001; Saltmarsh 2007; Sleeter 2008; Casey 2013), and the relationship that exists between the two (Apple [1986] 1988; Weiler, 1988; Luke 1992; Coffey and Delamont 2000; Miller 2005) significantly informs the research on neo-liberalism, gender and teaching presented in this study. However, it is important to acknowledge that while neo-liberalism is an extension and intensification of capitalism in the arenas of policy formation, ideological discipline and modes of internalised governing (Connell 2008; Foucault [2004] 2008; Brown 2015), neo-liberalism and capitalism are by no means interchangeable entities. As such, the analysis presented here is situated against the backdrop of this scholarly work around capitalism, gender and teaching as well as the literature concerning neo-liberalism and teaching and seeks to extend these analyses considering the ways in which discourses of neo-liberalism are particularly gendered and functioning in the working lives of teachers.

There are very few studies investigating the manifestations of neo-liberalism in the daily lives of teachers in the United States (see Duncan 2007; Watkins 2007; Ball and Olmedo 2013 for examples of this type of analysis). I contend there is a need to investigate the entanglement of gendered and neo-liberal discourses from the ground-up perspective of women teachers, as material and discursive entities produce the conditions for what becomes possible in how people might live (Foucault [1984] 1997; St. Pierre 2004; May 2005). Through this investigation, we can also look for ways of resisting damaging subjectification that is often implicit in the gendering effects of neo-liberal discourses.

In this paper, I share data from a year-long study investigating the sociopolitical, embodied, discursive and material manifestations of neo-liberalism in the working lives of five women elementary school teachers in the Southeastern United States. One aim of this study was to theorise how gendered and neo-liberal discourses contribute to what counts as *good enough* in teaching while simultaneously producing and upholding the pervasive yet impossible subject position of the *good enough (woman) teacher*. The concept of the good enough teacher serves as an analytical tool for deconstructing and problematising the impossible situations in which teachers find themselves in current sociopolitical contexts and is further discussed throughout this paper.

Early in the course of the study, conversations with participants revealed a surprising market created by teachers for teachers that is largely promoted through Pinterest[©]:[3] TpT[©]. I discuss data from interviews and websites concerning TpT[©] and Pinterest[©] to provide an example of one way neo-liberalism manifests itself in the gendered work of teaching as well as its role in persistently making over what counts as good teaching.

I use new materialist feminist theory (Braidotti 2000; Dolphijn and van der Tuin 2012) to analyse how women elementary school teachers *intra-act* (Barad 2007) with curricular *material actants* (Bennett 2010) produced for and consumed via TpT[©] and argue that these material actants have the capacity to alter the course of events in teachers' lives. Further, these material actants, which are most often obtained in the technological spaces of Pinterest[©] links to TpT[©], further entangle the material-discursive and virtual-real production of subjectivity and influences women elementary school teachers in variegated but particularly gendered ways that ultimately serve to reinforce feminist understandings of neo-liberal subjectivity (Walkerdine 2003; Gill 2008). In later sections of the paper, I describe new material feminism and the unique analytical perspective it offers around the mutual constitution of material and discursive entities (Barad 2007). But I first outline the methods of data generation and provide a briefly introduce the participants in this study.

Methods of data generation and participant overview

As discussed above, this paper analyses data from a broader study around the gendered nature of neo-liberalism and its manifestations in the work of teaching. Once I obtained approval from the institutional review boards at both my university and the local school district, I began the process of soliciting participants via email communication with three local school administrators with whom I was personally acquainted asking them to distribute my initial invitation to participate in the study to teachers who worked in their schools. As a result of the initial email solicitation, all three administrators agreed to distribute the letter of invitation, and five teachers from two schools, Creekview and Townsend Elementary Schools, ultimately agreed to participate. Figure 1 provides general information about each teacher.

Because Creekview was one of the schools in which I worked during my career as a teacher, three participants were former colleagues of mine. These interpersonal relationships are important to note because they impacted my position as a researcher as well

Participants	Years of Experience	Current School	Years at Current School	Highest Degree
Gretta	15	Creekview Elementary	15	Educational Specialist
Joplin	8	Creekview Elementary	8	Masters
Natasha	17	Townsend Elementary	4	Masters
Rose	6	Creekview Elementary	6	Doctorate
Taylor	5	Townsend Elementary	3	Masters

Figure 1. General information about study participants.

as the conversations that were possible with each participant in unique ways. Specifically, I was a participant in Rose's doctoral study, so she readily volunteered to participate. Another participant, Joplin, and I stayed in touch after I left teaching to pursue graduate work full time and often had discussions about her work and life, so our conversations for this study were familiar and comfortable from the start. Finally, I knew Gretta from our experience as colleagues from my earliest days teaching. Joplin, Rose, Gretta and I had a foundation upon which to begin our discussions and each of the women were eager to share their opinions about the state of education in both local and national contexts.

I did not personally know Natasha and Taylor who worked at Townsend Elementary prior to beginning the study. Much of our time together in the beginning of the study was spent getting to know each other and building trusting relationships. Both Natasha and Taylor seemed to become comfortable in our conversations after the first few meetings, and they each noted how they looked forward to what they called our bi-weekly 'therapy' sessions.

While each of the women in the study at one point or another discussed engagement with Pinterest[©] and TpT[©], Joplin, Rose and Taylor are centred in this analysis, as they were most actively engaged in the buying and selling on TpT[©]. I can conjecture several reasons for their engagement including but not limited to years of experience and age. Gretta and Natasha had been teaching many years longer than the other participants, and they had saved curricular materials from over the years that they could use as supplemental resources. They were also hesitant to consider purchasing curricular materials with their own money. It is also possible that Joplin, Rose and Taylor being in their 30s are demographically situated in an age range more likely to engage the social media space of Pinterest[©], which is the primary advertising platform for TpT[©] sellers.

Pinterest[©] and TpT[©]

Pinterest[©] is a popular social networking site outnumbered only by Facebook[©] and Twitter[©] in its number of users (Phillips, Miller, and McQuarrie 2013) (Figure 2).

Based on techniques of collecting *ideas* or *things* made possible by constructing bulletin boards, collages or scrapbooks, Pinterest offers a virtual space to construct similar collections but in the context of the practically infinite space of the Internet. The overwhelmingly feminised user base uses the application to 'pin' images on different 'boards' about topics in which they are interested. The user-created boards on Pinterest[©] house images about topics ranging anywhere from decorating ideas to recipes to inspirational quotes – and pretty much anything else imaginable.

For example, a user who is a teacher might go to Pinterest[©] for ideas about lesson planning, bulletin boards and classroom décor in addition to other 'Pinteresting' topics relevant to them such as parenting advice, party planning or gardening. A teacher looking for specific lesson ideas could enter a search for it using keywords such as '5th grade math fractions ideas.' Like Google[©], Pinterest[©] will suggest other typical words or categories that complement, extend or narrow the search. Once users decide on a search, they scroll through pictures in the results and decide which ones to pin on the board titled to describe the topic at hand on their personal Pinterest[©] page. The boards on a

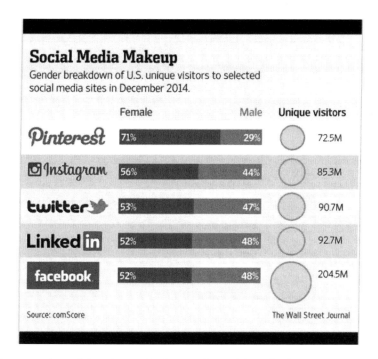

Figure 2. Data on unique visitors by gender for popular social media sites.

user's page-make-up projects, products or ideas that users think is appealing in some way. Users can also follow other people's boards and 'like' their pins similar to how one might 'like' a post on Facebook© or 'favorite' something on Twitter© (Figure 3).

Soon after beginning this study, I decided to try using Pinterest© myself. At the time, I was teaching math to a group of four home school students ranging from fifth to ninth grade one day per week. I thought trying Pinterest© might provide me with new instructional ideas from the perspective of a practicing teacher as well as prove beneficial in my upcoming conversations with women elementary school teachers regarding the possible influence of Pinterest© in their teaching lives. In learning to use Pinterest© from the perspective of a teacher, I began to recognise three prominent types of pins regarding teaching: curricular materials such as lesson plans and anchor charts, classroom décor such as themed classroom bulletin boards and matching door decorations, and inspirational or funny quotes about teaching (Figure 4).

Through searching for curricular materials to support my instruction with my home-school students, I noticed that many resources that seemed like they may be helpful almost always linked to TpT© website, and I was reminded of the conversation I had with Joplin described above and other conversations that I had with other women teachers in my study. In finding out more about this website that seemed to keep coming up, I learned that TpT© is an online, user-generated marketplace where merchants who are almost always teachers upload and sell lesson plans for other teachers to purchase.

Users can choose to filter content by categories such as grade level, subject area and price. Each seller is scored by consumer rankings from one to four stars, and shoppers

Figure 3. Personal Pinterest© page that was used when looking for materials to support instruction.

can create wish lists much like any other retail site. TpT© 'makes "resource sharing" into a full-featured shopping experience, where teachers can simultaneously be an entrepreneur and a customer' (www.edsurge.com, 2014). Additionally, it is widely recognised

Figure 4. Two screenshots from the TpT© website.

among TpT© sellers that the primary and 'required' (www.tptschool.com, 2014) marketing tool for TpT© merchants is Pinterest©. According to blogger, author and teacher Chris Kesler who after selling on TpT© for a little over a year was making '4-figure monthly pay-checks' (www.tptschool.com, 2014), Pinterest© is essential in driving

> the majority of traffic to TpT. You can't upload a product and expect it to take off if you're relying on the TpT search function to get it noticed. Pinterest is my only method of marketing, so I'm really deadly serious about it. (www.tptschool.com, 2014)

In other words, it is common knowledge among TpT© merchants that Pinterest© is essential to a successful business.

Success on Pinterest© can mean six figure salaries for teachers previously making a mere fraction of that annually. For example, Deanna Jump, a private school kindergarten and first-grade teacher (who continues teaching in Georgia, USA) has made over a million dollars selling lesson plans on TpT©, and the newly appointed CEO of TpT© (formerly the CEO of Etsy.com©) does not think the revenue will slow down any time soon (http://mashable.com/2012/05/17/teachers-pay-teachers/). He describes the TpT© market as 'massive and growing' as the site possesses over 22 million pieces of educational material that have generated over $86 million dollars in revenue since the site's launch in 2006 (http://mashable.com/2012/05/17/teachers-pay-teachers/).

The implications for such phenomenon seemed potentially wide reaching and game changing concerning the work of teaching. While millions of people participate in social media on a daily basis, there is almost no literature discussing social media and teaching. I was interested in finding out if and how the social media site Pinterest© was influencing the working lives of the women teachers in my study. Based on my own experiences and with the ultimate aim of informing broader questions of how neo-liberalism influences the subjectivity of women elementary school teachers, I anticipated that TpT© might come up in discussions with participants about Pinterest©. However, I was surprised when four out of five of the women in the study mentioned Pinterest© or TpT© before I asked specifically about either one.

For example, TpT© came up three times in my first interview with Rose, another fifth-grade teacher at Creekview with whom I had also worked previously. As a part of the first discussion with each participant, I asked about general background information such as how and when each of them decided to become teachers, their experiences as a teacher such as describing a typical day at work, and their lives outside of work such as social supports and roles outside of teaching.[4] When I asked Rose to tell me about her responsibilities outside of work, she mentioned schoolwork for her doctoral degree, household chores, weekend festivals where she promoted and sold a children's book that she authored, and complicated family relationships with her parents, sister and niece. In addition to each of these responsibilities, she concluded by adding, 'I opened my teachers pay teachers store – which is really exciting because even though I'm only making, like, 30 cents, 50 cents at a time, I'm still just – the fact that someone else wants my stuff – I like that.'

Rose mentioned TpT© a second time when I asked her to walk me through a typical day in her life in noting that on any given day she might make a new lesson for her TpT© store. She brought up TpT© a third time when I asked about when she feels most accomplished. Rose began by explaining that she has 'different definitions of accomplishment for everything' that she does. After explaining what makes her feel accomplished as a partner, an author, a doctoral student and as a teacher and colleague, her voice got louder and more lively as she concluded by describing accomplishment as a TpT© seller:

> Seeing the email from teachers pay teachers saying, 'Congratulations! You've made a sale on Teachers Pay Teachers!' I'm like, *Yes!* That feels like a *huge* accomplishment, you know? I don't know why. That's so weird, because it's like, 30 cents. [laughing] Seriously. But its just that whole: I've made something, do you want it? *Yes! I want that.*

After explaining that earning 30-cents selling one TpT© lesson felt like more of an accomplishment than selling 9 of her books totalling approximately $130 in earnings at a recent weekend festival, Rose comments on how she is not quite sure why she felt this way. Then, in theorising why the feeling she gets when selling lesson plans as a teacher might be different than the feeling she gets when selling books as an author, Rose continued,

> It's very foreign to me from a teacher's point of view. Cause, I get it as an author, but that's a different – That's a different me. You know? And so … from a teacher's perspective, I'm making these things and other teachers want it – for their classroom. I'm like, *Okay!* Like, that feels really good.

For Rose, selling lesson plans is seemingly more valuable than selling copies of her book because even though it might provide less money per transaction, there is something about successfully selling the TpT© lessons that makes her feel more accomplished. It was as though, for Rose, authors were *supposed* to make money selling their books, but teachers, on the other hand, were not supposed to make money selling lesson plans. However, if they did, as she had selling lesson plans on TpT©, that was in many ways going above and beyond the expectations she had for herself as a teacher. Promoting educational materials on Pinterest© to subsequently sell on TpT© was rewarding for Rose in a significantly different way than other types of teaching-related work accomplishments. The personal satisfaction Rose experienced becomes more intelligible when presented within the context of neo-liberal subjectivity.

Neo-liberal subjectivity

Following feminist educational scholars Walkerdine (2003) and Davies (2005), I use the term *neoliberal subjectivity* to refer to what Foucault ([2004] 2008) described as a fundamental shift from earlier classical liberal understandings of the *homo economicus* in that with neo-liberalism, labourers are no longer considered separated from labour power but are considered 'active economic subject[s]' (Foucault [2004] 2008, 223). With this shift, the 'wage is an income, not the price at which he sells his labor power' (223). With this economic analysis of labour, the neo-liberal subject embodies 'capitalization of existence itself' (Davies and Bansel 2007, 252), and 'the new worker is totally responsible for their own destiny and so techniques and technologies of regulation focus on the self-management of citizens to produce themselves as having the skills and qualities necessary to succeed in the new economy' (Walkerdine 2003, 240).

In other words, neo-liberal subjectivity is legitimised through the production of an individual who is capable of responsibly choosing the most efficient means to market oneself in ways that will be most economically profitable. On the one hand, with liberal ideology, workers were produced in the image of the factory so that they were efficient in their work while they were in the enclosed spaces of the factory. On the other hand, with neo-liberal ideology, an income includes a wage but also extends beyond the money a person makes to include the subject positions that become available through their work – subject positions that, in the case of teachers creating curriculum for individual monetary profit, were formerly only available to textbook publishers or other educational companies who sell curricular materials. Additionally, neo-liberal work is no longer enclosed in spaces like the factory because neo-liberal societies are not closed off by space and time. Workers can always check their email, work from home and produce income outside of any fulltime job.

With this understanding of neo-liberal subjectivity, Pinterest© is an interesting and important site of study concerning teaching, as images in the form of *pins* overwhelmingly link users to websites where they can purchase the items being pinned. With the understanding that the neo-liberal subject is considered most successful when they properly 'sell' themselves, it becomes possible to recognise different explanations for Rose's feelings of accomplishment than otherwise could have been imagined.

Rose was no longer just another teacher who sells her labour power in exchange for the wage provided through the work of teaching. She instead was distinguished from other teachers with the same educational qualifications and pay grade because she had successfully sold lessons that were unequivocally hers to other teachers who, by way of their purchasing power, had proven that they wanted what she had to offer.

As I became more familiar with TpT© via Pinterest©, I realised that Rose and other teachers like her were at the forefront of creating and maintaining what counts as *good enough*[5] in elementary school teaching. I was learning to recognise what 'Pinterest worthy' classroom materials looked like, and if teachers could not re-create these ideas because of lack of ability or time, they could still gain access to *good enough* – if they were willing and able to pay for it. In the next section, I discuss new material feminist theory and why it is useful in analysing the material and embodied production of what counts as good teaching within neo-liberalism and neo-liberal subjectivity.

New material feminist theory

New material feminist theory is a recent hybridisation of post-structural and feminist theory that allows researchers to remain committed to feminist understandings of embodied materiality while simultaneously drawing from post-structural understandings of discourse, power and space. Specific to the data presented here, new material feminist theory offers interesting ways to think about how virtual spaces like Pinterest© and TpT©, as well as materials such as lesson plans and student activities, have the capacity to alter what teachers understand as possible in the production of their subjectivity. The user-generated search results found on Pinterest© that link to a teacher's TpT© store produce conceptual and literal re-configurations of teachers' understandings of what counts as *good enough* within the context of teaching. This version of neo-liberal subjectivity is constantly in motion through material and discursive collisions and negations – or what has been called *intra-action* (Barad 2007; Taguchi 2012) in new materialist feminist research.

Barad (2007) defines the concept of *intra-action* as 'the mutual constitution of entangled agencies' (33), so in the example presented above, technology (that is most often, by the way, accessed via smartphones and tablets which are increasingly considered necessary appendages to the body) provides access to a kind of monetary and professional satisfaction previously unavailable. In other words, through intra-action with products she sells on TpT©, discourses of neo-liberalism, and her virtual production of subjectivity, it became possible for Rose to experience a new kind of accomplishment.

Taguchi (2012) extends the concept of intra-action in positing that intra-active entities are 'understood *not* to have clear or distinct boundaries from one another' (271, emphasis in the original). In new materialist feminist research there are no subject/object, no mind/body, no material/discursive binaries, as none of these entities have predetermined agency outside of intra-action. Drawing again from Rose's feelings of accomplishment produced when she was notified that another teacher purchased her lessons on TpT©, it was the combination of the lesson plan, the TpT© website, the Pinterest© application where she advertises her lessons, the email notification from the TpT© website and the monetary reward intra-acting in that moment to produce the feeling of accomplishment she described – an event that none of the events or materials could produce without their intra-action with the others.

With the continuously moving target of what counts as *good enough* in teaching and the shiftiness inherent in neo-liberal subjectivity, it is increasingly difficult to pin down exactly how various material-discursive entities operate in the lives of women elementary school teachers. In other words, the target of *good enough* follows the pattern of the neo-liberal, capitalist education market's perpetual changing requirements because this change fuels the need for an endless supply of products to buy and sell. With new materialist feminist theory, subjectivity is understood as always *becoming* (Deleuze and Guattari [1980] 1987) through *intra-actions* (Barad 2007) with technological, material, discursive, virtual and spatial apparatuses in unpredictable ways, prompting new material feminist Braidotti (2000) to call for 'new frames of analysis' (163) that might be capable of analysing this more rhizomatic understanding of subjectivity. This call is particularly timely for me as a researcher who is interested in studying the material effects of discourse in women's lives to investigate the macro- and micro-levels of critique that might create the conditions necessary for women teachers to imagine and thus create more equitable and ethical ways of being and knowing both within and against neo-liberal modes of governance.

Finally, as I discuss below, pin boards on Pinterest© along with lessons and activities sold on TpT© contribute to the production of the subjectivity through what new material feminists have called *material actants* (Bennett 2010). These non-human material actants can produce a shift that changes what becomes possible. In this onto-epistemological re-configuring, a person's knowing-through-being is altered through an ongoing process of *becoming* (Deleuze and Guattari [1980] 1987). In other words, the entanglement of the ethics of knowing and being is continuous in how we live together in the world. As Goodings and Tucker (2014) have pointed out, 'Socially mediated bodies emphasise the ways that technologies ... have the capacity to shape people, places and things through the joint enactment of humans and technologies' (40).

Put another way, subjectivity and agency in new material feminist theory are understood as part of the ongoing process of *becoming* (Deleuze and Guattari [1980] 1987; Ivinson and Renold 2013). While a subject cannot rationally *will* her own becoming (as she exists only with other material and discursive entities), subjects *can* experience a shift in what Foucault ([1976] 1990, 93) has called their *grid of intelligibility* – what they understand to be thinkable and thus possible. These moments of imagining the previously unimaginable lead to the ability to think and thus live differently. In what follows, I describe how the materials on TpT© change what counts as *good enough* in teaching in neo-liberal times.

In the next section, I return to Joplin's explanation of her intra-actions with TpT© which produced very different effects than those described by Rose. Then I turn to another participant, Taylor, who also had intra-actions with TpT© materials in her experiences teaching fifth grade at Townsend Elementary, another school in the same district as Creekview.

Teachers talk about materials

Like my first interview with Rose, TpT© came up in my first discussion with Joplin as well, but Joplin mentioned Rose in response to my asking what she does when she has time for herself. She began by explaining that she usually does not take work home on the weekends and continued:

> This is what I'm doing now. Instead of trying to create things – Cause I have found that is not my strong suit: creating meaningful activities. I have started to buy tons of crap off of Teachers Pay Teachers and today I spent $20 … Now, Rose goes home and creates things to put on Teachers Pay Teachers … But if I can use somebody else's stuff that is good, I will do that now. I am not … I'm [laughing] – I pay for stuff.

Because Joplin does not feel like she is good at 'creating meaningful activities,' she turns to purchasing them instead. Additionally, she brings up the fact that her colleague, Rose (who is discussed above) has her own TpT© store implying that she is good at creating meaningful activities. Further, she makes it clear that she does not spend her time on the weekend creating activities.

Joplin mentioned both Rose and TpT© again in our second meeting for this study. As described in the opening section of this paper, she first discussed using TpT© as her way of getting 'crafty' in coming up with lesson planning since it has in her opinion become increasingly difficult to find curricular materials to support her instruction since the implementation of the new CCSS curriculum. Later in that same discussion, I pointed out that when she, Rose and I worked together that we almost never bought curricular materials with our personal money. We sometimes bought supplies required for lessons such as food items or brought things from home like extra construction paper, but I could not recall a single time that any of us bought formal curricular materials such as worksheets or practice activities either in a store or online. I was curious about this shift to purchasing lesson plans. She responded:

> I needed stuff like this [pointing down to the thick binder filled with lessons and *task cards* that go with each lesson], and then I just kind of felt like Rose makes these great freaking lessons [when she's] in charge of writing and stuff, and I was in charge of the reading, and I just didn't feel like they were up to par, so I just got on Teachers Pay Teachers and I'm like, look at all this stuff. I'm just going to buy it.

The fifth-grade teachers at Creekview divided the lesson planning among each member of the team with one or two people working to plan each subject area. Each Tuesday, all grade-level teams across the school met to discuss pedagogical strategies that might be needed to enhance or extend the lessons each teacher had already planned for the upcoming week, and lesson plans were due to administration by 4 p.m. each Friday for the following week. In her statement above, Joplin feels like her lessons for reading are not 'up to par' with Rose's lessons in writing. Wanting to be an equal contributor to the team lesson planning, she began buying lessons on TpT[©].

Trying to find out more, I asked her if anything had changed as far as the curricular materials the district provided and if she thinks that any of these changes had anything to do with her shift to buying lesson plans. She responded,

> I mean, even I thought this would be good' as she points to a workbook-style resource that the district did, in fact, purchase for the 5th grade students in lieu of another previously provided resource that teachers did not find useful at all. She continues explaining that she thought that as a result of the new resource she wouldn't 'have to buy anything.

However, the workbook turned out to be not as useful as the team thought it would be in addressing the required standards. Joplin compared it to a Basal reader and explained, 'I guess I just don't like Basals.' Then, turning to the binder of TpT[©] resources she continues, 'And who is going to make task cards on a certain – I mean, I could do this. I'm not going to do it. Rose would do it. Because she's creative like that. I would not do it.'

Of course, teachers have always bought supplies such as books, markers, glue and paper with their own money. The difference in the current technological and neo-liberal context is that the curricular materials are not the only things for sale. The teaching materials being created, bought and sold via Pinterest[©] and TpT[©] are bound up in the discursive production and maintenance of what counts as *good enough* in teaching which is ultimately bound up in the very subjectivities of women teachers buying, selling, pinning and creating lesson plans on TpT[©]. Again, teachers have always created lesson plans that they possibly shared with colleagues or their entire district of teachers or maybe even the state department of education.

However, with the understandings of success outlined in neo-liberal subjectivity, teachers' intra-actions with curricular materials via Pinterest[©] and TpT[©] provide a wider audience of customers within this specialised market. In other words, those who have the necessary extra resources can buy access to what counts as the *good enough* teacher within neo-liberal educational discourses. Further, it is not just the materials that are being bought, but an image of who gets to count as good enough in addressing mandated standards.

Joplin introduced me to the idea that good teaching is something that can be bought. She positions herself as being able, but unwilling to put the extra time into creating lessons that she thinks will be perceived as up to par or *good enough* within the context of the Common Core Standards, her students and fellow teachers. Joplin approached the pressure to produce curricular materials as a task that she could forgo by purchasing meaningful activities instead of creating them.

Another participant, Taylor, also bought lessons from TpT[©]. She made it clear from the very first interview that her 11-month-old child was her top priority and that she definitley relies more on her teammates more than before for lesson planning ideas. At the time of our third meeting, it was nearing the end of the school year and Taylor talked a lot about being reflective around that time of year and how she was thinking about how to do things better next year. She comments that on the one hand, 'good instruction takes planning' but on the other how she was 'tired of finding things' – meaning curriculum materials. She continues, 'Granted, you're never going to find a textbook or anything that has everything, or has it all the way you want it to, but it sure would be a starting point.'

When I asked her if she used TpT© in planning her instruction, she responded, 'Oh, god yes. Bless the people who have the time to put things on that website. It's a beautiful thing.' She continues, 'I have definitely found task cards from Pinterest – Like somebody pinned it on their board and then the link takes you to Teachers Pay Teachers ... ' As she trails off she gets up and points me to at least six piles of laminated envelopes stacked behind her desk in crates. The sheer number of these envelopes shocked and perplexed me[6] (Figure 5).

Taylor explained that each of these envelopes contained lessons she has bought on TpT© to use,

> because we have limited resources – because we, in the year 2014, still have to find all of our goddamn resources ... Mary [her teammate] and I have bought a lot [of lessons off of Teachers Pay Teachers©] ... I don't have to make it, but I still have to assemble it.

She continues discussing how her teammate, Mary, makes lessons to sell on TpT©. I ask how her teammate finds the time to make all the lessons, pin them on her Pinterest© page and then sell them in TpT© store. Taylor responds, 'Well, its like if she's making them, you might as well make money for it.'

Figure 5. Photograph of some of Taylor's TpT© lessons.

In this way, Pinterest$^©$ turns out to be understood as empowering for many teachers who share ideas that people like and make money for these ideas in return. Their ideas are *valued* in ways they might not be in the school or classroom (or other places in their lives). It could be argued, on the one hand, that this is one way teachers are resisting neo-liberal policy initiatives that strip funding for public services like education to in turn, pad the pockets of corporations providing consultation services, curricular materials and testing products. Following this rationale, teachers selling lesson plans could be understood as simply finding a way to take their own cut of the public money that is being funnelled into the private sector. Many teachers could see this as an opportunity to finally be compensated for the hours of formerly unpaid labour time spent developing lessons and activities after school. It also provides a way for teachers who do not feel as creatively inclined to have access to new ways of conceiving how to teach a particular lesson on a particular topic.

However, on the other hand, as Connell (2008) points out, 'Neoliberalism seeks to make existing markets wider, and to create new markets where they did not exist before' (175). Further, 'Markets are often presumed to be gender-neutral, and the neoliberal agenda should in that case have the effect of eliminating gender inequalities, over time' (Connell 2008, 177). With this, teachers have in fact created a market where it did not previously exist, and even though TpT$^©$ has recently added a purchase ordering option so that schools can buy lessons with tax dollars, the overwhelming majority of customers on TpT$^©$ are teachers spending their own money to purchase curricular materials for their classrooms. In this context, the emergence of TpT$^©$, as a source of producing both income and curricular resources, has fulfilled twin needs.

Further, the teachers who *do* somehow find the time and energy to work this second job communicate a sense of accomplishment in the moments when as Rose put it, 'someone wants my stuff.' TpT$^©$ signals a dimension of entrepreneurial opportunity related to the profession of teaching that is entirely new, as the act of producing curriculum has not previously been conceived in terms of either its monetary value or in terms of the personal satisfaction of creating a product that someone else is willing to spend money to get. Teachers are all of a sudden thrust into a profitable domain previously limited to the sphere of textbook producers and curriculum writers. This supports Connell's understanding of neo-liberalism extending the market into previously unexplored domains.

However, this issue is further complicated for both the buyer and the seller. According to another participant, Greta, schools are beginning to tell teachers that the lessons they produce are not their own because they fall under intellectual property rights of the district. Additionally, teachers buying materials from TpT$^©$ have to agree that they will not share the lessons they have bought with anyone else, so while some women teachers who are Pinterest$^©$ users produce themselves online via the Pinterest$^©$ boards they construct based on the pins of others, others are pinning items they personally create and then intend to sell in the market of TpT$^©$.

Implications

The technological space of Pinterest$^©$ and the site of each TpT$^©$ store intra-acts with the curriculum materials being put up for sale and the very subjectivity of the teacher who makes these materials available. With this gendered production of subjectivity within the context of neo-liberal education, she is not only constructing the teaching materials, but these material actants work, at the same time, on the material and discursive production of her subjectivity. This perpetual making-over of what counts as good teaching influences how other women and teachers produce and makeover themselves. In other words, for many women on Pinterest© selling items in TpT©, these material actants represent part of 'who they are' or who they want to be in the case of teachers who purchase rather than sell curricular materials. And within the context of neo-liberalism, these gendered and neo-liberal subjectivities are constructed as freely chosen and even sometimes empowering. Whether the teacher is buyer or seller, each teacher participating in Pinterest© boards about teaching and TpT© is continuously reproducing or making over what counts as good enough in teaching through representations of who they want to be and how these *things* could help them makeover their lives as teachers – even if that means making enough money to leave the teaching profession all together.

Feminist educational scholars Walkerdine and Ringrose (2006) have theorised how women are overwhelmingly the subjects called on to re-make themselves and how the idea of the makeover is different within neo-liberal discourses. They posit, 'The makeover is hardly new, but we would argue that these incitements have intensified and work in important ways to normalize the neo-liberal ethos of continuously maximizing, bettering and reinventing the self' (36). While women have practically always been the ones who are called upon to monitor themselves in addition to the material objects in their immediate surroundings, what is different with neo-liberalism is that women are not only being acted upon and disciplined by these external material actants but they are also taking part in this disciplining through the active production of themselves as the idealised feminine subject who is understood to be 'empowered' by the ways she 'chooses' to present herself in both real embodied ways and in virtual ways in online spaces. In neo-liberal discourses, empowerment and choice are held up as endless opportunities. However, feminists have pointed out how this discourse around empowerment and choice only works to further narrow the choices available to women (Walkerdine and Ringrose 2006; Gill 2008).

While the work of curricular production via Pinterest© and TpT© provides feelings of empowerment for some teachers, it serves to marginalise others who either do not feel like their curricular materials are *good enough* to post on TpT© or simply do not have or prefer to give the time it takes to essentially work this second job. Further, it also marginalises teachers who do not have the means to purchase these additional curricular materials. There are potentially damaging consequences for teachers when what counts as *good enough* can be bought because the women who cannot afford to purchase these materials or have time to produce 'Pinterest worthy' lessons may ultimately not have access to what counts as *good enough* in teaching.

Additionally, TpT© provides an example of teacher subjectivity is constructed and perpetually made-over through intra-action of these material and discursive productions. The highly visual space of Pinterest© and TpT© is online for anyone to view, thus the good enough teacher subject position that is both produced and maintained through these resources could potentially drown out other ways teachers are able to feel successful in their jobs.

Finally, this paper highlights just how swiftly *good enough* targets change or get made-over within the context of neo-liberalism. The vast differences in curricular materials from 2011 to 2014 at Creekview Elementary demonstrates how the moving targets of good enough are increasingly modelled after moving targets in the market, for both women and teachers. These perpetual changes that require women to consistently revise and reimagine how to be successful in their work and lives has very real implications for women teachers. Participants engaged in conversations about products many of them look at all the time without thinking about the ways they impact their lives because it is easy to get swept up in discourses of *good enough* and other enticing aspects of neo-liberalism's elusive grasp. I have noticed a similar trend with my teacher education students, and I am personally committed to assisting preservice teachers in questioning what counts as *good enough* in teaching and who gets to decide.

Understanding what becomes (im)possible in the lives of women using the conceptual tool of intra-action helps new materialist feminist researchers see the convergence of forces at work on and through the production of women's bodies and subjectivities against the particular backdrop of the gendered nature of neo-liberalism. Researchers interested in opening up more ethically oriented possibilities for how women teachers might live in neo-liberal society, must therefore persistently question and critique how neo-liberalism gets normalised in the work of teaching. Through this persistent critique, we can push back against neo-liberalism and offer more possibilities for what counts as *good enough* for women teachers.

Notes

1. All participants and school names are pseudonyms.
2. While not technically a requirement, many states applying for and receiving Race to the Top grants included the implementation of CCSS in their applications. Ultimately, forty-two of the 50 states in the United States have adopted the CCSS (www.corestandards.org).
3. Pinterest[©] is a social media website and smartphone application that allows users to browse content using a search function. All content are images that often link to an external website. Users then 'pin' images to their boards which they can sort by areas of interest. Figure 2 is a screenshot of a board on Pinterest.
4. Though I knew both Rose and Joplin prior to the study, I asked each participant the same questions in the first interview. These questions can be found in Appendix.
5. I have elsewhere (Author) theorized the *good enough teacher* subject position within the context of the neo-liberalisation of education. The *good enough teacher* is what Walkerdine (2003) calls an 'impossible subject position' that is nonetheless constantly 'held up as possible.' The *good enough* teacher discourse is further maintained through the production of curricular materials, as discussed here.
6. Figure 5 is a photograph of some of Taylor's TpT[©] lessons. It was her idea to spread them out as they are in the image. She, too, seemed surprised at the amount of the floor in her classroom they covered, as she ran to get Mary to show her.

References

Apple, M. [1986] 1988. *Teachers and Texts: A Political Economy of Class and Gender Relations in Education*. New York: Routledge.

Apple, M. 2001. *Educating the Right Way: Markets, Standards, God, and Inequality*. New York: Routledge.

Ball, S. J. 2012. *Global Education Inc.* New York: Routledge.

Ball, S. J., and A. Olmedo. 2013. "Care of the Self, Resistance and Subjectivity Under Neoliberal Governmentalities." *Critical Studies in Education* 54 (1): 85–96. doi:10.1080/17508487.2013.740678.

Baltodano, M. 2012. "Neoliberalism and the Demise of Public Education: The Corporatization of Schools of Education." *International Journal of Qualitative Studies in Education* 25 (4): 487–507. doi:10.1080/09518398.2012.673025.

Barad, K. 2007. *Meeting the Universe Half Way: Quantum Physics and the Entanglement of Matter and Meaning.* Durham, NC: Duke University Press.

Bartky, S. 1990. *Foucault, Femininity, and the Modernization of Patriarchal Power. From Feminism and Foucault: Paths of Resistance, L. Quimby & I. Diamond.* Lebanon, NH: University Press of New England. (Reprinted in McCann, C. R. and S. Kim. eds. 2013. *Feminist Theory Reader: Local and Global Perspectives.* 3rd ed. New York: Routledge.

Bartlett, L., M. Frederick, T. Gulbrandsen, and E. Murillo. 2002. "The Marketization of Education: Public Schools for Private Ends." *Anthropology & Education Quarterly* 33 (1): 5–29.

Bennett, J. 2010. *Vibrant Matter: A Political Ecology of Things.* Durham, NC: Duke University Press.

Biken, S. K. 1995. *School Work. Gender and the Cultural Construction of Teaching.* New York: Teachers College Press.

Braidotti, R. 2000. "Teratologies." In *Deleuze and Feminist Theory*, edited by I. Buchanan, and C. Colebrook, 156–172. Edinburgh: Edinburgh University Press.

Brown, W. 2015. *Undoing the Demos: Neoliberalism's Stealth Revolution.* Brooklyn, NY: Zone Books.

Casey, L. M. 2013. "The Will to Quantify: The 'Bottom Line' in the Market Model of Education Reform." *Teachers College Record* 115 (9): 1–7. Accessed July 2, 2014. http://www.tcrecord.org.proxy-remote. galib.uga.edu/library. ID Number: 17107.

Coffey, A., and S. Delamont. 2000. *Feminism and the Classroom Teacher: Research, Praxis, Pedagogy.* New York: Routledge Farmer.

Connell, R. 2008. "The Neoliberal Parent and Schools." *Our Schools, Our Selves* 18 (1): 175–193.

Costigan, A. T. 2013. "New Urban Teachers Transcending Neoliberal Educational Reform: Embracing Aesthetic Education as a Curriculum of Political Action." *Urban Education* 48 (1): 116–148.

Davies, B. 2005. "The (im)Possibility of Intellectual Work in Neoliberal Regimes." *Discourse: Studies in the Cultural Politics of Education* 26 (1): 1–14. doi:10.1080/01596300500039310.

Davies, B., and P. Bansel. 2007. "Neoliberalism and Education." *International Journal of Qualitative Studies in Education* 20 (3): 247–259. doi:10.1080/09518390701281751.

Deleuze, G., and F. Guattari. [1980] 1987. *A Thousand Plateaus: Capitalism and Schizophrenia.* Translated by Brian Massumi. Minneapolis, MN: University of Minnesota Press.

Dolphijn, R., and I. van der Tuin. 2012. *New Materialism: Interviews & Cartographies.* Ann Arbor, MI: Open Humanities Press.

Duncan, J. 2007. "New Zealand Free Kindergartens: Free or Freely Forgotten?" *International Journal of Qualitative Studies in Education* 20 (3): 319–333. doi:10.1080/09518390701281926.

Foucault, M. [1976] 1990. *The History of Sexuality, Volume 1: An Introduction.* Translated by R. Hurley. New York: Vintage Books.

Foucault, M. [1984] 1997. The Ethics of the Concern of the Self as a Practice of Freedom. In *Michael Foucault Ethics: Subjectivity and Truth.* Edited by Paul Rabinow and translated by Robert Hurley et al. (Vol 1 *of Essential works of Foucault, 1954-1984*), 281–301. New York: The New Press.

Foucault, M. [2004] 2008. *The Birth of Biopolitics.* Edited by Michel Senellart and translated by G. Burchell. New York: Palgrave MacMillian.

Gabriel, R., and J. N. Lester. 2013. "Romance Quest of Education Reform: A Discourse Analysis of the *Los Angeles Times'* Reports on Value-Added Measurement Teacher Effectiveness." *Teachers College Record* 115 (12): 1–32.

Gill, R. 2008. "Culture and Subjectivity in Neoliberal and Postfeminist Times." *Subjectivity* 25 (1): 432–445. doi:10.1057/sub.2008.28.

Giroux, H. A., and P. McLaren. 1988. "Teacher Education and the Politics of Democratic Reform." In *Teachers as Intellectuals: Towards a Critical Pedagogy of Learning*, edited by H. A. Giroux, 158–176. New York: Bergin & Garvey Publishers.

Goldstein, D. 2014. *The Teacher Wars: A History of America's Most Embattled Profession*. New York: Doubleday.

Goodings, L., and I. Tucker. 2014. "Social Media and the Co-production of Bodies Online: Bergson, Serres and Facebook's Timeline." *Media, Culture & Society* 36 (1): 37–51. doi:10.1177/0163443713507813.

Grumet, M. R. 1988. *Bitter Milk: Women and Teaching*. Amherst: University of Massachusetts Press.

Harvey, D. 2005. *A Brief History of Neoliberalism*. New York: Oxford University Press.

Ivinson, G., and E. Renold. 2013. "'Valleys' Girls: Re-Theorising Bodies and Ageny in a Semi-Rural Post-Industrial Local." *Gender and Education* 25 (6): 704–721. doi:10.1080/09540253.2013.827372.

Klein, N. 2007. *The Shock Doctrine: The Rise of Disaster Capitalism*. New York: Picador.

Kumashiro, K. K. 2012. *Bad Teacher! How Blaming Teachers Distorts the Bigger Picture*. New York: Teachers College Press.

Luke, C. 1992. "Feminist Politics in Radical Pedagogy." In *Feminisms and Critical Pedagogy*, edited by C. Luke, and J. Gore, 120–137. New York: Routledge.

Maher, F., and M. K. Tretreault. 2000. "Knowledge Versus Pedagogy: The Marginalization of Teacher Education." *Women's Studies Quarterly* 28 (3/4): 194–201. doi:128.192.114.19.

May, T. 2005. *Gilles Deleuze: An Introduction*. New York: Cambridge.

Miller, J. I. 2005. *Sounds of Silence Breaking: Women, Autobiography, Curriculum*. New York: Peter Lang.

Munro, P. 1998. *Subject to Fiction: Women Teachers' Life History Narratives and the Cultural Politics of Resistance*. Philadelphia, PA: Open University Press.

Nias, J. 1989. *Primary Teachers Talking: A Study of Work as Teaching*. New York: Routledge.

Ong, A. 2006. *Neoliberalism as Exception*. Durham, NC: Duke University Press.

Peck, J. 2013. "Explaining (with) Neoliberalism." *Territory, Politics, Governance* 1 (2): 132–157. doi:10.1080/21622671.2013.785365.

Phillips, B. J., J. Miller, and E. F. McQuarrie. 2012. "Dreaming in Pictures: Pinterest and the Visual Imagination." Presentation at the American Academy of Advertising Conference.

Saltmarsh, S. 2007. "Cultural Complicities: Elitism, Heteronormativity and Violence in the Education Marketplace." *International Journal of Qualitative Studies in Education* 20 (3): 335–354. doi:10.1080/09518390701281934.

Sleeter, C. E. 2008. "Teaching for Democracy in an Age of Corportocracy." *Teachers College Record* 110 (1): 139–159.

St. Pierre, E. A. 2004. "Care of the Self: The Subject and Freedom." In *Dangerous Coagulations?: The Use of Foucault in the Study of Education*, edited by Bernadette Baker, and Katharina E. Heyning, 325–358. New York: Peter Lang.

Steger, M. B., and R. K. Roy. 2010. *Neoliberalism: A Very Short Introduction*. New York: Oxford.

Taguchi, H. L. 2012. "A Diffractive and Deleuzian Approach to Analysing Interview Data." *Feminist Theory* 13 (3): 265–281. doi:10.1177/1464700112456001.

Taubman, P. T. 2009. *Teaching by Numbers: Deconstructing the Discourse of Standards and Accountability in Education*. New York: Routledge.

Walkerdine, V. 2003. "Reclassifying Upward Mobility: Femininity and the Neo-liberal Subject." *Gender and Education* 15: 237–248. doi:10.1080/09540250303864.

Walkerdine, V., and J. Ringrose. 2006. "Femininities: Reclassifying Upward Mobility and the Neo-liberal Subject." In *The Sage Handbook of Gender and Education*, edited by B. Francis, and L. Smulyan, 31–46. Thousand Oaks, CA: Sage.

Watkins, M. 2007. "Thwarting Desire: Discursive Constraint and Pedagogic Practice." *International Journal of Qualitative Studies in Education* 20 (3): 301–318. doi:10.1080/09518390701281900.

Weiler, K. 1988. *Women Teaching for Change: Gender, Class, and Power*. South Hadley, MA: Bergin & Garvey Publishers.

Appendix

Thank you so much for agreeing to speak with me! I am excited to begin working together, and I am particularly interested in knowing more about the working lives of women elementary school teachers. If at any time you are uncomfortable answering any of the questions presented, please feel free to decline to answer. Please know that I have been a teacher myself and have the most possible respect and appreciation for your time and responses to the following questions.

Background Information:
- How/When did you decided to become a teacher?
- Thinking back on how you thought teaching would be when you initially decided to teach and the reality you live now, what are some of the main differences?
- Did you ever want to be anything other than a teacher? Tell me about the process of deciding to become a teacher and the struggles/joys around that decision.

The Life of a Teacher:
- What is something you just never have the time left over to do that you'd like to get done?
- What are some things that you have to do that you feel take away from what you'd like to be doing as a teacher?
- Remember a time recently when you've felt appreciated (either by a colleague, a student, an administrator, etc). What did they say or do that made you feel as though you are appreciated?
- Remember a time recently when you've felt underappreciated at work. What happened (what was said or not said/did or not done) that made you feel this way?
- What is the most frustrating part of teaching for you right now?
- What are your other responsibilities (outside of work)?
- Walk me though a typical day in your life.
- What do you love to do when you have free time?
- Who would you say are your main sources of support when you are struggling with balancing it all or when you are having a horrible day?
- What is the most frustrating part of trying to balance work and your other obligations?
- What comes to mind as something you are struggling with right now in balancing all of your roles?
- How do you make time for yourself?
- What do you enjoy doing when you have a free afternoon or evening?
- What does an excellent day look and feel like?
- When do you feel most accomplished?

Neoliberalism and higher education: a collective autoethnography of Brown Women Teaching Assistants

Ileana Cortes Santiago*, Nastaran Karimi* and Zaira R. Arvelo Alicea

ABSTRACT

The neoliberal conceptualisation of institutions of higher education positions them as transnational corporations of knowledge production that sell services internationally. In this context, realities are experienced differently based on attributes such as class, gender, race, region, and increasingly religion. As a result, women in academia, but particularly Brown Women Teaching Assistants (TAs), encounter restrictions in exercising their agency. This systematic *othering* of minority women through unfair assessment of their work and the silencing of their voices leaves them in a de-powered and vulnerable position. As women of colour in higher education, we draw upon comparable and unique life stories as a data source for a *collaborative autoethnography*. Furthermore, we adopt an arts-based lens through which we make sense of our narratives. Our aggregated stories reflect a constant negotiation for status as TAs in business-driven institutions of higher education.

Context and theory

Oftentimes when we think of underrepresented bodies, we envision urban settings in the United States or unjust practices in a faraway land, on the other side of the globe. Some way along this conceptualisation of the *other*, we tend to overlook how our institutions create caste systems that position women, international students, and ethnic, religious, racial, and sexual minorities in the lower tiers (Asmar, Proude, and Inge 2004; Cole and Ahmadi 2003; Gonzalez et al. 2002; Lee and Rice 2007; Seggie and Sanford 2010; Spencer-Rodgers and McGovern 2002). These systems, for the most part, are inconspicuous (see Marginson 2006). In this article, we situate the experiences of minority women teaching assistants (TAs) as examples of othering and existing in the caste system of academia. We also locate these experiences within the broader conversation of the market-driven mentality that has changed higher education. According to this conceptualisation, the university strives to be profitable, knowledge and research are packaged and commercialised as commodities, and people are workers supporting this enterprise (Marginson 2011; Rizvi 2011; Torres 2011).

---

*Both authors are first author.

To recognise these practices at the institutional level, we need to understand the context in which these sites function. The university exists in a global, national, and social milieu that operates alongside politics, the economy, technology, and human movement (Torres 2011). As Marginson (2011) puts it, and certainly as we have experienced it, the very nature of higher education is policy-determined. In fact, education in general cannot be understood without the recognition that educational policies and practices are strongly influenced by an increasingly integrated international economy (Apple 2011).

To further engage with conversations about the complex webs shaping institutions of higher education, we need to conceptualise globalisation in connection with the economy. The concept of globalised educational institutions and discourses was coined after Theodore Levitt's 1985 *globalisation*, where changes in the international economics affecting production, consumption, and investment were described (Spring 2008). Neoliberalism offers a useful lens to understand how globalisation and economics create norms that percolate into public and private institutions (Torres 2011).

The neoliberal conception of globalisation interconnects people, communities, institutions, and governments in a complex set of marketing practices (Rizvi 2011). According to Torres (2011), neoliberal governments promote open markets, global free trade, the reduction of the public sector, decreased state intervention in the economy, and the deregulation of markets. He further argues that globalisation has had a major impact on education, as international institutions promote finance-driven reforms, which often clash with equity-driven ones.

In this landscape, higher education prescribes knowledge and research as products and universities as businesses that aggregate self-interest (Marginson 2011). In the last two decades, universities have been positioned at the forefront of selling services internationally; as such, they have been transformed into transnational institutions of knowledge production, change, distribution, and consumption (Torres 2011). This phenomenon has turned higher education into a robust set of market practices, enabling it to become 'an industry' in which constituencies compete for funds and students (Rizvi 2011). For example, colleges and universities nationwide and internationally are increasingly using marketing slogans such as 'best value for your money' and 'great education at great ticket prices' to attract students, who respond to these discursive strategies. According to Giroux (2002, 426), the aforementioned practices are indicative of 'the dystopian culture of neoliberalism'. Overall, we share a fundamental idea with these scholars: the value of a college education as the pursuit of knowledge and active citizenship has steadily dissipated and has been replaced by competitive models.

In this context, realities are structured and experienced differently around markers such as class, gender, race, region, and increasingly, religion; identities are transformed as individuals build lives in higher education (Apple 2011). In particular, graduate students become low-level wage earners in a corporate enterprise (Torres 2011), who experience exploitative practices at the institutional level (Rizvi 2011). These practices are in direct contradiction with concepts of fairness, inclusion, and social justice, some of the more recent additions to the list of essential tenets of a college education (Brennan and Naidoo 2008). It is in this light that women in academia, particularly Brown Women TAs, are restricted in exercising their agency (Marginson 2012).

This systematic *othering* of minority women through unfair assessment of their work and the silencing of their voices leaves them in a de-powered and vulnerable position.

In their groundbreaking work on gender and racial inequities, Gutiérrez y Muhs et al. (2012) explore the experiences and challenges of women of colour in higher education. As Brown Women TAs pursuing doctoral degrees in a large research-intensive institution, we are increasingly compelled to tell our stories. In this article, we aim to address the following questions: How does the neoliberal mentality of research universities inform our experiences as Brown Women TAs? How do we navigate our responsibilities as teachers while understanding our positionality and value within this system?

Through our narratives, we strive to make sense of our own place in the larger scene of the university as a finance-driven business. Our methodological choice was a means to reclaim our voice in the aforementioned context. Thus, our aggregated or *collective auto-ethnographies* (Cloke, Crang, and Goodwin 2013) further reflect a constant negotiation for status as TAs with limited bargaining power in the stock market we call the university.

Methodology

As academic subjects, we have been socialised to follow strict definitions of research, what it looks like, and who is considered a researcher (Butz and Besio 2004). After years of navigating this academic landscape, engaging with seminal research in our fields, and critically questioning what it means to produce 'valid' research, we began to recognise discourses aiming to connect qualitative research to positivist epistemologies (see Lin 1998). The desire to conform seemed to subtly make its way into conversations, expectations, and even the methods we were to use in our academic work. For peoples whose embodied selves did not fit the definition of the 'Scholar', we found it ever hard to comply, both personally and professionally (Butz and Besio 2004).

The dominant discourse around research contributes to an epistemological stance that favours positivistic notions of research; these approaches, which are perceived to be traditional or canonical, are rooted in European traditions developed during the Enlightenment period, where research could be measured using a predetermined set of standards (Gandhi 1998). These standards continue to be 'The Way' to access and produce knowledge, and academia remains a colonised space reproducing this framework (Marginson 2011). Moreover, there is a gendered bias to this research, as it was developed by a select group of European upper class men whose underlying principle was objectivity (Spivak 2006).

Hence, to decolonise our mindsets and craft the type of work that resonated with our voices, we decided to experiment with alternative approaches. These choices mean that we are given an opportunity to showcase our authentic selves and narratives through research. We are lured by the ingenuity of thinkers whose work challenges ritualistic research that constantly compares itself to a positivistic ideal (Ellis, Bochner, and Adams 2011). Their ideas undergird our intention to write differently and through a rather unorthodox methodology. Such *intentionality* drives the 'consciously driven ideological, political, pedagogical, and theoretical motives behind the desire to tell a chosen story of self' (Rodriguez 2005, 121). As subjective, racialised beings in higher education, we acknowledge these motives and celebrate the agency and authenticity they provide.

Our collective, resonant, and diverse narratives would, at first glance, seem unfit within such prescriptive frameworks. Together and separate, they are not a narrative or a case; rather, they form a collective consciousness of ideas that aim to disrupt the rigidity of dominant structures – the ones that call for predetermined and 'valid' forms of research (Chang, Ngunjiri, and Hernández 2013). It is within these conversations that *autoethnography* becomes a powerful tool to individuals whose voices are often silenced (Young and McKibban 2014), as it happens in the current business-driven university. For instance, the voices of Brown Women TAs do not fit the general conceptions of the 'privileged academic', that is, the white male scholar in the ivory tower (see Waring and Bordoloi 2012). Authoethnography, thus, allows for the careful uncovering and exploration of the intricate stories self-determined by underprivileged, gendered, and racialised individuals (Ellis and Bochner 2006). In other words, it provides an opportunity for the voiceless, a most-needed approach where the researched becomes a researcher with agency and point of view (Ellis, Bochner, and Adams 2011).

It is a scary enterprise, precisely because it dares to defy the privilege of the dominant genres and the construct of the researcher (Roth 2005). As individuals, it provides a canvas for self-reflexivity, determination, and episodic recounting (Ellis, Bochner, and Adams 2011), and as a group of voices, that is, the *collective autoethnography*, it offers a space for convergence of experiences that still maintains the agency and interconnectedness of the self (Cloke, Crang, and Goodwin 2013). A group of brown women doctoral students sitting together, sharing those moments within close-door conversations, is in fact a perfect fit for the construction and reconstruction of collective understandings and divergent moments (Chang, Ngunjiri, and Hernández 2013). This *collective autoethnography* of an Iranian hijabi Muslim woman and two Puerto Rican women, one Catholic and one agnostic, draws upon multiple engaged discussions on student evaluation reports, community-building conversations, reflections on how to improve classroom practice, and a retrospective account of our journeys as TAs in the Midwest. The aforementioned 'data' were the catalyst for profound and vulnerable dialogues where unique and similar experiences ensued.

We acknowledge that autoethnography requires a level of criticality, an authentic exploration of personal biases and negotiation (Ellis and Bochner 2006). Nonetheless, as previously mentioned, our epistemological stance draws upon Kuhn's (2012) scholarship that rejects the notion of an objective 'Truth' accessed by a distant independent researcher. In this paradigm, all research including positivist ones are biased in nature, as they are filtered through a human being. Hence, our attempt to decolonise knowledge includes accepting and claiming the biases inherent to research. Thus, we draw upon reflection as a means to embrace this subjectivity in both research and practice.

In general, Zeichner's (2014) approach to reflection guided our dialogues and conversations; during these times, we posited questions and considered the personal, pedagogical, and socio-political dimensions of being a Brown Woman TA. This method encouraged us to explore the multiple layers that compose our narratives while offering a framework for the in-depth analysis of our experiences. Moreover, the reflective process assisted us in improving our teaching at multiple levels which, combined with autoethnography as methodological approach, offered a unique lens to problematise our experiences from an educator's standpoint (Jacobs 2005; Zeichner 2014).

In this article, the unfolding ethnographic accounts are shaped by *microaggressions*, or subtly discriminatory statements, that are presented as creative devices and intermissions showcasing our lived tensions and disruptions (Lee and Rice 2007; Wing Sue 2010). Student evaluations, lived experiences, and collective reflections serve as our data sources for the excerpts and interregnums that highlight and complement important moments in our narratives. We intentionally repurpose and appropriate student evaluations, the only source that is not self-developed and serves as a seminal assessment of our perceived value as TAs. It is no secret to women of colour what these evaluations can do to our professional identity and future opportunities (see Lazos 2012). Thus, we approach our analysis of these evaluations as an opportunity to tell a different side of the story.

Embracing our liberal arts backgrounds as English educators, we further position our story within a complex discourse that engenders feelings of frustration, shame, isolation, guilt, and confusion, as we crafted research creatively. In this context, we also recognise autoethnography's value as a tool for critical self-reflection that connects individuals with a system of dominant ideologies where questions such as 'maybe I am doing something wrong?' are challenged (see Rodriguez 2005). In conjunction, our methodology and theoretical framework provide the conditions to position and improve our practice with the understanding that our future and success will always be anchored in a system that is not in our favour. Thus, authentic professional learning goes beyond the personal and cannot be disengaged from the larger socio-political context (Gutiérrez y Muhs et al. 2012).

We recognise the privilege that accompanies those of us who have made it to the ivory tower. Beyond recognising such advantage, we understand the importance of ethical considerations. In our case, we must be aware of a possible us-versus-them binary creation that can oversimplify the complexity of lived experiences; for instance, we do not wish to antagonise our students but to position them, and their perspectives, as part of a larger systemic conversation that creates castes of people (see Gutiérrez y Muhs et al. 2012; Rodriguez 2009). Garnering our stories also brings to light other people who are part of them; to care for their well-being, we consciously de-identified information that could connect to specific individuals. We embrace the professional risk associated with autoethnographic work, as we see vulnerability as an integral aspect of growth (see Waring and Bordoloi 2012). We hope that sharing our stories as political, cultural, and social selves can help other Brown Women TAs feel validated and positioned as subjects with agency to claim their voice and ameliorate the negative assumptions that can curtail their success.

Arts-based research

To further question the structural positivism prevalent in educational research and enhance our current approach of autoethnographic work, we draw upon components of *arts-based research* (Barone and Eisner 2012; Finley 2008, 2014). Our work embeds poetic devices and related techniques as meaningful 'research tools' that can showcase complex messages. Similar to autoethnography, which acknowledges emotionality as a form of knowing, *arts-based research* uses a multiplicity of artistic mechanisms to convey the emotive quality of human experience (Faulkner 2009). In our stories, these cases would include the ephemeral moments of covert and overt discrimination and their connection with systemic injustices (see Finley 2014).

Arts-based research interjects and complements autoethnographic work. Artistic techniques provided us with the opportunity to creatively explore meaning making as a humanising approach to fieldwork (Faulkner 2009; Finley 2008). From a socio-political perspective, it is a medium to resist dominant structures (Pelias 2004, 2005) and problematise stereotypical portrayals of underserved communities (Faulkner 2006, 2009). Moreover, there is a social justice imperative about arts-based inquiry that guides our actions (Finley 2014). The use of excerpts and interregnums helps us to address the constant struggles and make sense of our stories.

Like any inquiry approach, *arts-based research*, if used as a method, calls for a commitment with *craftsmanship* and the rigorous attention to developing the art form; therefore, we are not claiming arts-based inquiry as a primary methodology, but rather as a tool to enhance our narratives, to most meaningfully tell our stories (Faulkner 2009). The Brown Woman TA is a collaged piece to which each of us contributes as part of an interconnected autoethnography interlaced with reflections (see Cord and Clemens 2010). Three reasons inform our decision to composite our stories into one character: first, it is an attempt to minimise the risk associated with sharing our individual stories openly and discreetly; second, it is a means to tackle systemic biases larger than individual stories; and third, it fits the creative license afforded by an art-based lens. An additional license we take is allowing for the narrative voice to flow interchangeably between 'we', three individuals with unique perspectives and experiences, and 'I', the Brown Woman TA as a systemic other. This constructed identity or main character serves as an overarching narrative voice that provides a thread to the seemingly separate lives and layered lived experiences of three women of colour in academia.

Introducing the Brown Woman TA

I woke up one day in a land of cornfields, red barns, and tall water towers. It seemed like a distant reality to the one I had lived in my native land. The landscape appeared flat, and it was; the noises of the town were rare and tamed. Let me explain, I came to the Midwest to do a Ph.D. in Education. My family is proud. I am alone and accompanied; I am a citizen but needed a visa to come into this country. My skin is brown, sometimes darker and other times lighter, so much so that I nearly look white. My religion is none and all, but if I pray, I pray to God. I am a hijabi and sometimes I am not. When I am, I wear colourful veils that break the misconceptions about those who wear them; when I am not, my hair hits the wind all dark and long, as expected from the Caribbean spirit in me. I am tall and short, full figured and slim, serious and comical.

This truth I know: the day I woke to a life in the Midwest, I began to recognise more vividly the watchful eye of systemic surveillance that walks with us (Foucault 1995) and started looking at my life as a constant negotiation of demand, offer, and market value. I became an ethnic trope defined in relation to capital terms like efficiency, production, and industriousness (see Apple 2011). Who I am, a Brown Woman TA, has been constructed and preconceived through the gaze and consciousness of those who have only met me in passing, those who have only heard constructed stories of detriment, chaos, and unruliness. In academia, I have become a constellation of the 'other', one that needs to be labelled, dissected, explained, made to fit (see Gutiérrez y Muhs et al. 2012). But I do not fit, because the ruler with which I am measured employs a prescribed metric of majority standards. As a result, I have come to experience the best and the worst of me in higher education: that my first language is not English, that my racial identity is not set, that I am not competitive enough, that my spirituality is a hindrance, that the way I make sense of the world, talk, think, and construct meaning is not an asset. As a woman of colour in this context, my identity and body disrupt the status quo.

My choice to study education is not coincidental. I love teaching; I am here to do just that. Although it is uncommon for me to dwell on my accomplishments, I need you to know I came to this country with a complex set of experiences and professional prowess. But those values seem to stay inside the walls of my beige graduate student office every time I teach. Some years ago, I arrived at the academic venue where I would cultivate my voracious craving for knowledge. Like many others, I became a TA who was (and was not) a teacher. I was handed a list of students, obligations, and strict policies. I was offered a rigid framework and benchmarks through which I was to interact and communicate with Anglo students. Since all my preparation and academic experiences were intricately attached to becoming a teacher educator, most of my story in Midwest town can be told from a Brown TA lens.

It is precisely at the junction and aggregation of attributes such as graduate student, TA, woman of colour, and cultural and linguistic minority that I narrate my experiences and invite all the multifaceted voices within me (see Karimi, forthcoming; Karimi, Akiyama, and Deng, forthcoming). As a Brown Women TA, I reside between *too little and too much, but never enough*, and more often than not, I am *the brown elephant in the room*. I exist in the consonant tones of the collective autoethnography of three Ph.D. students of education in a Midwest university, but I also come undone to celebrate the moments of unique individuality and positionality that each of these voices has to offer. As I share snippets of my story, I draw upon *microaggressions*, student evaluations, and poignantly cruel comments to convey the emotional toll we forgo and the *deprofessionalisation* we endure in this neoliberal system (see Gutiérrez y Muhs et al. 2012). By sharing these intertwined narratives, I wish not 'to come across as whiny', as a white, heterosexual, middle-class, cisgender fellow male educator once said. Rather, I invite you to walk with me and share a conversation.

Let me tell you about the time I was 'the brown elephant in the room'

As I navigate the halls of academia, sit through classes, participate in discussions, hand in papers, and teach lessons, I sense a strange cloud of reactions – as if there were a questionable character that did not belong. I look around but see no one. Yet, there is a lingering question: 'if there is someone strange, what are they doing here?' People look puzzled, and I cannot point to what it is. Yet, I feel it all around. I see it in the questioning gazes of classmates, colleagues, students, faculty, and even staff. This cannot be a coincidence, and I was determined to figure out the mystery. I follow the looks and the glances. They are all pointing at something around me. I look to my left, then I look to my right; there is no one else around, nothing else to be precise. Then realisation strikes: 'it's me, I am the "brown" elephant in the room'.

> *Stand up straight, young Latina!* 'I think it all has to do with confidence,
> if you walk with confidence, then people will treat you differently'. Later, she was reminded:
> 'you have what it takes to be a better teacher, but lack confidence'.

Remembering the advice given to me by an in-service teacher and a staff member, both white women, I considered how very little majority groups understand the experiences of their minority peers, especially in predominantly white institutions (Rodriguez 2009). This conundrum stems from the fact that individuals in the majority do not have to actively see themselves as different, as they are protected by privilege (Delpit 2013). Come to think of it, perhaps brown elephants are not born with a strong sense of self-assurance. Or is it elegance? The capacity to walk around unnoticed? At the risk of tiring the metaphor, you cannot expect a three-ton mammal to walk like a gazelle. The pondering continues.

That semester, I was to start working as a TA for a course on diversity and education, which has been documented to cause additional challenges for TAs of colour (Waring and Bordoloi 2012). I remember it as if it were yesterday: It is my first day of class, and I am ready to go. I have prepared and over prepared what I want to do during class time. I am excited and enthusiastic to start. I enter my first classroom and try to incorporate all this excitement and eagerness into my tone, body gestures, and class atmosphere. However, I am taken aback by the same suspicious questioning gaze and by the constant apprehensive facial gestures that followed thereafter. Now, after years of teaching young college students of majority backgrounds, I think about Lazos (2012) who explains that students typically cannot accept women of colour in positions of power, as such models do not fit the stereotypes to which they have been exposed. Subconsciously (and sometimes consciously too), a brown woman cannot possibly be a knowledgeable and qualified educator (Pittman 2010).

'The instructor was very hard to connect to. Especially in this type of class,
I think that is important. I found her awkward.'
The reviews are in for the Brown Woman TA: 1 out of 5 stars!

Let us be frank, 'awkward' is a bad review, particularly when it comes out of student evaluations. For women of colour, lower scores and strong worded feedback in end-of-semester evaluations are a common trend; yet, they are perceived to be an unbiased and reliable assessment that can affect our employability and performance reviews (Lazos 2012). When students as the institution's customers complain about the Brown Woman TA's performance, the system attempts to normalise itself by requesting she becomes more efficient. In fact, in the corporate zeitgeist presented by Rhoads and Rhoades (2005), she could be seen as a mistake, a slide occurring in an otherwise well-organised system that promises customers the highest possible value. Understanding how a situated *microaggresion* connects to a complex system of business values required a series of dialogical reflections, moving from the personal to the socio-political (see Zeichner 2014).

I convince myself that I am attributing too much to simple looks and student comments, but I feel the obligation to convince them of my capabilities – what many teachers feel the urge to do at the beginning of each class (see Gutiérrez y Muhs et al. 2012; Waring and Bordoloi 2012). Thus, I start talking about my background, my teaching experience, my academic credentials. I also make sure to mention that I have lived and studied in international settings. But the gaze does not seem to diminish. And even though I face a lot of resistance throughout the semester from topics that would otherwise be considered typical in this type of class, I try to convince myself that this is a common experience among all TAs assigned to this course. After all, don't we all laugh when reading the challenges faced by the 'typical' and most popular characters in the successful Ph.D. comics website (http://phdcomics.com/comics.php)?

At this point, I search for evidence that I am not alone, that underrepresented TAs get a smaller piece of the pie. The findings from the International Teaching Assistant (ITA) scholarship are reassuring albeit unfair. Research on instructor evaluations shows that women of colour are still held to a US unattainable standard: the white teacher (Anderson 2010). Moreover, the ITA is normalised in college campuses as 'a problematic character' (Fitch and Morgan 2003, 306). These assessments on ITAs' attributes show that our identities heavily inform how we are evaluated.

Emotional crushers as they may be, these studies suggest that markers beyond our control – being a woman, non-white, and non-native language speaker – contribute to negative student perceptions (Campbell, Gerdes, and Steiner 2005; Campbell, Steiner, and Gerdes 2005). Minority status has been negatively associated with students' valorisation of the course, our teaching ability (Pittman 2010; Smith 2009), and even the level of attention they pay in our classes (Basow, Codos, and Martin 2013). In such difficult scenario, I feel obliged to assert my scholarly competence because I am quite aware that my teaching effectiveness is monitored in this system (Basow, Codos, and Martin 2013). The story becomes more problematic as progress and evaluations peak in the horizon.

In the middle of the semester, I try to do an informal instructor evaluation to understand what I can do better, how I can improve the class activities, and where my students stand in relation to me. The evaluations are paper and pencil and anonymous. After collecting them, I skim through sheets out of curiosity and cannot resist the urge to discuss them face-to-face. I open up the conversation and promise them a safe space to express their thoughts. What takes me back at first is the tone they use in expressing these thoughts. I find it very disrespectful, but I give them the benefit of the doubt. In regard to their comments, on the other hand, I cannot.

Their basic claim is that I do not understand 'the American norm'. Initially, I had anticipated this might happen, so I ask for concrete examples. Most of the points they bring up are related to the logistics of running the classroom, which are clearly stated on the syllabus. I cannot help but think if it were another TA running this session, one whose hijab is not a visible reminder of minority status, would they have the same reaction? After all, I did not write the syllabus. It was written by the course supervisor who coincidentally happens to be American, and the syllabus is typically the same across all sections. That semester, and others following it, my student evaluations reflected how deeply rooted were their perceptions of me as a racialised woman and how much their assessment of my work could negatively affect my life.

Tearing up inside her shared office, the Brown Woman TA comes face to face with the undisclosed discourse of antagonism in her course evaluations. With her dignity in shatters, she turns on the Internet radio, and waits for the music to start:

> *Igualada,* your ethnicity and culture are overbearing. You are very judgmental when we, the students, talk of those outside the American Norm. You do not belong here.

de la Riva-Holly (2012) adopts the term *igualada* – a concept used for the *subaltern* who aims to climb the hierarchical ladder – in reference to women of colour's attempt to navigate and raise above the unfair treatment in academia. As a Brown Woman TA, this flashback to a course evaluation reminds me of meritocracy's mirage as it is constructed and perpetuated by the US business model. As an eager teacher with a new classroom, I saw the mirage and walked to it, only to see myself holding sand. Reflecting more on the concept *igualada* provided me with a language to name and position my experience alongside other tokenised bodies, a critical moment that deepened my understanding of interconnections (see Jacobs 2005; Zeichner 2014).

I wish I could end the story here, draw the curtain right now. But it goes on. My other encounter occurred while teaching a multicultural literature course. Largely, books were conceived by many of my students as familiar and enjoyable and as possessing great didactic potential. In fact, they recalled with profound excitement the titles and authors that made them feel warm, safe, and at home. Their view on reading, early literacy, and literary texts reflected those of American majority culture (Dyson 2015; Nelson 2010). Because reading is such an important part of these students' lives, I was committed to teaching them what diverse literary choices and reading may do for understanding others. Growing up with particular titles and authors, mainly from privileged backgrounds, certainly helps to establish perceptions of acceptable literature that is enjoyable (see Van Dongen 2004). My avid readers were unsure why they had to read voices outside 'their Norm'. These cultures had already been allotted a marginal space where low-currency knowledge dwells as a by-product of a market-driven system. Why must they also be read outside of the heritage months designated to hyphenated Americans? The larger (and difficult) issue here was to come face to face with how majority culture is ever present in the classroom: in instructional choices, in student–teacher interactions; it ripples in our words, in our actions (see Margolis 2001).

My class, which required them to read from diverse groups inside and outside the US, was perceived as my personal agenda. Of course, these students were less apprehensive of their own cultural biases; as such, they did not question why majority culture must be the universal literature, the transparent and neutral text. Why it had become the equivalent of a normal life, whether physically experienced or vicariously lived through books. The course's multicultural book list was automatically linked to my cultural background. Simply put, I wanted them to read about non-white, non-English-speaking characters, because I was one of them. As a TA, this naturally evidenced my ineffectiveness to practise their former teachers' literary objectivity.

> It is about that time, a day after grades are turned in and the Brown Woman TA is ready to click on the 'view student responses' button; her thoughts going high speed, and her senses in alert, she awaits for the evaluations to load: 'She has to work on being unbiased, in certain things, and not bringing her cultural identity so much in class discussions'. She keeps scrolling down. 'I just think minorities are given so many opportunities; I just think that if you live in America, you need to learn English'.

For those of us who are visible minorities, many of these troublesome traits are part of who we are and aspects we cannot change (Hamermesh and Parker 2005; Pittman 2010). What does this say about neoliberal, market-driven institutions that assign and appoint TAs based on student evaluations, most of which are crafted as customer satisfaction surveys? (see Lazos 2012; Lugo-Lugo 2012) How are Brown Women TAs ever going to compete in a context driven by such evaluations? What happens when, as Lazos (2012) problematises, these assessments are heavily dependent on factors beyond teaching, such as *charisma*? What does this say about Brown Women TAs who may not necessarily satisfy students' thin sliced socialised judgement of aesthetics and cultural values?

That time I was too much and too little, but never enough

It became evident quite soon that my *otherness* would follow me into every US educational setting. My language learner marker or bilingual persona mattered in all the wrong ways. What I perceived as an asset was considered a deficit when I taught a course on English language learning. To increase my efficiency in the system, I had to deal with this recently discovered shortcoming. I had no other options, my funding, my academic career, even my legal status in the US depended on it. But 'how could I, the language learner, tell English-speaking pre-service teachers how to speak to their future students?' Somehow, I became the unreasonable instructor asking them to do extra work; in their view, this work would only serve a handful of students who, like me, were inadequate anyway. I could not even speak 'good' English, as one student shared in the evaluations. Under these auditing and assessment processes, such as perceptions of linguistic ability, we internalise a neoliberal academic self; thus, Anglo-American hegemony and its constituencies are maintained through nuanced practices – in this case, the valorisation of the English language (Dowling 2009).

> That day, the Brown Woman TA turned on the news only to be bombarded by a lesson on her own inadequacy: More immigrants coming into the US! Now, does this mean we need to start learning Spanish in schools? We have a panel of experts here today.
> This was a reminder of what she had been told all along as a teacher: 'I hope our instructor becomes a better English speaker, so that she can relate better to us'.
> As a graduate student, she had also received the kind of face-to-face 'praise' that reminded her of being an English learner: 'wow! You can write well; I'm surprised'.

Women of colour who are also linguistic minorities are constantly compared and measured up to an ideal English heritage language speaker (Karimi, Akiyama, and Deng, forthcoming; Sherry, Thomas, and Chui 2010). Receiving this type of assessment became a common indicator of the type of media and social rhetoric that my students and I were exposed to (Stewart, Pitts, and Osborne 2011). These messages draw on and perpetuate unfounded stereotypes of minority groups, such as their resistance to learning a new language.

Around this same time, I supervised a practicum in a school district with a large influx of Latino/a children, most of them English learners. In this context, my ethnic identity would matter too, but in this case to the school administration. They were evidently not accustomed to seeing a Brown woman walking down their hallways, clipboard in hand. I guess the backlash should not have surprised me. A month before starting this collaboration, I had driven down to introduce myself, meet the school personnel, and be subjected to an informal background check by one of the school principals. She was deeply interested in unravelling my credentials: my country of origin, years of residence in the United States, language background. It seems the accountability culture was also alive and well outside the ivory tower. Thus, in the principal's eyes, my presence needed to be justified and validated.

Our students and administrators see us! Who we are comes into play in subtle in-class student comments when they marvel and remark 'your English is so good professor!' It also resurfaces when a *microaggressor* school principal contacts the campus to complain about their brown woman, who is alarmingly 'too self-confident and too professional'. It appears I had disrupted some essentialist trope of the docile, naïve, unprofessional, and caring Brown Woman TA – I had become too much, too soon. In such cases, we are reminded that our identities and subjectivities are created, enacted, and debated in this neoliberal context (Dowling 2009). Therefore, if I want to compete, to remain marketable in this vigilant landscape, I need to embody the ideal worker through my language and discourse and the 'costumes' I wear; in doing so, I engage in a constant negotiation of how to increase my status as a worker to keep my current position (Vander Kloet and Aspenlieder 2013).

Perhaps to my own dissatisfaction, I did learn how to accomplish such exhausting task. First, I needed to lower my visibility, a strategy highly recommended by Lazos (2012). I tried very hard to be caring by embracing the female perceptions of meeting needs and providing tailored support. I also followed Lazos's suggestion to be tactful when handling authority to avoid being perceived as 'too angry' or 'too pretentious' for my own kind. Basically, I paid extra attention to the individualistic identity of my American students and collaborators, who as Lugo-Lugo (2012) rightfully describes, yearn for the recognition and relief only a good service person can provide. At the end of the day, I was only a salesperson in the highly competitive corporate enterprise known as the university.

This unfortunately meant embracing my own *deprofessionalisation* (see Gutiérrez y Muhs et al. 2012). I switched from Ph.D. candidate to the roles described by Lugo-Lugo (2012) as: the *customer service representative* and the *prostitute*.

> After her best performance yet, the Brown Woman TA finally got a standing ovation from her students. The 'accomplishment' was bittersweet, as it came with an unnecessary sexual innuendo: 'I loved how willing she was to help in any way she could. I felt like she would bend over backwards for me, if I asked her to'.

For a Brown Woman TA like me, lessening this type of visibility is a necessary vice. These modifications did yield more positive student evaluations. It certainly paid off to emulate the caring brown woman model promoted in academia (Lazos 2012), even if it was not my own. However, despite my efforts, it seems I never measured up. In one case, I am considered too professional. In another instance, I am viewed as overly emotional – too soft, too cute. During the times that I expressed emotions beyond the established polite norm, I felt the need to apologise for showcasing what was considered unprofessional and unbecoming behaviour for an academic setting.

There he was, the new mentor. Making a distressing hand gesture towards the Brown Woman TA, he attempts to appease her high-energy account:

> 'I just cannot deal with all this energy right now'. In his eyes, these moments of *vulnerability* implied a flaw in character, one that could ultimately reflect on his scholarly demeanor and poise; these subjective traits had to take a backseat or be avoided. (see Brown 2015)

After this episode of candid openness with the aforementioned mentor, sometime during my second year, I learned when and where to remain silent. Onwuachi-Willig (2012) writes about the inherent power of silences for minority scholars, some bringing about positive outcomes while others yield negative or unpardonable results. Pondering on this scholar's teaching, I have learnt how such moments of silence interplay in my academic life, distressing my personal and professional identities. Reflecting deeper on my adopted silences, I have come to learn that most of them were not by choice, because the risks associated with minorities disrupting the status quo have been widely discussed in research (Gonzalez et al. 2002; Rodriguez 2009; Waring and Bordoloi 2012). So, I began having these vulnerable conversations inside the protective walls of my office space, with other Brown Women TAs. In fact, such support networks have been identified as crucial to the success of graduate students from minority backgrounds (Ceja and Rivas 2010) and, indeed, they supported me in many ways.

One closed-door conversation comes vividly to mind now. I had been feeling frustrated and unsettled after receiving the instructions for a new course I was to teach that semester. There were pages after pages of policies, instructions, and regulations, and I was to follow them to a 'T'. During the times the syllabus was discussed, I felt overwhelmed with many statements that went against my teacher personae; none of these classroom policies was outrageous or outside the norm when it comes to US higher education. Yet, many of them had resonated with the strict US educational policies that had failed a majority of underserved students. I was told to rigorously follow all aspects of the document throughout the semester; it was, after all, our 'contract' with students, yet another business transaction connecting to the aforementioned framework of the neoliberal university. With such a stern 'welcome' to a classroom, you can imagine the types of relationships and sometimes prescribed exchanges that ensued with students. I remember seeing my friend, another Brown TA, in the hallway of our department and exchanging with her a look that signalled misery. We went into her office, and we closed the door. I paused; I felt my throat contracting. I found it very difficult to convey that I, a reasonably experienced educator, would work under an illusion of agency. In this manner, instead of becoming an 'agent of change', I became an 'instrument of reproduction' (Dowling 2009).

As this friend-to-friend conversation proceeded, we found ourselves nodding and validating experiences when silence had become a resource; we also unpacked the multiple instances of subtle and conspicuous discrimination we had endured in our short careers as TAs in the United States. While we, Brown Women TAs, were not overtly marginalised by the policies in our syllabi, these official documents implicitly sent the message that there was 'a way', 'The Way' to do things right in prestigious academic institutions (Gutiérrez y Muhs et al. 2012). These standards, including those used to develop an effective syllabus, have been in place for such a long time it is easy to forget who created them and whose ideologies they represent: the majority (Delpit 2013). My friend and I would constantly talk about what it meant for us to remain silent, sometimes because negotiation was beyond our reach. As a TA, even if you bring a repertoire of experiences and a set of assets from your home institutions, the system here is different. You are, as Apple (2011) so aptly puts it, perceived and labelled *labor*. I was immediately reminded of my status as cheap labour when in the online thread for a large educational association someone asked about good transcription software, to which a prominent scholar answered: 'Whatever happened to graduate students? They work for pennies and a half-eaten banana'. These experiences were indicative of a broader problem beyond the construct of labour.

Finding our voices displaced or vanished from the normative talks on standards, strictness, and 'controlling' students can be quite frustrating, to say the least. In the aforementioned neoliberal context where racial and gender majority values are the 'Standard', the voices of Brown Women TAs have little to no room. The first time I was called out for being 'too soft … a softie', I had been compared to a standard of objectivity and reason, one against which the binary is labelled subjective, emotional, unstructured. Back in the closed office, my friend puts her hand over mine and tells me about the 'tools of the trade', what Harris and González (2012) explain as the institutional strategies women of colour lack to navigate majority-based academic systems.

If I am perfectly honest, I now tend to cringe when I hear majority stakeholders talk about the need to recruit more minorities at multiple tiers of higher education. I wonder if we are truly ready to accept the profound implications of (meaningfully) fostering diversity within work and educational spaces. What about enacting change and creating the necessary infrastructures? Are we ready or do we just want to increase our numbers? My answer is 'yes and no', as I hear a friend tell me about a white male colleague's complaint of the job market: ' … I think I have not been able to find a job because I'm a white male in academia'.

My colleague's inner reflections on such unsolicited remarks point to a broader conversation on the effects of neoliberal benchmarks in higher education combined with a perceived change in the system's oppressive mechanisms (see Norton and Sommers 2011). Consider it this way: when competing for the limited number of faculty positions available, these same individuals cannot help but default to the highly problematic misconceptions of 'minorities taking over American jobs' as the root cause of the problems; thus, disregarding the probability of a more qualified women of colour being hired, for instance (Chomsky 2007). This is another issue Brown Women TAs face throughout their careers. Yet, as a friend to many amazing and caring white colleagues, it is also important to understand that they (i.e. white males) struggle, like we do, with maintaining their biases in check, especially in these difficult times. Thus, reducing these issues to us-versus-them can only make the path towards equity all the more difficult.

Closing reflection

At the end of our narrative and throughout, our constructed character posited questions that are vital to understanding how we conceptualise the role of minority women amidst the neoliberal mechanisms that govern our universities. Recounting some of our most personal experiences as Brown Women TAs was no easy task, as it required a level of vulnerability that we are constantly advised to conceal and be ashamed of (see Brown 2015). A further layer of challenge was presented as we positioned ourselves in a macro system of market value. How did this relationship come to be? How did it help perpetuate the othering of non-conforming diverse peoples? It always seems that, as emerging scholars, we still hold dear the concept of an untouched institution that is true to the values of fairness, the pursuit of knowledge, and an equitable treatment of all its members. However, this was not the case for us.

Our aggregated narratives showcase the discrimination and unfair treatment that people of colour, particularly women, face as they slowly make their way into the 'pipeline' of a better future and reclaim pieces of their agency. Reflecting on our research findings, we cannot ignore the significant role *othering* has had in shaping our experiences and creating challenges with majority students, faculty, and staff – the allegory of 'the brown elephant in the room' serving to expand an established frame of reference to further problematise identity markers such as race, ethnicity, and religion. This systemic condition also creates a state of uncertainty and exhaustion that positions Brown Women TAs at the crossroads of various expectations that often disconnect with their identities (see McLaren 1988); in our work, we encompassed these ideas in 'that time I was too much and too little, but never enough', as the verbal representation of how these cultural and socio-political negotiations ensued in our lives in the business-driven academia.

In neoliberal academic spaces where the quest for knowledge and investigation translate as currency aiding the corporatisation of higher education (Marginson 2011), individuals working in and within this system must engage in conscious reflection on how the self can be an entryway to understand larger systemic conditions affecting underserved communities (Jacobs 2005; Zeichner 2014). The current national and international rhetoric of competition and corporatisation are used to reiterate power and nationhood (Apple 2011); they also inform how students, faculty, and administrators conceptualise academia, in general, and Brown Women TAs, in particular, as subjects in higher education. As showcased throughout this article, these discourses impose new challenges on us, such as increased xenophobia, stereotyping, and silencing.

Our decision to create a fictional character to represent our aggregated voices is also connected with claiming agency amidst a constellation of dominant discourses. This alternative persona dwelled in environments shaped by business-driven ideologies that, in many ways, subtracted her cultural, emotional, and intellectual assets (see Gutiérrez y Muhs et al. 2012). Therefore, it was imperative to show how the complex layers of who she is – teacher, doctoral student, colleague, racialised woman, linguistic minority – are intricately connected to the larger socio-political conversation. As we recollected episodes from our lived experiences, a humanising process took place, one that was mediated by the methodological depth of the *collective authoethnography* and an arts-based lens. These inquiry tools provided an opportunity for reflection on our practice and how we are positioned in relation to others in a highly competitive environment (Zeichner 2014).

One thought that kept lurking during conversations was the possibility that, like this collective piece, our experiences are threaded in more ways than we acknowledge. Perhaps the Brown Woman TA narrative is an implicit call to action in order to identify and resist patterns of domination; patterns that keep women of colour at multiple hierarchical tiers from reaching parity, succeeding, and embodying their full intellectual, emotional, and spiritual selves. Perhaps this repositioning can provide a platform for change in relation to the neoliberal underpinnings of higher education.

Disclosure statement

No potential conflict of interest was reported by the authors.

References

Anderson, Kristin J. 2010. "Students' Stereotypes of Professors: An Exploration of the Double Violations of Ethnicity and Gender." *Social Psychology of Education: An International Journal* 13 (4): 459–472.

Apple, Michael W. 2011. "Democratic Education in Neoliberal and Neoconservative Times." *International Studies in Sociology of Education* 21 (1): 21–31.

Asmar, Christine, Elizabeth Proude, and Lici Inge. 2004. "'Unwelcome Sisters?' An Analysis of Findings from a Study of How Muslim Women (and Muslim men) Experience University." *Australian Journal of Education* 48 (1): 47–63.

Barone, Tom, and Elliot Eisner. 2012. *Arts Based Research*. Thousand Oaks, CA: Sage.

Basow, Susan, Stephanie Codos, and Julie Martin. 2013. "The Effects of Professors' Race and Gender on Student Evaluations and Performance." *College Student Journal* 47 (2): 352–363.

Brennan, John, and Rajani Naidoo. 2008. "Higher Education and the Achievement (and/or Prevention) of Equity and Social Justice." *Higher Education* 56 (3): 287–302.

Brown, Brené. 2015. *Daring greatly: How the Courage to be Vulnerable Transforms the Way We Live, Love, Parent, and Lead*. New York: Avery.

Butz, David, and Kathryn Besio. 2004. "The Value of Autoethnography for Field Research in Transcultural Settings." *The Professional Geographer* 56 (3): 350–360.

Campbell, Heather E., Karen Gerdes, and Sue Steiner. 2005. "What's Looks Got to Do with It?: Instructor Appearance and Student Evaluations of Teaching." *Journal of Policy Analysis and Management* 24 (3): 611–620.

Campbell, Heather, Sue Steiner, and Karen Gerdes. 2005. "Student Evaluations of Teaching: How You Teach and Who You Are." *Journal of Public Affairs Education* 11 (3): 211–231.

Ceja, Miguel, and Martha Rivas. 2010. "Faculty-student Interactions and Chicana PhD Aspirations." *Journal of the Professoriate* 3 (2): 75–101.

Chang, Heewon, Faith W. Ngunjiri, and Kathy-Ann C. Hernández, eds. 2013. *Collaborative Autoethnography*. Walnut Creek, CA: Left Coast Press.

Chomsky, Aviva. 2007. *"They Take Our Jobs!" And 20 Other Myths about Immigration*. Boston, MA: Beacon Press.

Cloke, Paul, Phillip Crang, and Mark Goodwin. 2013. *Introducing Human Geographies*. New York: Routledge.

Cole, Darnell, and Shafiqa Ahmadi. 2003. "Perspectives and Experiences of Muslim Women Who Veil on College Campuses." *Journal of College Student Development* 44 (1): 47–66.

Cord, Bonnie, and Mike Clemens. 2010. "Reward Through Collective Reflection: An Autoethnography." *E-Journal of Business Education & Scholarship of Teaching* 4 (1): 11–19.

Delpit, Lisa. 2013. *"Multiplication is for White People:" Raising Expectations for other People's Children*. New York: The New Press.

Dowling, Robyn. 2009. "Geographies of Identity: Landscapes of Class." *Progress in Human Geography* 33 (6): 833–839.

Dyson, Anne Haas. 2015. "The Search for Inclusion: Deficit Discourse and the Erasure of Childhoods." *Language Arts* 92 (3): 199–207.

Ellis, Carolyn S., and Arthur P. Bochner. 2006. "Analyzing Analytic Autoethnography: An Autopsy." *Journal of Contemporary Ethnography* 35 (4): 429–449.

Ellis, Carolyn, Arthur P. Bochner, and Tony E. Adams. 2011. "Autoethnography: An Overview." *Forum Qualitative Sozialforschung* 12 (1). http://www.qualitative-research.net/index.php/fqs/article/view/1589/3095.

Faulkner, Sandra L. 2006. "Reconstruction: LGBTQ and Jewish." *International and Intercultural Communication Annual* 29: 95–120.

Faulkner, Sandra L. 2009. *Poetry as Method: Reporting Research through Verse*. Walnut Creek, CA: Left Coast Press.

Finley, Susan. 2008. "Arts-based Research." In *Handbook of the Arts in Qualitative Research: Perspectives, Methodologies, Examples, and Issues*, edited by J. Gary Knowles and Ardra L. Cole, 71–82. Thousand Oaks, CA: Sage.

Finley, Susan. 2014. "An Introduction to Critical Arts-based Research: Demonstrating Methodologies and Practices of a Radical Ethical Aesthetic." *Cultural Studies/Critical Methodologies* 14 (6): 531–532.

Fitch, Fred, and Susan Morgan. 2003. "'Not a Lick of English': Constructing the ITA Identity through Student Narratives." *Communication Education* 52 (3–4): 297–310.

Foucault, Michel. 1995. *Discipline and Punish: The Birth of the Prison*. New York: Vintage Books.

Gandhi, Leela. 1998. *Postcolonial Theory: A Critical Introduction*. New York: Columbia University Press.

Giroux, Henry A. 2002. "Neoliberalism, Corporate Culture, and the Promise of Higher Education: The University as a Democratic Public Sphere." *Harvard Educational Review* 72 (4): 425–464.

Gonzalez, Kenneth P., Patricia Marin, Mark A. Figueroa, Jose F. Moreno, and Christine N. Navia. 2002. "Inside Doctoral Education in America: Voices of Latinas/os in Pursuit of the PhD." *Journal of College Student Development* 43: 540–557.

Gutiérrez y Muhs, Gabriella, Yolanda Flores Nieman, Carmen G. González, and Angela P. Harris. 2012. *Presumed Incompetent: The Intersections of Race and Class for Women in Academia.* Boulder: University Press of Colorado.

Hamermesh, Daniel S., and Amy Parker. 2005. "Beauty in the Classroom: Instructors' Pulchritude and Putative Pedagogical Productivity." *Economics of Education Review* 24 (4): 369–376.

Harris, Angela P., and Carmen G. González. 2012. "Introduction." In *Presumed Incompetent: The Intersections of Race and Class for Women in Academia*, edited by Gabriella Gutiérrez y Muhs, Yolanda Flores Nieman, Carmen G. González, and Angela P. Harris, 1–16. Boulder: University Press of Colorado.

Jacobs, Walter R. 2005. *Speaking the Lower Frequencies: Students and Media Literacy.* Albany: State University of New York Press.

Karimi, Nastaran. Forthcoming. "The Internal Privileged Me Against My Constructed Oppressed Image: The Experiences of an International Iranian Muslim Female in the Midwest." In *Research for Social Justice: Personal~Passionate~Participatory Inquiry.* Charlotte, NC: Information Age.

Karimi, Nastaran, Reiko Akiyama, and Yuwen Deng. Forthcoming. "Sociocultural Alienation of Female International Students in a Predominantly White College." In *Internationalizing Teaching and Teacher Education for Equity: Engaging Alternative Knowledges Across Ideological Borders.* Charlotte, NC: Information Age.

Kuhn, Thomas S. 2012. *The Structure of Scientific Revolutions.* 4th ed. Chicago, IL: University of Chicago Press.

Lazos, Sylvia R. 2012. "Are Student Teaching Evaluations Holding Back Women and Minorities?: The Perils of 'Doing' Gender and Race in the Classroom." In *Presumed Incompetent: The Intersections of Race and Class for Women in Academia*, edited by Gabriella Gutiérrez y Muhs, Yolanda Flores Nieman, Carmen G. González, and Angela P. Harris, 164–185. Boulder: University Press of Colorado.

Lee, Jenny, and Charles Rice. 2007. "Welcome to America? International Student Perceptions of Discrimination." *Higher Education* 53: 381–409.

Lin, Ann Chih. 1998. "Bridging Positivist and Interpretivist Approaches to Qualitative Methods." *Policy Studies Journal* 26 (1): 162–180.

Lugo-Lugo, Carmen R. 2012. "A Prostitute, a Servant, and Customer-service Representative: A Latina in Academia." In *Presumed Incompetent: The Intersections of Race and Class for Women in Academia*, edited by Gabriella Gutiérrez y Muhs, Yolanda Flores Nieman, Carmen G. González, and Angela P. Harris, 40–49. Boulder: University Press of Colorado.

Margolis, Eric. 2001. *The Hidden Curriculum in Higher Education.* New York: Routledge.

Marginson, Simon. 2006. "Dynamics of National and Global Competition in Higher Education." *Higher Education* 52 (1): 1–39.

Marginson, Simon. 2011. "Higher Education and Public Good." *Higher Education Quarterly* 65 (4): 411–433.

Marginson, Simon. 2012. "Including the Other: Regulation of the Human Rights of Mobile Students in a Nation-Bound World." *Higher Education* 63 (4): 497–512.

McLaren, Peter L. 1998. "The Liminal Servant and the Ritual Roots of Critical Pedagogy." *Language Arts* 65 (2): 164–180.

Nelson, Katherine. 2010. "Developmental Narratives of the Experiential Child." *Child Development Perspectives* 4: 42–47.

Norton, Michael I., and Samuel R. Sommers. 2011. "Whites See Racism as a Zero-sum Game that They Are Now Losing." *Perspectives on Psychological Science: A Journal of the Association for Psychological Science* 6 (3): 215–219.

Onwuachi-Willig, Angela. 2012. "Silence of the Lambs." In *Presumed Incompetent: The Intersections of Race and Class for Women in Academia*, edited by Gabriella Gutiérrez y Muhs, Yolanda Flores Nieman, Carmen G. González, and Angela P. Harris, 142–151. Boulder: University Press of Colorado.

Pelias, Ronald J. 2004. *A Methodology of the Hearth: Evoking Academic and Daily Life*. Walnut Creek, CA: Altamira Press.

Pelias, Ronald J. 2005. "Performative Writing as Scholarship: An Apology, an Argument, an Anecdote." *Critical Studies – Critical Methodologies* 5 (4): 415–424.

Pittman, Chavella T. 2010. "Race and Gender Oppression in the Classroom: The Experiences of Women Faculty of Color with White Male Students." *Teaching Sociology* 38 (3): 183–196.

Rhoads, Robert A., and Gary Rhoades. 2005. "Graduate Employee Unionization as Symbol of and Challenge to the Corporatization of U.S. Research Universities." *Journal of Higher Education* 76 (3): 243–275.

de la Riva-Holly, Francisca. 2012. "Igualadas." In *Presumed Incompetent: The Intersections of Race and Class for Women in Academia*, edited by Gabriella Gutiérrez y Muhs, Yolanda Flores Nieman, Carmen G. González, and Angela P. Harris, 287–299. Boulder: University Press of Colorado.

Rizvi, Fazal. 2011. "Beyond the Social Imaginary of 'Clash of Civilizations'?" *Educational Philosophy and Theory* 43 (3): 225–235.

Rodriguez, Alberto. 2005. "Unravelling the Allure of Auto/Biography." In *Auto/Biography and Auto/Ethnography: Praxis of Research Method*, edited by W. M. Roth, 119–130. Rotterdam: Sense.

Rodriguez, Dalia. 2009. "The Usual Suspect: Negotiating White Student Resistance and Teacher Authority in a Predominantly White Classroom." *Cultural Studies – Critical Methodologies* 9 (4): 483–508.

Roth, W. M. 2005. "Auto/Biography and Auto/Ethnography: Finding the Generalized Other in the Self." In *Auto/Biography and Auto/Ethnography: Praxis of Research Method*, edited by W. M. Roth, 3–16. Rotterdam: Sense.

Seggie, Fatma N., and Gretchen Sanford. 2010. "Perceptions of Female Muslim Students Who Veil: Campus Religious Climate." *Race, Ethnicity and Education* 13 (1): 59–82.

Sherry, Mark, Peter Thomas, and Wing H. Chui. 2010. "International Students: A Vulnerable Student Population." *Higher Education* 60: 33–46.

Smith, Bettye. 2009. "Student Ratings of Teaching Effectiveness for Faculty Groups Based on Race and Gender." *Education* 129 (4): 615–624.

Spencer-Rodgers, Julie, and Timothy McGovern. 2002. "Attitudes toward the Culturally Different: The Role of Intercultural Communication Barriers, Affective Responses, Consensual Stereotypes, and Perceived Threat." *International Journal of Intercultural Relations* 26 (6): 609–631.

Spivak, Gayatri C. 2006. "Can the Subaltern Speak?" In *The Post-colonial Studies Reader*. 2nd ed., edited by Bill Ashcroft, Gareth Griffiths, and Helen Tiffin, 28–37. New York: Routledge.

Spring, Joel. 2008. "Research on Globalization and Education." *Review of Educational Research* 78 (2): 330–363.

Stewart, Craig O., Margaret J. Pitts, and Helena Osborne. 2011. "Mediated Intergroup Conflict: The Discursive Construction of 'Illegal Immigrants' in a Regional U.S. Newspaper." *Journal of Language and Social Psychology* 30 (1): 8–27.

Torres, Carlos Alberto. 2011. "Public Universities and the Neoliberal Common Sense." *International Studies in Sociology of Education* 21: 177–197.

Vander Kloet, Marie, and Erin Aspenlieder. 2013. "Educational Development for Responsible Graduate Students in the Neoliberal University." *Critical Studies in Education* 54 (3): 286–298.

Van Dongen, Richard. 2004. "Reading Across Cultural Borders: Indigenous Influences on Diversity in Children's Literature." Paper presented at the meeting of the IBBY Congress, September 5–9, Cape Town, South Africa.

Waring, Chandra D. L., and Samit Dipon Bordoloi. 2012. "'Hopping on the Tips of a Trident:' Two Graduate Students of Color Reflect on Teaching Critical Content at Predominantly White Institutions." *Feminist Teacher* 22 (2): 108–124.

Wing Sue, Derald. 2010. *Microaggressions in Everyday Life: Race, Gender, and Sexual Orientation*. Hoboken, NJ: Wiley.

Young, Stephanie, and Amie R. McKibban. 2014. "Creating Safe Places: A Collaborative Autoethnography on LGBT Social Activism." *Sexuality and Culture* 18 (2): 361–384.

Zeichner, Kenneth. 2014. *Reflective Teaching: An Introduction*. 2nd ed. New York: Routledge.

Encountering gender: resisting a neo-liberal political rationality for sexuality education as an HIV prevention strategy

Andrée E. Gacoin

ABSTRACT

Globally, sexuality education is framed as a key programmatic strategy for achieving HIV prevention among youth. In particular, sexuality education is positioned as a way to address gender inequalities and promote youth empowerment in relation to gendered identities. In this paper, I argue that the focus on *what* content should be taught and *what* is the effectiveness of that content serves to mask how sexuality education itself is always a political project. Specifically, I problematise a neo-liberal 'political rationality,' following Wendy Brown, operating through sexuality education in this particular globalised moment. Drawing on data from an ethnographic study conducted in South Africa, I use the notion of encounters *with* gender to mobilise understanding of gender with(in) the inevitable risks of knowing and being known through educational research and practice. I argue that holding sexuality education responsible to the complexity of lived lives necessitates proposing alternative political rationalities to guide its encounters.

Introduction

Globally, sexuality education is framed as a key programmatic strategy for achieving HIV prevention among youth. In particular, sexuality education is positioned as a way to address gender inequalities and promote youth empowerment in relation to gendered identities (Bhana and Pattman 2009). The premise is that messages related to gender equality can be scripted into sexuality education curricula and then taught to youth in a range of contexts (Senderowitz and Kirby 2006; UNESCO 2009b). The effectiveness of this content can then be measured in terms of (and reduced to) supposedly neutral HIV prevention outcomes, such as the increased uptake of condom usage in heterosexual relationships.

While there is recent evidence that HIV prevention programmes addressing gender relations are more effective than those that do not (Haberland 2015), the overwhelming focus on *what* content should be taught and *what* is the effectiveness of that content in terms of measurable health outcomes (Aggleton and Crewe 2005; Baxen 2010) simultaneously masks how sexuality education, and *what* is taught, is always a political project. Any measure of 'effectiveness' is already entangled in multiple relations of power and knowledge, including what kinds of subjects (such as educators and youth) are created, and potentially disciplined, in measures of 'effectiveness'. In this paper, I argue that making the political claims of sexuality education explicit is crucial for problematising how 'gender' has been taken up in relation to HIV prevention with youth. In particular, I problematise a neo-liberal 'political rationality' (Brown 2003) guiding sexuality education in this context in order to turn attention to the 'imaginaries of gender, sexuality and relationships' being offered to educators and youth (Lesko 2010, 282). As such, the question is no longer *what* should be taught, or how *effective* that content is in terms of pre-defined outcomes, but rather *how* sexuality education is already entangled in relations of power and knowledge that settle into, and have lived effects for, conceptions of self, Other and their relations.

This paper uses the notion of encounters *with* gender to mobilise gender with(in) the inevitable risks of knowing and being known through educational research and practice. These encounters took place during an ethnographic research study conducted with love-Life, South Africa's largest national HIV prevention programme for youth (see www.lovelife.org.za). By using the notion of encounters with gender, I am specifically resisting an analytic approach that would seek to identify what gender 'is' (in the *belief* of the educator, for example), even as I recognise the inevitable analytic pull into what can/should be 'known' about gender. To work with this tension, I begin from the view that what gender 'is' in any moment is 'charged and enacted in the sticky materiality of practical encounters' (Tsing 2005, 1). As such, when gender is understood as a 'becoming' (Butler 2004), the question is not only what understandings of gender are articulated in a particular moment, but also how sexuality education is implicated in what understandings of gender come to be coherent *and* what political rationalities these understandings both draw upon and mobilise. This view foregrounds the focus on gender as something to 'teach' through sexuality education as extremely problematic, at the same time as it takes that focus as providing a unique opportunity to work with multiple and contested meanings of the very notion of gender. What is at stake is what kind of political project might be available around notions of gender when these notions are seen to be both unsettled, and unsettling, with(in) any articulation of sexuality education.

Encountering 'gender' within this globalised moment

Within sexuality education as an HIV prevention strategy, the explicit focus on gender roles and expectations aims to address how gender inequalities 'shape people's behaviour and limit their choices' (UNAIDS 2004, 9), such as young women's ability to negotiate for condom usage. In South Africa, for example, young women aged 15–19 have 8 times the HIV prevalence as their male peers (Human Sciences Research Council 2014). However, while the 'problem' of gender aims to address the social inequalities at play within these statistics, this paper begins from the position that it is precisely the multiple and complex realities of these inequalities that necessitates engaging the 'problem' (of gender relations) and the 'solution' (of sexuality education) as a 'meeting-up of histories' (Massey 2005, 4) within global space. Over the course of the HIV and AIDS epidemics, scientific prevention discourses have enacted particular understandings of gender and heteronormative relationships coupled to the 'safety' of chastity, fidelity and marriage

(Wilton and Aggleton 1991; Treichler 1999) and ideologies of caring partnerships (Bedford 2009). Furthermore, while the discursive focus on gender may appear 'new', contemporary 'global' guidance on 'local' educational initiatives extends through colonial encounters that targeted 'Africa' with medicalized discourse that was 'heavily gendered and sexualized in its language' and effects (Vaughan 1991, 21). These histories refuse knowledge about 'gender' as a neutral object of knowledge to be taught through sexuality education. In order to encounter gender within these histories and imagined futures, I first briefly contextualise the coherence of a preventative model of sexuality education, including how it may draw on and extend a neo-liberal political rationality.

The de-politicisation of 'gender' within a preventative model of sexuality education

Broadly, models of sexuality education have been based on two underlying, and interlinked, conceptualisations: first, the way in which sexuality is understood (Britzman 1998) and, second, how the development of youth is conceptualised (Gilbert 2007). In the North American context, this has led to two dominant models of sexuality education: 'the normal' and 'the critical' (Britzman 1998, 66). While this analysis cannot be simply extended to the South African context, educational responses to HIV in South Africa are deeply embedded in North American readings of the epidemic (Lees 2008; Baxen 2010). Indeed the mobility of these understandings can be seen as part of the power relations, and their implicit political aims, that move across what are taken to be 'local' or 'global' contexts.

Within the first model, a 'normal' paradigm, sexuality is broadly conceptualised as a 'natural' part of human development, and youth consists of a series of biological or psychological stages (Britzman 1998). As such, the purpose of education is to transmit supposedly neutral information to young people in order to support the development of what is taken to be a (hetero)normative sexuality. In contrast, and in reaction to historical traces of eugenic and racist notions of development within the 'normal' paradigm (Britzman 1998; Lesko 2001; Glaser 2005), a 'critical' paradigm of sexuality education draws on social constructionist views of sexuality and youth, whereby understandings of sexuality and youth emerge as 'an effect of discourse, history, culture and the social' (Gilbert 2007, 49). Here, sexuality education has the potential to either reproduce normative ideas of sexual identities and behaviours, or provide a space for youth to challenge those constructions and engage in conversations around 'who' they are within relations of power (Pattman 2005; Fields 2008; e.g. Campbell and MacPhail 2002).

While these models and their political projects may appear distinct, in terms of whether they propagate a particular construction of 'normal' or whether they critically engage with social norms that script what 'normal' is seen as, I argue that the HIV and AIDS epidemics have given form to a particular moment in which these models are yoked together, particularly as attention has turned to the 'problem' of gender for HIV prevention outcomes. Broadly, HIV prevention discourses deploy a preventative model of sexuality education that in and of itself is not 'new' (Britzman 1998). Historically, debates around sexuality education for youth have coalesced around outbreaks (whether real or perceived) of disease (Vaughan 1991; Adams 1997; McLaren 1999; Jeeves 2001). However, and what I argue is 'new', is how the current articulation of sexuality education as prevention operates within a discursive tightening around gender that relies simultaneously on normative and critical models of sexuality education. Drawing on a normative model, there is such a thing as neutral and universal information about 'gender' that can be transmitted from teacher to youth. 'Cultural relevance', or 'local adaptation', is a matter of 'fit': making sure that activities designed to transmit a pre-defined body of content are 'sensitive to community values', for example (UNESCO 2009a, 19). This is coupled with a critical model by simultaneously positioning sexuality education as a site within which all youth will rationally engage with gendered norms and act for more equitable gender relations.

As these models are yoked together in the name of 'prevention', the risk is that 'gender' is depoliticised at the same time as the underlying political rationality of this model is masked. For example, framing 'participation' (from a critical model) around pre-defined outcomes has been critiqued as a de-politicising move within international development discourses (Leal 2007). Taken to a preventative model of sexuality education, students are expected to challenge power relations at the same time as a particular 'truth' of bodies and their relations form the basis for this action. Furthermore, the ideology of 'good health for all' (Lupton 1995, 2) makes a preventative discourse particularly hard to critique, foreclosing attention of what political rationality might be at play within it. As explored in the rest of this paper, what is at stake here is both how a preventative model of sexuality education may draw on and extend neo-liberal relations of international development (Cornwall 2007) *and* what effects these relations may have on the youth that they claim to help.

Targeting gender within a neo-liberal political rationality

Within a preventative model of sexuality education, that focus given to 'gender' can be seen to enact how neo-liberal development discourses are not just concerned with what people 'do', but also who they are, and what relations they have to one another. In the context of HIV prevention initiatives, this has played out in the privileging and normalising of particular identities 'especially those associated with individualism and economic rationality' (Kerr and Mkandawire 2010, 459). This includes the focus on 'responsibility' for sexual decision-making (Adam 2005), particularly among youth who, as not-yet-adult (Lesko 2001), are not 'set in their ways' (Boler and Archer 2008, 36). Within these constructions, the critique is not only that neo-liberal discourse constructs the (supposedly) gender-neutral economic individual through gendered norms and expectations that privilege masculine subjects (Elson 1999). It is also that an 'inclusive neo-liberalism' mobilises notions of gender through 'governance practices' of 'empowerment, self-government and responsibility' (Bedford 2009, xv). For example, in the context of World Bank policies, Bedford (2009) argues that economic policy is intimately connected to the promotion of a 'normative model of heterosexuality' (1) propagated through ideological constructions of 'loving couples' (28). Here, the figures of the empowered women and caring man can be seen to work in the service of resolving 'tensions between paid work and social reproduction' that have been created through neo-liberal economic policies.

Read through this lens, framing 'gender' as something to 'teach' across a range of 'local' contexts is inseparable from global restructuring as 'the construction, reconstruction, and transformation of categories of knowing' (Marchand and Runyan 2000, 2). Sexuality education as an HIV prevention strategy is thus a particularly dense site for exploring both (1) what kinds of gendered subjects are mobilised within it as well as (2) how it might rely upon and set the conditions for a particular kind of relation between gendered subjects. In order to explore this site, I work with neo-liberalism as a 'political rationality' (Brown 2003). As a political rationality, neo-liberalism extends a market rationale into 'all aspects of thought and activity' (Brown 2003, para. 19). This includes a mode of governmentality of subjects whereby the very 'freedom' of the subject to act becomes their regulation, based on the *moralization* of the consequences of this freedom' (Brown 2003, emphasis original, para. 17). This lens provides a way to explore the traces of neo-liberalism within 'local' places, while simultaneously resisting deterministic readings of neo-liberalism on the subjects and relations it targets. In South Africa, for example, there have been complex and competing moves to reconstitute the 'nation' post-apartheid (Hart 2014).[1] By 'encountering' gender within sexuality education, my goal is thus to ask what effects a neo-liberal political rationality might have on the imaginaries of gender being offered to youth *through* sexuality education as an HIV prevention strategy, while simultaneously *provoking the limits* of that rationality through its encounters with particular educators and learners.

Methodology

The encounters with gender presented in this paper are drawn from an ethnographic research study that was carried out from 2012 to 2013 with the South African non-governmental organisation loveLife. The purpose of the study was to explore the experiences of South African educators and youth as they teach and learn about gender, gender relations and empowerment in the context of sexuality education as an HIV prevention strategy. Over the course of one year, I worked with staff educators (known at the time as 'Regional Programme Leaders') in the Western Cape region of South Africa as they selected, trained and supported a group of youth peer educators (known as 'groundBREAKERs'). Data were drawn from three ethnographic methods: field notes from participant observation (at regional training events as well as educational activities within particular communities), individual semi-structured interviews (with staff educators and youth peer educators) and artefact analysis (including curricular documents, other educational materials and media and research documents related to loveLife). Data were analysed using the qualitative research software AtlasTi, with a focus on open coding as a dynamic process where 'new connections spark among words, bodies, objects and ideas' (MacLure 2013, 229). Writing was then engaged as a mode of analysis, using juxtaposition of a diverse range of source materials to 'make something new and different of what we think we already know' (Ellsworth 2005, 13). Specifically, I wove observational data into a series of vignettes. The fragmentary form of the vignette works against the interpretive authority of a 'full' and linear story within traditional ethnographic texts (Britzman 2000). As evocative scenes, the vignettes are grounded in a 'stubborn materiality' (Lather 2007, 10) that is irreducible to a single story, including the inevitable interpretive power of research stories. The 'reality' of the vignettes took form through a research encounter with and through a particular time and place. Instead of quotes, I have used italics to represent the collection of quotes, translations and remembered moments from these particular encounters. I have then engaged each vignette for connections and tensions of with other threads of data as well as the broader research literature.

This description of how the research was 'done' is inseparable from a key dilemma within feminist and post-structural readings of ethnographic research: 'how does one act knowing what one does?' (Visweswaran in St. Pierre and Pillow 2000, 1). Within the ethnographic field as a 'contested and fictive geography' (Britzman 2000, 28), a white North American cisgender researcher studying 'gender' inevitably repeats the imperial histories of ethnography and Western hierarchies of knowledge that operate within HIV prevention discourses (Chilisa 2005). However, as will be explored below, this has provided an opportunity to explicitly engage with relations of power and knowledge that my body momentarily made visible in these encounters. Refusing to 'solve' this limitation is itself a political statement that there is not a 'global' truth of gender within sexuality education at the same time as it is impossible to hold forward a 'local' place (with 'local' subjects) as an educational solution to what it means to know and be known as gendered subjects.

I invite the reader to momentarily lose the received 'truth' of gender by going into the 'middle of things' (Tsing 2005, 1). This particular 'middle of things' picks up from when Lu, a groundBREAKER who described his own gender as a 'son of the world' (Interview, 15 August 2013), and I co-facilitated a session entitled 'Gender'. This session is part of love4-Life, loveLife's 'core programme aimed at empowering young people with knowledge, attitudes and skills' (loveLife 2012, 4). My aim is not to evaluate the impact of this session (in terms of behavioural outcomes, for example). Instead, I seek to problematise the political rationality shaping these encounters while simultaneously attending to how the encounters may exceed their stated intentions.

Three encounters with gender

An encounter through definition

The first activity in the love4Life 'Gender' session is entitled 'How we learn gender roles'. The broad aims of the activity are to 'understand how socialization can trap us into certain roles as men and women' and 'challenge some stereotypes about men and women' (loveLife 2012, 154). Lu began by introducing the topic:

> Lu asks: *what is gender?* One boy says male and female. I continue: *are there different ways that boys and girls are brought up?* Most of the learners say yes – parents allow boys to go out at night, guys think ladies are weak. Next question: *why are there differences?* One male learner explains that guys have a penis. No, says another male learner, *we are all human.* (Fieldnotes, August 2013)

This introduction began with a definitional question: *what is gender?* Within the logic of the script, whereby sex refers to 'certain physical differences between males and female' and gender refers to 'the way we are brought up and socialized' (loveLife 2012, 157), the response given by the learner is incorrect. Following a sex/gender binary, dominant within international development discourses (e.g. World Health Organization 2015), the learner should have responded that gender refers to 'men' and 'women', or brought in some discussion of social roles. This focus on *what* is being defined draws attention to the learners need for 'correct' information, regardless of how these terms are often used interchangeably in English and the educator and learners were English second-language speakers. Furthermore, the way that the slippage between sex and gender quickly passed unchallenged by both Lu and myself can be seen as an effect of the binary construction of these terms. While a sex/gender binary explicitly distances 'gender' from biological bodies (sex), the binary remains tethered to a biological truth of bodies through that binary (Butler 1990). In other words, gender may be a social construction (norms of masculinity and femininity), but the illusion of two fundamentally separate bodies (male and female) is necessary in order to enact those gender roles. Furthermore, those binary constructions are already implicated in the validation of one term through the 'subsumption and exclusion' of the other (Sedgwick 2008, 10). This includes the 'truth' of biological bodies as male/female and the establishment of masculine/feminine as 'expressive attributes' of those bodies (Butler 1990, 283). The risk is thus that relying on a distinction between 'sex' and 'gender' to teach gender equality, as seen in this encounter as well as in loveLife's definition of 'gender roles' as 'largely determined by the world we are brought up in' (loveLife 2012, 157), may actually reify and mask the very power relations that it explicitly aims to address. Working with and engaging the potential effects of this risk necessitates not only analysing *what* is taught, but also *how* that 'answer' becomes coherent within the pedagogical encounter.

Each of the 'answers' given by learners in this particular encounter revolved around a definitional question: *what is gender?* This question is built on the assumption that there is a knowable answer, and indeed this is the explicit aim of this activity: making sure that learners understand what gender 'is' before the session continues. The issue, however, is that the move to fix gender into something that 'is' has already relied upon, and in doing so redeployed, particular ways of understanding gendered identities within relations of power and knowledge. For example, in the second part of this vignette, I relied upon an underlying binarised construction of gendered identity to ask the question: *are there differences in the ways that boys and girls are brought up?* Following the love4Life script (loveLife 2012), the aim of this discussion is to disrupt gender roles as 'natural' and challenge 'stereotypes that unfairly put people into categories that rob them of their personhood' (157). Yet, the coherence of the question about differences in the ways boys and girls are brought up is reliant upon particular and binarised conceptions of personhood: *boys/girls*. Learners are thus already being understood in terms of categories based on gender (speaking as *boys* or *girls*) as well as age (as youth who are still *being brought up*). Learners are then expected to take up these positions to speak about how parents treat children differently – *boys are allowed to go out at night* – as well as articulate particular gendered identities – *ladies are weak*. In contrast, and in line with their role of 'trying to eliminate gender bias' (loveLife 2012, 156), the educator is positioned as being able to step outside of any *bias* that they themselves might have. This positioning relies upon, at the same time as it reifies, a view of educators as 'deliverers of an uncontested, sanitized and agreed upon body of content' (Baxen 2010, 17). It also props up a view of education as the solution to the 'problems' of upbringing, drawing coherence from long histories of sexuality education as a corrective to the racialized and classed (and non-western) family (Stoler 1995). At the end of this encounter, a learner potentially resisted the understandings of gender at play when he spoke back to a biological definition of gender (*guys have a penis*) by stating that *we are all human*. However, within the definitional logic of the session, humanistic conceptions of identity mark a 'self-contained, authentic subject' (Alcoff 1988, 415) in tension with the 'extent to which subjectivity in South Africa is a raced, cultured, gendered and classed experience' (Soudien 2009, 41). The risk is thus not only that being 'human' fails to achieve a gender-neutral subject, but also that it simultaneously works to mask the power-laden discursive norms that make gendered subjects intelligible.

These definitional moves can be seen to operate within and redeploy a neo-liberal political rationality on two registers. For one, the definition of 'gender' draws coherence from and redeploys a reproductive heterosexuality, whereby economic development is coupled with the nuclear family unit (Bedford 2009). Definition drew on gender as a binarized identity pivoting around the 'truth' of biological bodies. Secondly, the pedagogical practice of definition enacts the moral imperative for rational, and individual, decision-making. Once gender is clearly defined, any learner (boy or girl) can, and must, overcome gendered norms by being empowered through knowledge. Indeed, by getting to 'the' answer, the struggles over knowledge already at play within any act of definition were masked. Furthermore, while seemingly contradictory, these two registers enact a struggle over subjectivity within neo-liberalism whereby the gendering of the individual is masked through the imperative for the individual to overcome social identities in order to act. In other words, pedagogical practices of definition are a limiting act: an impossible division of self from Other in the claim to know what gender 'is'. In this particular session, those divisions were scripted through the western epistemologies of the English language: what can be defined (gender as sex/gender), who controls the definition (the 'correct' answer according to an English script) and the deployment of particular 'aspirations' within that definition (here: gender equality). The question then becomes how the pedagogical approach meets and engages the power-laden limits that it inevitably repeats.

An encounter within the pedagogical approach

Lu and I held the class outside, sitting on a concrete slab surrounded by overgrown grass. There were long silences, and wanting to boost the energy of the group, I started an agree/disagree activity from the love4Life script. As the facilitator, I read a statement from the script, such as *a girl wearing a short skirt is asking to be raped*. In response, learners moved to opposite sides of class space depending on whether they agreed or disagreed with the statement.

> *Agree or disagree?* Lu translates for me as the learners speak. While the translations help me follow the session they also feel like an interruption, pausing the discussion as well as the movement of the activity. I keep reading the statements – *A girl wearing a short skirt is asking to be raped*. A group of boys agree: *she is showing off her body and guys are attracted*. *No*, disagrees most of the class, including all of the girls, *it is just how she is dressed*. I read another statement: *It is our culture that men have more than one wife*. Most of the boys and one girl agrees. A girl who disagrees explains: *you don't know if those men have an infection*. Another statement: *A man is head of the household*. Most of the boys agree: *they pay ilobola*[2] *and work*. The girls disagree: *women can also work*. (Fieldnotes, August 2013)

My first reading of gender in this vignette focused on finding gender: exploring the session for how learners understood gendered identities and relations. This has been a dominant way of engaging 'gender' in educational research with youth, including in South Africa, and has been crucial for destabilising individualistic and (supposedly) gender-neutral HIV prevention messages aimed at youth. In this vignette, for example, the comment that boys *pay ilobola and work*, and are therefore the *head of the household*, draws on the discursive construction of a 'provider' masculinity that is constituted through coexisting discourses of 'tradition' and 'modernity' and draws on multiple and contested struggles over identity within histories of capitalism, colonialism and Christianity (Hunter 2010; Jewkes and Morrell 2010). As part of hegemonic masculinity (Connell 1987), a dominant and highly valued form of masculinity that is 'structured along lines of gendered domination' in South Africa (Jewkes and Morrell 2010, 3), these understandings of gendered identity are in tension with HIV prevention messages that expect young men and women to equally embrace an empowered modern subjectivity. Furthermore, and as seen in the ways that learners make sense of femininity within this vignette, already contested understandings of gendered identities are at play. On the one hand, social norms of femininity and masculinity that position men as active and women as passive (Walker, Reid, and Cornell 2004), together with a normalisation of violence as a part of masculine control of women's bodies (Jewkes and Morrell 2010), allows a group of boys to collapse being *attracted* to girls wearing a short skirt to possessing her body through force. On the other hand, there are moments when girls actively resist these constructions. For example, one girl draws on public health's 'modern' individual (Lupton 1995), saying that *you don't know if those men have an infection*, to speak back to cultural (and implicitly 'traditional') expectations: *men should have more than one wife*. In contrast, the girl who agreed with these expectations may have found being one of several partners to be a space of negotiation for gendered expectations within her sexual relationships (Jewkes 2009) or a means to achieve economic aims (Winskell and Enger 2009). The language of multiple concurrent partners, while framed as a 'key driver for HIV infection' (UNAIDS 2008), may also be appropriated as a woman also having the right to multiple partners. Overall, as moments that highlight contested and power-laden understandings of masculinity and femininity, these readings contribute to problematising simplistic understandings of youth's worlds that plague HIV and AIDS prevention work (Bhana and Pattman 2009).

At the same time, attending to these notions *within* the pedagogical approach speaks to the risk of separating understandings of masculinity and femininity from the conditions that have enabled them to be articulated. In other words, the pedagogical approach can be engaged as setting the conditions for *what* is said in terms of *who* speaks, *what* is expected to be spoken about, and *how* that speaking occurs (Lodge 2005; Bragg 2007; Gacoin 2010). In the case of this agree/disagree activity, *who* spoke was invited through a pedagogical 'mode of address' (Ellsworth 1997): an address through curricula and pedagogies that 'invite their users to take up particular positions within relations of knowledge, power and desire' (2). As the educator, I invited youth into this encounter by asking them to embody gendered positions grounded on shared cultural definitions of gender. By taking cultural definitions as an underlying 'truth', the pedagogical approach foreclosed consideration of how cultural understandings of 'gender' are entangled in understandings of other social identities, such as race and class. Simultaneously, it took the discursive separation of gender from other social identities as a condition for participating in the session: there are mutual (agree), even if contested (disagree), understandings of *who* men and women are said to be. This was extended when *what* was talked about was 'gender'. As a topic, a particular articulation of gender (gender roles and expectations) was centred through the pedagogical act of definition, as discussed in the previous section. *How* that speaking occurred, in turn, was invited through the pedagogical approach. As I facilitated the activity, I watched as learners physically embodied the gendered binary of the activity: it was us against them; *boys* against *girls*. A few learners did break the gendered space, but no one stepped into the physical space in-between the groups that had been instructed to *agree* or *disagree*. The pedagogical use of space worked in the service of particular lines of intelligibility for gendered identities and their relations where *agree* and *disagree* became about the right and wrong answers of gender equality.

Reading these lines of intelligibility against my own body in this encounter provides a way to attending to traces of a neo-liberal political rationality within them. Standing before this group of learners, my body was a material enactment of the 'colonially established framework of homogeneity in the search for answers and solutions to the HIV/AIDS epidemics' (Chilisa 2005, 668). I was a white North American cisgender researcher who wanted to 'find' gender and who found my own coherence in the focus on heterosexual relationships. I was using an English script designed to get youth to 'understand' and 'challenge' gender roles, with the ultimate goal of caring intimate partnerships. Centred around gender, this address foreclosed attention to the specificities of the learners in front of me, black isiXhosa-speaking learners from a poor township outside of Cape Town, and the entanglement of gender with other social identities. My very ability to travel into this 'local' space was shaped through neo-liberalism's free-floating global citizen. Of course, it could be argued that I should not have been the educator in the first place – that I am an outsider, that it was not appropriate. However, removing my body does not erase the relations of knowing and being known that were already at play. These were the dividing lines of what could be coherent as gender, and gender relations, in this encounter: researcher/participant; north/south; white/black; foreigner/national; homosexuality/heterosexuality. Driven by its own binary logic, a pedagogical approach based on equality/inequality became part of the repetition of the very terms it claimed to challenge.

Encountering gender within the pedagogical approach is an encounter with that approach as an always-political act. Engaging this particular encounter within a neo-liberal political rationality foregrounds how the pedagogical approach constituted the 'right' answers of gender equality at the same time as it set the rational conditions for achieving that answer. However, the point here is not that the pedagogical approach is a (supposedly neutral) tool for transmitting a political project. Rather, my aim is to draw attention to how the pedagogical approach is itself what Foucault calls a technology of power: a 'whole set of instruments, techniques, procedures, levels of application, targets' that 'assures an infinitesimal distribution of the power relations' (Foucault 1995, 216). In this particular encounter, and drawing on gender as a definable object of knowledge, the pedagogical approach mobilised particular relations of power and knowledge and settled them into what can be 'known' about gender. Supported by the ideological language of equality, the approach potentially reified understandings of social identities and their relations that have unequal and violent effects in people's lived lives. These are lives that are already exceeding a neo-liberal political rationality that seeks to target them through the ideological language of gender empowerment.

Encountering gender equality with(in) words

Lu and I had 50 minutes for the 'Gender' session. At the end, Lu gave a summary of the key messages for the learners.

> Guys have rights, he says, but should also help at home. In my culture, men are the head of the household (I used to think this, he explains to me after the session, but I don't agree with it now). Girls weren't allowed to work in the mines, but now they can. There is nothing that women can't do. There is no specific duty for each and every gender. (That is my role, he later tells me, making sure they know about inequality and equality). (Fieldnotes, August 2013)

In these final words, Lu enacted a particular pedagogical vision of gender empowerment, organised into a linear and rational flow of identities and their forms of knowledge. Within this vision, youth should first recognise that there are unequal gendered expectations within their communities – *such as men being head of the household.* Secondly, youth must understand that these roles can change, as seen in the example that girls can now *work in the mines.* Finally, youth will accept that there is *no specific duty* for each and every gender. In this imaginary, the notion of gender is reduced to power relations that circulate through social norms and stereotypes. The problem is power imbalances between gender roles. The solution is education: understand and challenge unequal power relations (within a set amount of time, here 50 minutes).

Part of the discursive power of this approach is how it draws on ideologies of critical pedagogy that seeks to transform the consciousness of learners (Apple 2004). Lu himself embodied this transformation when he told me that he changed his own views because of the loveLife training and defined his own sexuality in terms of a rejection of 'male dominance' (Interview, 15 August 2013). Armed with this transformation, he was ready to embody his perceived role as educator – making sure that learners *know about inequality and equality.* As we worked together throughout the year, I saw his commitment to 'learn from' the learners: listening to feedback from learners after a session, coming up with topics based on issues he saw in his community, trying to make the sessions fun and engaging. In my notes, I remarked upon the sense of rapport that he seemed to have with the learners, and I continue to admire the way that he resisted addressing learners at this school as deviant and unruly subjects. However, there are many parts of this encounter with the discourse of gender empowerment that continue to trouble me. I had suggested this session, and Lu may have been performing the 'good' educator in relation to gender and my research interests. What he thought I wanted to know, as well as what I can claim to know, were a constitutive part of this encounter and my readings of it. Furthermore, the stark binary of *inequality* and *equality* carried with it implicit judgements of those who failed to step into the side of equality, an enactment of the moralising effects of a neoliberal political rationality. Pivoting around a binary construction of gender (masculine/feminine), a further effect was the silencing of other inequalities that young people might be facing in their lives, such as racism, poverty and homophobia. This silencing was a troubling enactment of how neo-liberalism may appropriate alternative political rationalities, such as those underlying critical pedagogy (McLaren 2001), and draw credibility through the ideological power of terms such as 'equality' and 'empowerment' (Cornwall 2007).

As I have thought about these silences, I have re-encountered gender in the words of the educators as they spoke with me during interviews. I find gender in responses to questions about how they would address issues such as gender and gender relations in their work. Gender should be about 'equality' (Gustav, Interview, 6 August 2013), teaching learners that it is a '50/50 situation' (Nkunzi, Interview, 29 June 2013). Gender relations are about the 'facts' and making youth aware of 'what is happening' within communities

(Drifter, Interview, 28 May 2013; Nyla, Interview, 17 May 2013) – teenage pregnancy, rape, stereotypes of men and women. Gender power plays out when learners do not live up to particular expectations, such as taking up the risky position of 'independent women' leading to 'being abused' or 'being excluded' (Makaziwe, Interview, 15 July 2013). Once found, these words can be used to argue for the importance of speaking about gender relations with youth in sexuality education.

At the same time, the educators and I continually lost what we could articulate as gender with(in) our words. One groundBREAKER, Gustav, told me that answering the question 'how do you define your gender' was difficult. Makaziwe, a Regional Programme Leader, said that the very notion of gender needed 'unpacking', noting that most conversations about gender happened within jokes rather than a particular session (Interview, 15 July 2013). This ongoing difficulty of articulating what gender 'is' was particularly evident in the interview with Varni, a Regional Programme Leader. Varni first defined gender as 'male and female' and as something that can be 'taught' (Interview, 10 June 2013). However, as she continued to speak, she said that it is a 'broad topic if you really go into [it]'. At that point in the interview, trying to understand what she meant by 'broad', I asked her about an image from the love4Life manual that represents gender as a spectrum. The image, which has the potential to disrupt binarised understandings of gender, was a new addition to the curriculum in 2013, and was part of a loveLife session that had been revised by a North American woman introduced to me as the 'gender expert' (Fieldnotes, January 2013). In response, Varni said that she had not seen the image. It is possible that she did intend to read this session before using it, although the interview took place several months into the 'implementation' of the programme. It is also possible that she had disregarded the new session as irrelevant, resisting the foreign 'expert' and/or process of top-down curricular change. At the same time, as she continued to speak, she invoked gender as a 'complex topic' and said that the curriculum only takes young people through a 'very small part of gender'. She also pointed to the complexity of gender when she defined her gender as female, but then said that this definition was something that she had grown up with: 'you're either male or you're female'. Throughout the interview, I found myself chasing this 'complex topic', wanting Varni to articulate exactly what she meant. In doing so, I slid into my desire for knowledge and definition and potentially shut down the very complexity I was seeking.

If the interviews marked a failure to 'find' gender, they were also exceeded by already complex and contested understandings of gender. Consider, for example, the pseudonym of one participant: Nkunzi. During the interview, Nkunzi responded to my question of 'how do you define your gender' by evoking the pseudonym: 'a person with the name that I gave you, Nkunzi which means "a bull"' (Interview, June 29, 2013). Through the research act of choosing a pseudonym, Nkunzi marked a way of understanding identity that exceeded the concerns of research confidentiality. He named himself by drawing on an understanding of identity within the isiXhosa language, whereby a name is drawn from and locates a person within social relations (Ubuntu Bridge, n.d.). This naming exceeded the imaginary of a free-floating gendered individual at the same time as it exceeded the binary of man/woman that settles through the western epistemologies of the English language.

In re-encountering gender within these interviews, I have come to ask how the difficulty of finding gender might be part of the condition for beginning to think outside of a neoliberal political rationality guiding sexuality education as an HIV prevention strategy. Across these encounters with(in) words, it was the moments we (learners, educators, researcher) failed to 'speak' gender that notions of gender may have escaped their definitional weight. This encounter is always an incredibly murky space. *Rights*, *culture* and *equality* are themselves contested terms (Cornwall 2007). Yet, sexuality education relies on these words in the promise of gender empowerment. I am not arguing that we need to get rid of these words, but I am asking what it might mean to take them as part of the limits of what comes to be articulated as gender within sexuality education, operating at the limits of multiple relations of power and knowledge, rather than a description of gender's truths.

Discussion: gender, youth and the lived effects of a neo-liberal political rationality

The encounters with gender discussed in this paper problematise how 'gender' is defined and engaged within a neo-liberal political rationality. Within a scripted curriculum, the 'problem' of gender was targeted through pedagogical acts of definition that drew on and mobilised heteronormative and Westernised understandings of gendered subjects. As a technology of power, the pedagogical approach extended these definitional acts in terms of particular imaginaries of gender relations. Across these encounters with gender, and through the 'solution' of sexuality education, the complexity of social identities and their relations was met with the imaginary of a free-floating individual subject. This subject is central to loveLife's pedagogical imaginary: from the accounts of educators who framed their task to as getting youth to discover themselves as 'individuals' to senior staff members who told me that the core of programme was about 'self-awareness' (Grace Matlhape, Personal Communication, 7 August 2013) and valuing young people's 'own sense of themselves' (Scott Burnett, Personal communication, 3 October 2013). While loveLife's approach was developed in resistance to individualistic and moralistic abstinence-based messages (Robbins 2010), the imaginary of the individual remains tethered to the claim that knowing the self will enable the self to act. Mobilised within the context of inequitable gender relations as a 'problem' for HIV prevention, knowing the gendered self becomes crucial to this action. In other words, a sense of personal (gendered) identity is key for action *and* this action (here: being in charge of his or her own life) serves as the moral compass of identity.

What is at stake within this rationality is not only the individualisation of responsibility for health decisions. What is also at stake is what happens to the gendered subject at the limits of their intelligibility. Following Butler (2004), a feminist politics committed to the 'social transformation of gender relations' (204) is not just about making already knowable gendered subjects (such as particular articulations of 'man' and 'woman') and their relations more equitable. It is about working at the limits of the discursive norms of gender, and asking how, and at what expense, particular articulations of gendered identities become intelligible. This intelligibility is crucial for having what Butler terms a 'livable life' (224): a life that embodies particular norms, such as understandings of masculinity and femininity, which in turn make that life intelligible (and by extension valuable) in specific discursive contexts. Lives that do not fit within these understandings are positioned outside of what is considered 'real' in terms of the categories that are needed to make sense of the world. Within the discursive context of sexuality education as a global HIV prevention strategy, this raises disturbing questions related to whose lives are made to count within a neo-liberal political rationality that mobilises gender identity as a universal target and knowable target and goal. Sexuality education as an HIV prevention strategy is filled with stories of *who* youth are and what they need: imperialist stories concerned with the deviant African subject, development narratives diagnosing 'local' problems, international 'best practice' guides that promise the solution. As long as moral responsibility is equated with individual action, the tellers of these tales (such as 'expert' policy-makers, programme developers and researchers) will not be held to account for relations of power and knowledge deployed in the name of 'helping' youth. Furthermore, while the explicit goal is to save lives (HIV prevention), sexuality education within this political rationality is complicit in sacrificing lives that fall outside the discursive limits of who gendered subjects are already said to be as well as what kinds of relations they are presumed to have.

At the same time, perhaps these dilemmas may be the grounds for beginning to articulate different ways of thinking about how gender is engaged within sexuality education in this particular globalised moment. Here, I am specifically resisting what should be 'done' (in terms of revised curricula or learning objectives, for example). Throughout this paper, I have argued that the 'doing' of sexuality education is an *effect* of how power-laden understandings of self, Other and knowledge take form within its conceptual boundaries. What I am suggesting is that encountering gender *within* sexuality education already resists deterministic accounts of who youth are and what they need, including understandings of gendered identities and their relations. These encounters foreground teaching about gender is an always-problematic site, rather than a 'solution' to the dilemmas of knowing and being known. Working within this site, I suggest that one possible articulation for sexuality education would be formed through a political rationality of vulnerability. When understandings of self are understood as intimately connected with understandings of Other, this co-constitutive relation becomes the condition of responsibility for one another (Butler 2001). This vulnerability extends through understandings of multiple social identities (such as race, class and gender) as well as their mobilisation across 'global' and 'local' spaces. As notions of gender are encountered through sexuality education, it is these encounters themselves that may be an invitation to interrogate multiple relations of power and knowledge already at play in any articulation of what gender 'is'.

Conclusion

It is necessary, but not enough, to talk about complexity *within* notions of gender in sexuality education. While gendered meanings may be complex, the risk is that the analytic frame (the notion of gender) is somehow propped up as a neutral and universal concept that works in the service of particular political projects. This might not seem like a 'new' argument. The term 'gender' has sparked decades of feminist debates, including: the linguistic limits of the term (e.g. Haraway 1991); the distinction, or lack thereof, between sex and gender (e.g. Butler 1990; Rubin 2011); and what power relations are deployed and reified when gender is a 'problem' for international development initiatives (e.g. Saunders 2004; Cornwall, Harrison, and Whitehead 2007). However, and what I argue is 'new', sexuality education as a global HIV prevention strategy has the potential to both reify as well as challenge the power relations within these articulations of gender.

I recognise that by focusing on a neo-liberal political rationality in this analysis, I risk foreclosing attention to other political rationalities already at play in the particular context of South Africa. However, part of my argument is that opening space for alternative political rationalities requires de-stabilizing the hold that a neo-liberal political rationality has on the 'problem' of gender and the 'solution' of sexuality education at this particular moment. The United States Agency for International Development (USAID) is currently funding a five year 'School-Based Sexuality and HIV Prevention Education Activity' to be implemented across South Africa.[3] Scripted lesson plans are being developed based on characteristics of 'effective' programmes, including addressing gender norms, drawing on the 'expertise' of North American consultants (Wood and Rolleri 2014). These scripts will deploy multiple and power-laden understandings of gendered subjects and their relations as the 'solution' to the complexities that youth are already living.

Following notions of 'gender' into the pedagogical encounter foregrounds the impossibility of ever simply 'transmitting' them (such as through scripted curricula). Notions of gender are unsettled, and unsettling, within those encounters. They operate within relations of difference, even as they may be re-articulated in ways that challenge what that difference is said to be. Educators and learners (and researcher) are already struggling with the excesses of the 'small part' of gender that can be contained in any scripted session. I have argued that it is those struggles that invite an articulation of sexuality education that exceeds what can/is/should be known about gender identities and their relations. It is about beginning to articulate an alternative political rationality for sexuality education that is interested in what might happen to all social identities and their entangled relations in the pedagogical space between *agree* and *disagree*.

Notes

1. This includes discourses of re-nationalisation specific to the histories of South Africa. I take up these moves in a separate paper drawn from this study problematising the possibility of a stable (and "local") youth subject that can be targeted and empowered through sexuality education.
2. In South Africa, *ilobola* refers to the practice of a man providing compensation (such as cattle or cash) to the family of the woman he is marrying. It is considered to represent the customary negotiation of a marriage (Department of Justice and Constitutional Development 2015).
3. See http://www.ngopulse.org/opportunity/2015/08/25/curriculum-development-coordinator.

Acknowledgements

I would like to thank the participants of this study for welcoming me into your work, sharing your time with me, and for trusting me with versions of the worlds that you are living. Thank you as well to my doctoral committee, Drs Mona Gleason, Lisa Loutzenheiser and James Lees, for proving guidance and support through all stages of this project.

Disclosure statement

No potential conflict of interest was reported by the author.

References

Adam, Barry D. 2005. "Constructing the Neoliberal Sexual Actor: Responsibility and Care of the Self in the Discourse of Barebackers." *Culture, Health & Sexuality* 7 (4): 333–346.

Adams, Mary Louise. 1997. *The Trouble with Normal: Postwar Youth and the Making of Heterosexuality*. Toronto: University of Toronto Press.

Aggleton, Peter, and Mary Crewe. 2005. "Effects and Effectiveness in Sex and Relationships Education." *Sex Education: Sexuality, Society and Learning* 5 (4): 303–306. doi:10.1080/14681810500278030.

Alcoff, Linda. 1988. "Cultural Feminism Versus Post-structuralism: The Identity Crisis in Feminist Theory." *Signs: Journal of Women in Culture and Society* 13 (3): 405–436.

Apple, Michael W. 2004. *Ideology and Curriculum*. 3rd ed. New York: RoutledgeFalmer.

Baxen, Jean. 2010. *Performative Praxis: Teacher Identity and Teaching in the Context of HIV/AIDS*. New York: Peter Lang.

Bedford, Kate. 2009. *Developing Partnerships: Gender, Sexuality and the Reformed World Bank*. Minneapolis: University of Minnesota Press.

Bhana, Deevia, and Rob Pattman. 2009. "Researching South African Youth, Gender and Sexuality within the Context of HIV/AIDS." *Development* 52 (1): 68–74. doi:10.1057/dev.2008.75.

Boler, Tania, and David Archer. 2008. *The Politics of Prevention: A Global Crisis in AIDS and Education*. London: Pluto Press.

Bragg, Sara. 2007. "'Student Voice' and Governmentality: The Production of Enterprising Subjects." *Discourse: Studies in the Cultural Politics of Education* 28 (3): 343–358. doi:10.1080/01596300701458905.

Britzman, Deborah P. 1998. *Lost Subjects, Contested Objects*. Albany: State University of New York Press.

Britzman, Deborah P. 2000. "'The Question of Belief': Writing Poststructural Ethnography." In *Working the Ruins: Feminist Poststructural Theory and Methods in Education*, edited by Elizabeth Adams St. Pierre and Wanda S. Pillow, 27–40. New York: Routledge.

Brown, Wendy. 2003. "Neo-liberalism and the end of Liberal Democracy." *Theory & Event* 7 (1). doi:10.1353/tae.2003.0020.

Butler, Judith. 1990. *Gender Trouble: Feminism and the Subversion of Identity*. New York: Routledge, Chapman and Hall.

Butler, Judith. 2001. "Giving an Account of Oneself." *Diacritics* 31 (4): 22–40.

Butler, Judith. 2004. *Undoing Gender*. New York: Routledge.

Campbell, Catherine, and Catherine MacPhail. 2002. "Peer Education, Gender and the Development of Critical Consciousness: Participatory HIV Prevention by South African Youth." *Social Science & Medicine* 55: 331–345.

Chilisa, Bagele. 2005. "Educational Research Within Postcolonial Africa: A Critique of HIV/AIDS Research in Botswana." *International Journal of Qualitative Studies in Education* 18 (6): 659–684. doi:10.1080/09518390500298170.

Connell, Robert. 1987. *Gender and Power*. Stanford, CT: Stanford University Press.

Cornwall, Andrea. 2007. "Buzzwords and Fuzzwords: Deconstructing Development Discourse." *Development in Practice* 17 (4): 471–484. doi:10.1080/09614520701469302.

Cornwall, Andrea, Elizabeth Harrison, and Ann Whitehead. 2007. "Introduction - Feminisms in Development: Contradictions, Contestations and Challenges." In *Feminisms in Development: Contradictions, Contestations & Challenges*, edited by Andrea Cornwall, Elizabeth Harrison, and Ann Whitehead, 1–17. London: Zed Books.

Department of Justice and Constitutional Development. 2015. "Getting Married under Customary Law." Department of Justice and Constitutional Development. Accessed August 27. http://www.justice.gov.za/services/getting-married-cusmar-law.html.

Ellsworth, Elizabeth. 1997. *Teaching Positions: Difference, Pedagogy and the Power of Address*. New York: Teachers College Press.

Ellsworth, Elizabeth. 2005. *Places of Learning: Media, Architecture, Pedagogy*. New York: Routledge.

Elson, Diane. 1999. "Labor Markets as Gendered Institutions: Equality, Efficiency and Empowerment Issues." *World Development* 27 (3): 611–627. doi:10.1016/S0305-750X(98)00147-8.

Fields, Jessica. 2008. *Risky Lessons: Sex Education and Social Inequality*. New Brunswick, NJ: Rutgers University Press.

Foucault, Michel. 1995. *Discipline and Punish: The Birth of the Prison*. Translated by Alan Sheridan. Original ed., 1975. Reprint, 1975. New York: Random House.

Gacoin, Andrée. 2010. "Youth Voice and HIV Prevention: Discursive Opportunities, Limitations and Productive Impossibilities." *Discourse: Studies in the Cultural Politics of Education* 31 (2): 165–178. doi:10.1080/01596301003679685.

Gilbert, Jen. 2007. "Risking a Relation: Sex Education and Adolescent Development." *Sex Education: Sexuality, Society and Learning* 7 (1): 47–61. doi:10.1080/14681810601134736.

Glaser, Cliver. 2005. "Managing the Sexuality of Urban Youth: Johannesburg, 1920s–1960s." *International Journal of African Historical Studies* 38 (2): 301–327.

Haberland, Nicole. 2015. "The Case for Addressing Gender and Power in Sexuality and HIV Education: A Comprehensive Review of Evaluation Studies." *International Perspectives on Sexual and Reproductive Health* 41 (1): 31–42. doi:10.1363/4103115.

Haraway, Donna. 1991. *Simians, Cyborgs and Women: The Reinvention of Nature*. New York: Routledge.

Hart, Gillian. 2014. *Rethinking the South African Crisis: Nationalism, Populism, Hegemony*. Athens: University of Georgia Press.

Human Sciences Research Council. 2014. *South African National HIV, Behaviour and Health Study 2012*. Pretoria: Human Sciences Research Council.

Hunter, Mark. 2010. *Love in the Time of AIDS*. Bloomington: Indiana University Press.

Jeeves, Alan. 2001. "Introduction: Histories of Reproductive Health and the Control of Sexually Transmitted Disease in Southern Africa: A Century of Controversy." *South African Historical Journal* 45: 1–10. doi:10.1080/02582470108671399.

Jewkes, Rachel. 2009. "HIV and Women." In *HIV/AIDS in South Africa 25 Years On*, edited by Poul Rohleder, Leslie Swartz, Seth C. Kalichman, and Leickness Chisamu Simbayi, 27–40. New York: Springer.

Jewkes, Rachel, and Robert Morrell. 2010. "Gender and Sexuality: Emerging Perspectives from the Heterosexual Epidemic in South Africa and Implications for HIV Risk and Prevention." *Journal of the International AIDS Society* 13 (6): 1–11.

Kerr, Rachel Bezner, and Paul Mkandawire. 2010. "Imaginative Geographies of Gender and HIV/AIDS: Moving Beyond Neoliberalism." *GeoJournal* 77 (4): 459–473. doi:10.1007/s10708-010-9353-y.

Lather, Patti. 2007. *Getting Lost: Feminist Efforts Toward a Double(d) Science*. Albany: State University of New York.

Leal, Pablo Alejandro. 2007. "Participation: The Ascendancy of a Buzzword in the neo-Liberal Era." *Development in Practice* 17 (4): 539–548. doi:10.1080/09614520701469518.

Lees, James Carlton. 2008. "Rethinking AIDS Education: Laying a New Foundation for more Appropriate Practice in South Africa." Doctoral diss., University of the Western Cape, Faculty of Education.

Lesko, Nancy. 2001. *Act Your age! A Cultural Construction of Adolescence*. New York: RoutledgeFalmer.

Lesko, Nancy. 2010. "Feeling Abstinent? Feeling Comprehensive? Touching the Affects of Sexuality Curricula." *Sex Education: Sexuality, Society and Learning* 10 (3): 281–297. doi:10.1080/14681811.2010.491633.

Lodge, Caroline. 2005. "From Hearing Voices to Engaging in Dialogue: Problematising Student Participation in School Improvement." *Journal of Educational Change* 6 (2): 125–146.

loveLife. 2012. *love4Life*. Johannesburg: New loveLife Trust.

Lupton, Deborah. 1995. *The Imperative of Health: Public Health and the Regulated Body*. London: Sage.

MacLure, Maggie. 2013. "The Wonder of Data." *Cultural Studies, Critical Methodologies* 13 (4): 228–232. doi:10.1177/1532708613487863.

Marchand, Marianne H., and Anne Sisson Runyan. 2000. "Introduction: Feminist Sightings of Global Restructuring: Conceptualizations and Reconceptualizations." In *Gender and Global Restructuring: Sightings, Sites and Resistances*, edited by Marianne H. Marchand and Anne Sisson Runyan, 1–23. London: Routledge.

Massey, Doreen. 2005. *For Space*. London: Sage.

McLaren, Angus. 1999. *Twentieth-century Sexuality: A History*. Malden, MA: Blackwell.

McLaren, Peter. 2001. "Che Guevara, Paulo Freire, and the Politics of Hope: Reclaiming Critical Pedagogy." *Cultural Studies, Critical Methodologies* 1 (1): 108–131. doi:10.1177/153270860100100112.

Pattman, Rob. 2005. "'Boys and Girls Should not be too Close': Sexuality, the Identities of African Boys and Girls and HIV/AIDS Education." *Sexualities* 8 (4): 497–516.

Robbins, David. 2010. *Beyond the Billboards - the LoveLife Story*. Pinegowrie: Porcupine Press.

Rubin, Gayle. 2011. "The Traffic in Women: Notes on the 'Political Economy' of Sex." In *Deviations: A Gayle Rubin Reader*, edited by Gayle Rubin, 33–65. Durham, NC: Duke University Press.

Saunders, Kriemild, ed. 2004. *Feminist Post-development Thought: Rethinking Modernity, Post-colonialism and Representation*. London: Zed Books.

Sedgwick, Eve. 2008. *Epistemology of the Closet*. Original ed., 1990. Berkeley: University of California Press.

Senderowitz, Judy, and Douglas Kirby. 2006. *Standards for Curriculum-Based Reproductive Health and HIV Education Programs*. Arlington, VS: Family Health International.

Soudien, Crain. 2009. "'What to Teach the Natives': A Historiography of the Curriculum Dilemma in South Africa." In *Curriculum Studies in South Africa*, edited by William F. Pinar, 19–49. New York: Palgrave Macmillan.

St. Pierre, Elizabeth Adams, and Wanda S. Pillow. 2000. "Introduction: Inquiry among the Ruins." In *Working the Ruins: Feminist Poststructural Theory and Methods in Education*, edited by Elizabeth Adams St. Pierre and Wanda S. Pillow, 1–24. New York: Routledge.

Stoler, Ann Laura. 1995. *Race and the Education of Desire: Foucault's History of Sexuality and the Colonial Order of Things*. Durham, NC: Duke University Press.

Treichler, Paula. 1999. *How to Have Theory in an Epidemic*. Durham, NC: Duke University Press.

Tsing, Anna Lowenhaupt. 2005. *Friction: An Ethonography of Global Connection*. Princeton, NJ: Princeton University Press.

Ubuntu Bridge. n.d. *Let's Learn Xhosa with Craig Charnock*. Cape Town: Ubuntu Bridge.

UNAIDS. 2004. *AIDS Epidemic Update: December 2004*. Geneva: Joint United Nations Programme on HIV/AIDS.

UNAIDS. 2008. "How do Concurrent Partnerships Impact HIV Prevention?" In *HIV Prevention Toolkit*. Geneva: Joint United Nations Programme on HIV/AIDS. Accessed June 5, 2016. http://hivpreventiontoolkit.unaids.org/support_pages/concurrent_partnerships.aspx.

UNESCO. 2009a. *International Technical Guidance on Sexuality Education: An Evidence-Informed Approach for Schools, Teachers and Health Educators*. 2 vols. Vol. 1: The Rationale for Sexuality Education. Paris: UNESCO.

UNESCO. 2009b. *International Technical Guidance on Sexuality Education: An Evidence-Informed Approach for Schools, Teachers and Health Educators*. 2 vols. Vol. 2: Topics and Learning Objectives. Paris: UNESCO.

Vaughan, Megan. 1991. *Curing their Ills: Colonial Power and African Illness*. Stanford, CA: Stanford University Press.

Walker, Liz, Graeme Reid, and Morna Cornell. 2004. *Waiting to Happen: HIV/AIDS in South Africa, the Bigger Picture*. Boulder, CO: Lynne Rienner.

Wilton, Tasmin, and Peter Aggleton. 1991. "Condoms, Coercion and Control: Heterosexuality and the Limits to HIV/AIDS Education." In *AIDS: Responses, Interventions and Care*, edited by Peter Aggleton, Graham Hart, and Peter Davies, 149–156. London: Falmer Press.

Winskell, Kate, and Dan Enger. 2009. "A New Way of Perceiving the Pandemic: The Findings from a Participatory Research Process on Young Africans' Stories about HIV/AIDS." *Culture, Health and Sexuality* 11 (4): 453–467.

Wood, Lesley, and Lori A. Rolleri. 2014. "Designing an Effective Sexuality Education Curriculum for Schools: Lessons Gleaned from the South(ern) African Literature." *Sex Education: Sexuality, Society and Learning* 14 (5): 525–542. doi:10.1080/14681811.2014.918540.

World Health Organization. 2015. "Gender, Women and Health." Accessed August 25. http://apps.who.int/gender/whatisgender/en/index.html.

Contesting silence, claiming space: gender and sexuality in the neo-liberal public high school

Susan W. Woolley

ABSTRACT

Drawing on ethnographic research in an urban high school in the USA, this article highlights how schooling structures and practices produce and reinforce an ideology of heteronormative binary gender. The construction of gender and sexuality occurs in systematic ways, shaped through structural forces and mapped onto social spaces and bodies. Yet, through the ways that neo-liberalism operates, the production of gender and sexuality is made to appear as individual choice and expression rather than imposed and shaped by structures of inequality. In this context of neo-liberal individualism, educators and students negotiate structures of difference that construct gendered and sexualised bodies and social spaces. By using social semiotics to examine the ways sex, gender, and sexuality are read and written onto bodies and individuals, this research challenges us to think through how 'safe spaces' to be lesbian, gay, bisexual, transgender, queer, and questioning are marked and contested through semiotic means in the social landscape of the neo-liberal public high school.

Introduction

In this neo-liberal moment, schools have become active sites for the production of identity. The construction and assignment of gender and sexuality occur in systematic ways, shaped through structural forces and mapped onto social spaces and bodies. Yet, through the ways that neo-liberalism operates, the production of gender and sexuality is made to appear as individual choice and expression rather than imposed and shaped by structures of inequality. In this context of neo-liberal individualism and accountability, educators and students negotiate structures of difference that construct gendered and sexualised bodies and social spaces. Enduring particularly heightened surveillance of their gendered and sexualised embodiment, lesbian, gay, bisexual, transgender, queer, and questioning (LGBTQ) individuals and collectivities are subject to disciplining forces that reproduce heteronormativity and gender conformity and that punish those who fall outside particular norms.

Context for the research, or the air we breathe

As scholars have pointed out, neo-liberalism has been the defining social paradigm since the late 1970s and early 1980s, although its roots can be traced back to the crisis of over-accumulation that began emerging in the mid-1960s (Harvey 2007; Lipman 2011; Stern 2012). Neo-liberalism asserts that the free market is the solution to inequality and the need for individual freedom. In neo-liberalism, the provision of public goods – like education, welfare, healthcare, and employment – shifts towards their privatisation, open for bidders to compete over in the free market. In this article, I draw on Giroux's (2004) definition of neo-liberalism as a set of values, ideologies, and practices that work more broadly as a cultural field in which marginalised populations are increasingly denied the symbolic, educational, and economic capital necessary for engaged citizenship. In the current social, economic, and political moment of neo-liberalism, cultural ideals of individualism dominate and centre the individual as accountable for him- or herself.

The social paradigm of neo-liberalism is like the air we currently breathe, or the 'common sense' Marxist scholar Antonio Gramsci ([1971] 2012) articulated. 'Common sense' illustrates the traditional popular conception of the world – the incoherent set of generally held assumptions and beliefs common to society (Gramsci [1971] 2012). It is these assumptions and beliefs, this 'common sense', that when internalised and diffused can become all pervasive and hegemonic. Pauline Lipman (2011) argues that neo-liberalism has developed as a new social imaginary,

> a common sense about how we think about society and our place in it ... the way in which ordinary people 'imagine' their world – the common understandings, myths, and stories that make possible generalized practices and the widely shared legitimacy of a particular social order. In this sense, the power of neoliberalism lies in its saturation of social practices and consciousness, making it difficult to think otherwise (6).

Neo-liberalism is the dominant paradigm in which we operate, the 'common sense' we know but seldom name or examine, like the air we breathe and take for granted. This 'common sense' of neo-liberalism is the cultural, economic, and political context in which the US society and education are situated at the current moment.

In this article, I extend this notion of the 'common sense' of neo-liberalism to illustrate how what I call an ideology of heteronormative binary gender shapes the social imaginary of gender as a binary construct tied to heterosexuality and the ways this ideology structures possibilities for identity in public school spaces. Heteronormativity, like other forms of privilege that dominate the social order (e.g. White supremacy, ableism, and patriarchy), calls for particular forms of embodiment and interaction in order for subjects to receive public legitimation and acceptance. In this way, heteronormativity is contingent on violence and oppression. Neo-liberalism is an ideological project that reconstructs values, social relations, and social identities – to produce a new social imaginary (Lipman 2011). As such, neo-liberalism is a fertile ground in which the ideology of heteronormative binary gender can flourish and dominate the social imaginary. At this sociopolitical and historical moment, we are embedded in a neo-liberal social imaginary in which ideological projects, like heteronormative binary gender, structure social relations and identities as well as space. In this article, I analyse the ways heteronormative binary gender shapes the physical and social as well as the discursive space of schooling.

Foucault ([1977] 1995) illustrates that the school, like the prison and other state institutions, functions like Jeremy Bentham's 1791 panopticon. Operating as an unverifiable yet omnipresent means of surveillance, the panopticon offers a disciplinary mechanism through the conscious and permanent visibility of people. Foucault ([1977] 1995) demonstrated that being visible and potentially supervised can prompt people to self-regulate their own behaviour; internalising forms of discipline and surveillance can be even more effective than punishment. In this way, the panopticon serves as an apparatus of power that works on representations and on people's minds, instilling a fear of being watched and a responsibility to monitor one's own behaviour. Schools rely on such discipline and surveillance to regulate individuals, produce knowledge, and standardise learning. What happens when we consider the standardisation that schooling enforces in terms of one's learning about gender, sex, sexuality, and expression? Schooling practices and structures reproduce the mutually exclusive notion of two sexes which match onto two genders or forms of gender expression that fall within the binary of masculine and feminine, men and women, male and female. The disciplinary apparatus of the school produces knowledge, such as the conception of gender as binary, and in discourse we see power and knowledge joined together (Foucault 1980). In this case, bringing together power and knowledge in the discourse of heteronormative binary gender and affirming its power through institutional authority work to naturalise such binary distinctions.

The development of a legitimate and recognisable gender as tied to heterosexuality reflects the discipline that schooling structures and practices enforce on its students. Practices dividing students by biological sex and gender have been deeply ingrained in the institution of schooling (Connell 1996; Ferguson 2001; Goodwin 2006; Martin 1998; Thorne 1993). Organising and socialising students into discrete groups divided by sex begins during primary school and continues through high school. School contexts are coded as gendered and sexualised – that is, as heteronormative, as LGBTQ, as 'safe spaces' for difference, and as gendered along binary lines. Building on previous scholars' work, this research demonstrates that space is socially produced and thus gendered and sexualised, most often heterosexualised (Bell and Valentine 1995; Lefebvre 1991; Massey 1994).

In the context of neo-liberalism, the ideology of heteronormative binary gender standardises gendered expression, knowledge, and, thus, available subject positions. Scholars and teachers have pointed to neo-liberalism's ideologically driven hidden agenda, which includes intensified surveillance of students, abstinence-based sex education, and support for organisations with gay-exclusionary policies (Lipman 2007; TSJ 2004). True to neo-liberalism's colours, the hidden agenda of schooling reproduces binary gender and heteronormativity through mechanisms of surveillance and in line with purposes of education aimed at preparing a literate and disciplined workforce. I argue that literacy, as tied to control for social purposes, can include the reading of gender as binary and disciplined within boundaries, the delineation of those boundaries of gender normativity, and the surveillance of bodies and forms of expression that fall outside of such boundaries. In the context of neo-liberalism's focus on improving 'deficient' individuals, such reading and disciplining of gender put individuals, rather than the institutional structures that produce and reproduce inequality, under the magnifying glass for examination (Lipman 2004).

The purpose of education in the neo-liberal market has returned to training the future labour force like it once did in the early twentieth century. The commodification of education has meant that its intrinsic value once again rests in what kind of job your education can get you, and employment possibilities are gendered – binarily gendered – in that, boys are trained to be men and work in traditionally male-dominated fields, while girls are trained to be women and work in positions as high up as the glass ceiling will allow them or in feminised fields like education and nursing. The ideology of heteronormative binary gender disciplines and tries to squeeze people into one of two boxes so that they are legible, employable, and legitimately recognised by the state and future employers. Nowhere is this more apparent than in the staggering unemployment rates we see among transgender people, as White transgender people experience unemployment rates at twice the rate of the general population, with rates for transgender people of colour up to four times the national unemployment rate (Grant et al. 2011). Moreover, 78% of transgender employees report experiencing harassment, mistreatment, or discrimination on the job, with no federal law explicitly prohibiting such discrimination based on gender identity and expression (Center for American Progress and Movement Advancement Project 2015).

Taking as a starting point the Freirian notion of literacy as reading the word and the world around us (Freire [1970] 2006), this article uses social semiotics to examine the ways sex, gender, and sexuality are read and written onto bodies and social actors in the space of schooling. This work illustrates that meaning-making is social practice and that processes of signification and interpretation shape individuals and society. Here, I build on Saussure's ([1959] 1998) linguistic theory of the sign composed of the signifier which is what he called the 'sound-image' or the spoken word that points to and is connected with the signified or the concept we come to associate with the word. The relationship between the signifier and the signified is arbitrary and determined by convention. I extend Saussure's linguistic theory of the sign to think through the social semiotics of gender, sex, and sexuality norms as framed in what I call the ideology of heteronormative binary gender.

Sex is commonly believed to be biological, and gender, the social construction that correlates to this, such as social expectations, norms, and gender roles. Sex and gender are thought of as binary structures – that is, as male/female, boys/girls, men/women, and masculine/feminine. As such beliefs demonstrate, binary sex and gender are deeply entrenched organising principles for our society and serve as dominant paradigms, naturalised and made to seem enduring through reiterative practices including language (Butler [1990] 1999). Gender and sexuality operate as domains or intersecting axes of identification along which power relations are articulated (Collins 2000; Crenshaw 1991; Rubin [1984] 1993; Scott 1986). Gender and sexuality are organised into systems of power and as vectors of oppression, which intersect and are entangled with other lines of difference (Collins 2000; Crenshaw 1991; Foucault 1978; Rubin [1984] 1993). In other words, gender and sexuality – like race, ethnicity, class, citizenship status, age, language, and ability – operate as vectors along which people experience privilege and oppression and through which power relations are negotiated. Sexuality, as an axis along which power is negotiated, has been theorised as dense transfer points in relations of power (Foucault 1978). Gender and sexuality, as they intersect with other axes of difference, serve as domains and transfer points for the articulation and negotiation of power.

Binary structures of sex and gender are socially constructed norms used to discipline bodies and expression – particularly individuals with transgender identities, gender non-conforming expression and presentation, and intersex bodies. Research like that of biologist Anne Fausto-Sterling (1993, 2000) challenges the division of dimorphic sex and points out that biological sex is also a social construction, not simply an innate or essential state of being. Fausto-Sterling's argument is that we read biological sex onto bodies through various means, such as genitalia, chromosomes, hormones, and brain or neurological gender. The binary structure of sex is complicated by intersex bodies, or those who may be born with ambiguous genitalia, or an extra chromosome (XXY or XYY), or have more or less estrogen or testosterone than average for their assigned biological sex.

Binary gender is also complicated by transgender identities and experiences. I use the term 'transgender' when my participants identify as such and 'to refer to people who move away from the gender they were assigned at birth, people who cross over (*trans-*) the boundaries constructed by their culture to define and contain that gender' (Stryker 2008, 1). The term 'transgender' encompasses a range of trans-identities and practices that cross over, cut across, and move between socially constructed sex/gender boundaries of male/female, including male-to-female and female-to-male transsexuals, trans-identified women and men, genderqueer, gender bending, androgynous, as well as gender non-conforming presentation which includes bodies and identities that do not conform to social expectations about feminine or masculine gender expression. I use the term 'genderqueer' as my participants do to refer to their genders as fluid phenomena, experienced and expressed differently day to day and across a lifespan, as having both feminine and masculine qualities, or as entirely outside of the binary gender system, that is, neither male nor female – and as 'queer' implies, an intentional blurring and thwarting of boundaries, in this case, concerning binary gender.

Methodology

Drawing from three years of ethnographic research in a Northern California urban public high school in the USA, I focus on the ways schooling structures and practices produce and reinforce heteronormative binary gender. Through participant-observation, individual and focus group interviews, audio and video recordings, photography, questionnaires, and the collection of artefacts, I examine how gender and sexuality are constructed and contested in everyday practices of schooling. In my research, I look at various sites for such identity work including classroom interactions, the curriculum, common spaces, and gay–straight alliance (GSA) student club activities.

For three school years, Fall 2007–Spring 2010, I carried out ethnographic research at MacArthur High[1] across multiple sites of inquiry, examining the ways students and teachers construct, negotiate, and talk about gender and sexuality. Sites for inquiry included (1) the classroom – in particular, three freshman social studies courses that represent the school's curricular and pedagogical approach to the study of gender, sexuality, and LGBTQ issues; (2) the GSA – a student-led club that engages in activism, peer education, and awareness-raising efforts to target homophobia and transphobia in their school; and (3) communal spaces for student and teacher interaction such as the hallways, courtyards, and assemblies. The multiple sources of data I gathered – including ethnographic field-notes, audio-recorded interviews, student questionnaires, cultural artefacts generated by participants in this school, and audio and video recordings of classroom interactions

– enabled me to triangulate patterns and recurring themes in my data and research findings (Bogdan and Biklen 2007; Hammersley and Atkinson 2002).

The methods of analysis I used included ethnographic inquiry to examine patterns found through observation over time and applied linguistic methods of discourse and conversation analysis, specifically conversation analysis that is situated within ethnographic analysis of the social context (Moerman 1988). Because my research rests on the sociolinguistic insight that language both reflects and actively shapes the context in which it is used, I focused on how language is used in the negotiation of power and in the construction of identity (Cameron and Kulick 2005; Goffman 1981; Goodwin and Duranti 1992; Hanks 1996, 2006; Schegloff 1987). I also drew on proxemics to look at the spatial positioning and movement of people in school spaces (Hall et al. 1968).

My positionality as a researcher in this setting was that of an outsider – or perhaps as 'the outsider within' (Collins 1986) – in that I was not part of the school community in any way except as a doctoral student conducting research, positioned within MacArthur High in order to try to collect data that would answer research questions beneficial to both my endeavours and the school's interests. I came to this research having taught and tutored students ages 5–65 years for over a decade. This meant that my position as an educator was always at the forefront of what I did; yet I made a deliberate effort not to intervene in students' work, academic or otherwise. As a queer woman, my involvement with the GSA and in courses that addressed gender and sexuality was a political move. The students in the GSA understood me as an adult with experience starting a GSA in college and accustomed to tutoring and working with students. The students in the freshman social studies courses I observed understood me as an adult from the local university who was conducting research on gender, sexuality, and LGBTQ experiences in their high school. My status as a White, upper middle-class, cisgender, non-disabled, and native English-speaking academic from a nearby prestigious university marked my privilege and influenced my interactions with my participants and research site.

The ideology of heteronormative binary gender

Semiotics of heteronormative binary gender

Schooling practices and structures produce and reproduce the ideology of heteronormative binary gender. This ideology shapes possibilities for identity, which also means expression, a sense of belonging, and community. Such practices and structures operate at various levels – from the level of the built environment and how this structures participants' use of spaces and identity as mapped onto space, to the level of social interaction and discourse, or the everyday language students and teachers use in discussing and negotiating gender and sexuality. Students and teachers co-construct this ideology of heteronormative binary gender through their social interaction – through language practices such as joking, teasing, and the use of slang like 'that's so gay', which interpellate, or hail, and marginalise queer identities (Woolley 2013). Linguistic expressions like 'that's so gay' operate as microaggressions, which are brief everyday exchanges that send denigrating messages about people of colour, women, or LGBTQ folk (Nadal 2013; Sue 2010a).

The ideology of heteronormative binary gender operates through semiotic means, but with material consequences and with heterosexist and patriarchal stakes. This ideology aims to keep the signifier of gender and the signified of biological sex stable and intact for the production of heterosexuality as the legitimate sexuality. The ideology of binary gender is tied up with heterosexuality, or opposite sexual object choice. Heteronormativity insists that one desire someone of the opposite gender in order to maintain the stability of binary gender and to uphold its social norms. When the relationship between the signifier and the signified becomes threatened by the existence of gender non-conformity or by queer desire, things fall apart and the stability of heteronormative binary gender gets unsettled.

Although students and teachers find and carve out space for resistance, the ideology of heteronormative binary gender structures students' and teachers' gender and sexual identities as mapped onto space. Social interaction and discourse as well as the built environment itself shape participants' uses and meanings assigned to school spaces in addition to possibilities for LGBTQ representation and visibility across school contexts. By examining the social semiotics of the ways sex, gender, and sexuality are read and written onto bodies and social actors across the spaces of schooling, this research challenges us to think through how 'safe spaces' to be LGBTQ are marked and contested through semiotic means in the social landscape of the neo-liberal public high school.

Gender and sexuality in everyday life at a neo-liberal high school

At MacArthur High School, the ideology of heteronormative binary gender is dominant and largely influences LGBTQ students' daily experiences of 'safe space'. The students I observed and interviewed over the time I spent at MacArthur High shared numerous stories of abuse that spanned a range of experiences like backhanded joking comments, isolated incidents of harassment, and recurring forms of bullying and name-calling. In my interviews and questionnaires, students reported being called names such as 'faggot', 'tranny', and 'dyke' and hearing 'that's so gay' or 'no homo' at least once every class period. Such language disparages LGBTQ people regardless if the speaker intended to directly and personally target individuals or indirectly contributed to ambient experiences of homophobic and transphobic microaggressions (Nadal 2013; Sue 2010b).

The discipline of gender and sexuality can take the form of microaggressions as well as symbolic and physical violence (Bourdieu 1979), but is commonly a part of mundane everyday interactions, and thus normalised. Microaggressions are so named to describe the everyday oppression faced by groups – such as people of colour, women, and LGBTQ folk – which can be 'micro' or not immediately visible to the eye, insidious, psychologically and physically draining, and often difficult to define or redress (Sue 2010a). Racial microaggressions (Allen 2010; Ong et al. 2013), gender microaggressions (Capodilupo et al. 2010), and sexual orientation microaggressions (Nadal et al. 2011) may be so covert or subtle that they simultaneously deny the existence of racism, sexism, transphobia, and homophobia. Expanding on original conceptualisations of microaggressions and taking a more intersectional approach illuminate the fact that microaggressions can also target ability, language, religion, ethnicity, class, and other forms of difference (Collins 2000; Crenshaw 1991; Foucault 1978; Rubin [1984] 1993).

In my study, LGBTQ students experienced forms of intimidation including threats of 'corrective rape', that is, threats that they will be raped in order to turn them straight. One student, Nikola who self-identified as a White bisexual girl, recounted a moment when a classmate told her 'that he would take me home and show me how to be straight'. Some students heard their classmates make comments about gay bashing, while others were specifically told they were not welcome at this school. Students received threats and attempts towards getting beaten up at school dances and on school grounds. They also experienced various forms of physical assault. LGBTQ students at MacArthur High suffer what one student, Ty, a self-identified Black and Puerto Rican bisexual gender non-conforming boy, described as 'endless harassment, never-ending ridicule, and non-stop verbal abuse'. But, despite occurrences of physical assault and harassment, students expressed an ambivalent acceptance, as if microaggressions, name-calling, and teasing as well as much more blatant abuses were a part of the normal fabric of daily high school life. Kathryn who identified as White and lesbian said, 'I feel like MacArthur High is a physically safe place but I would say *emotionally* … it's not safe'.

The students' mixed feelings towards their school as a 'safe space' to be LGBTQ came across in their discussions. Despite such examples of abuse, the general consensus among LGBTQ students was that MacArthur High was 'the best place to be gay' because of its location in a liberal part of the country with considerable LGBTQ visibility in the surrounding community. That is, the 'common sense' social imaginary was that individual examples of name-calling, bullying, and harassment were just that – individual isolated cases rather than pervasive and structural. Individual microaggressions – if called out and so named – are seen as the problems of individuals, namely the offender and the offended, rather than symptoms of deeply embedded structural inequality and violence.

The 'common sense' of heteronormative binary gender shaped participants' expectations and assumptions of what was normal in terms of symbolic and structural violence. Heteronormative binary gender worked to discipline students' social relations, identities, and interactions across school spaces, and thus, experiences of marginalisation and violence were taken to be a normal part of high school rather than exceptional or noteworthy. The surveillance and discipline of heteronormative binary gender were so internalised that students expected to experience violence at some point. Ty explained,

> now that I am open about [my sexuality], that just means I'm due to experience homophobia. I know somewhere along the line before I graduate I will hear a homophobic comment thrown my way. But, you know, I am prepared for it. It happens.

In the neo-liberal moment when the focus is on improving deficient individuals rather than addressing structural problems in education, such symbolic violence is taken to be a part of the normal everyday experience of schooling – something that one is due to encounter at some time. The 'common sense' of heteronormative binary gender normalised symbolic and structural violence as well as the discipline and surveillance of queer bodies and identities while locating the problem in the individual and their deviance from norms.

The ideology of heteronormative binary gender is produced and reinforced through structures and practices of schooling. Such practices include dividing classroom and school spaces by sex or gender, arranging boys and girls into separate lines or groups, selecting a prom queen and king, or pairing opposite-sex students together into 'adopt an egg' or 'adopt a bag of sugar' activities as a proxy for taking care of a baby in home-economics classes or sex education lessons. In addition to structuring possibilities for identity, the ideology of heteronormative binary gender shapes spaces in schools such as gendered bathrooms and locker rooms, hallways and corridors, and the classroom, which illustrate the limits of 'safe space'. The built environment of schools reproduces binary gender and heteronormativity. For example, locker rooms and bathrooms are highly gendered spaces, designated exclusively for either girls or boys. Accessing and using such spaces pose their own set of issues for queer and gender non-conforming students. At MacArthur High School there were no safe gender-neutral bathrooms. Gender-neutral bathrooms are bathrooms for anyone, usually single stall rooms you can close and lock, designated by signs with both the 'male' and 'female' symbols on them. Instead, the transgender and gender non-conforming youth in my study chose to leave campus in order to use the public restrooms available at the local YMCA where they could access safe gender-neutral bathrooms.

Transgender and gender non-conforming students reported being subject to the scrutiny of others when they entered gendered bathrooms at their school. Such surveillance regulates which individuals, what kinds of bodies, and which forms of gendered presentation are permitted to occupy and use gendered bathroom spaces, namely those who are recognisable or legible as masculine male or feminine female. As one self-identified genderqueer student explained to me, 'You are forced to *choose* a gender when you go to use a bathroom'. That is, Siri, who identified neither as a boy nor as a girl, felt forced to choose a gendered identity and presentation in order to use school bathrooms. Safety concerns as well as assumptions about students' heterosexuality and the risks of heterosexual sexual activity occurring in bathroom and locker rooms – outside of the surveillance of school officials, security guards, and video cameras – dictate that these spaces be segregated by biological sex and gender. The ideology of binary gender as tied to heterosexual desire calls for these school spaces to be gendered and the practices that occur within these spaces to be heavily policed for gender normativity and heteronormativity. I consider this as a kind of literacy practice – the reading and writing of gender as tied to biological sex onto the body, and in this reading practice, students read one another's gender presentation and embodiment in order to figure out their biological sex (Woolley 2015). Transgender and genderqueer students' use of gendered bathrooms dictates that they confront the task of 'passing' as male or as female in order to enter and be sanctioned users at such spaces. So, I argue that reading gendered presentation as a signifier that points to the signified of biological sex engages in particular kinds of literacy practices that use bodies as texts for interpretation (Woolley 2015).

In the context of neo-liberalism, this is viewed as a choice – a choice to leave school and go to the bathroom elsewhere despite the presence of gendered bathrooms and locker rooms at school. Under the guise of individual choice, the onus for finding a safe place to go to the bathroom falls on the individual student – in this case, individuals who do not conform to binary gender norms and/or heteronormativity. Neo-liberal logic here supports the notion that the market can do all things better than public institutions. Individuals, especially those who 'choose' to violate heteronormative binary gender, are seen as responsible for taking care of themselves and for finding a safe place for them to take care of their bodily needs. Here, as in neo-liberalism, the market is the arbiter of social life – individuals can simply find a comfortable bathroom for their needs if they just shop around, rather than institutions being ethically responsible for taking care of all its subjects. After all, what is profitable about remodelling old communal bathrooms and locker rooms segregated by sex? Often the argument against installing gender-neutral bathrooms is that it will cost too much to retrofit old buildings and restructure bathroom spaces. Is the comfort of a few individuals worth the cost of remodelling old buildings with antiquated sex-segregated bathrooms full of stalls and lines of urinals?

At the time of this writing, North Carolina has passed a controversial new law – House Bill 2 – which now requires school systems to enact regulations on single-sex multiple-occupancy bathrooms and changing facilities in direct violation of the Department of Education and the Office of Civil Rights guidance. House Bill 2 now requires that transgender people use the bathrooms and changing facilities designated for people of the biological sex assigned on one's birth certificate. In doing so, North Carolina appears to be in violation of Title IX of the Education Amendments of 1972, which prohibits discrimination on the basis of sex in federally funded education programmes and activities. In the current neo-liberal moment, the responsibility for providing safe places for people of all genders to use the restroom or to change their clothes has shifted from public institutions like schools to individuals – in particular, to some of the most marginalised and vulnerable people in US society. That is, transgender and gender non-conforming people in North Carolina are now obligated by law to use restrooms designated for the biological sex they may not identify with, or to find their own safe space to go to the bathroom, or change while in public.

As Lipman (2011) has shown us, 'freedom', 'choice', and 'individual rights' are best guaranteed by the market under neo-liberalism, and in this case the personal responsibility for finding a comfortable or safe place to go to the bathroom falls on the individual rather than on institutions to provide structural accommodations for all. Also, the neo-liberal logic that the market is the arbiter of social life supports the argument that transgender and gender non-conforming students should seek out other institutions – specialised LGBTQ-friendly schools or ones that specifically cater to trans-students. Instead of public institutions shouldering the responsibility of accommodating the public and all kinds of students, again the burden falls on individuals to find a space in which they feel the most comfortable. We see this logic in the case of charter schools opened to cater to special needs, under the banner of a special theme, falling outside the purview of public regulations and not held accountable to the public or the common good. As we have seen,

> neoliberalism reframes all social relations, all forms of knowledge and culture in the terms of the market. All services established for the common good are potential targets of investment and profit-making. In the discourse of neoliberalism, the society becomes synonymous with the market, democracy is equated with consumer choice, and the common good is replaced by individual advantage. (Lipman 2007, 51)

Further challenging the notions of 'safe space', common spaces like hallways and corridors offer contested spaces for sexuality. Students describe particular hallways in MacArthur High as opportune places to make out and cuddle as they may be absent of traffic and far from the view of teachers and security guards. Students in the GSA identified other hallways as 'definitely not safe zones to be queer'. Hallway passing times as thousands of bodies methodically and chaotically passed through transitory spaces to get to the next destination in six minutes serve as unstructured and unregulated times during which bodies in close proximity touch and brush up against one another. The unmarked heterosexuality of hallways and corridors is reinforced through the policing of queer desire as one could frequently hear epithets like 'gay faggot' hurled down the hallway unfettered. The heterosexuality of hallways was also reinforced through the contested visibility of queer representations. Throughout the halls, the GSA club would post visibility materials like 'safe space' and 'ally' posters to index particular classrooms and hallways as LGBTQ-friendly. Frequently, however, club flyers were ripped down within the hour of being posted, and sometimes torn posters and signs littered the ground within minutes of their posting. This highlights the limitations of the GSA students' claims to safe space through the appropriation of a queer presence in the hallways. The ramifications of violence symbolised in the ripping down of LGBTQ presences can change school climate in a matter of minutes, erasing identities and communities. The students' claims of a safe space – a visual space in which queer identities and communities could be represented – both challenged dominant ideologies of heteronormativity and, like the posters in the hallway, faced immediate censure literally at the hands of their schoolmates.

Students' negotiations of the gendered spaces of bathrooms and locker rooms as well as the heterosexualised spaces of hallways reproduce the ideology of heteronormative binary gender. Social interaction in addition to the built environment itself shapes participants' uses and meanings assigned to school spaces as well as possibilities for queer representation and identity across school contexts. In school spaces, the ideology of heteronormative binary gender structures social interaction, the occupation and movement of bodies through school spaces, and possibilities for subjectivity and identity. These data show us how students have used literacy to read and write gendered comportment and sexual identity onto bodies, to read and interpret school spaces as safe or unsafe places to be queer, to occupy public spaces and presence within their school, and to seek representation and acknowledgement. As these data illustrate, MacArthur High is not physically or emotionally safe for the development and learning of all its students.

The process of standardising and normalising binary gender as tied to heterosexuality calls for the discipline and surveillance of bodies and individuals who deviate from gender and sexuality norms (Foucault [1977] 1995, 1978). In the context of neo-liberalism, the 'common sense' social imaginary that heteronormative binary gender constructs locate such deviance onto a few 'problem' individuals rather than oppressive structures. Within neo-liberalism, discourses of choice and freedom place the responsibility for dealing with social issues on the individual rather than public institutions. The neo-liberal state, or the market, is constructed as egalitarian and non-discriminatory because everyone is treated as having equal rights, access, and options (Spade 2011; Stern 2015). For some students in US public schools, issues around gender and sexuality are treated as deviations or 'problems' of individuals, rather than gender and sexuality as structural institutions that shape individual and social experiences (Foucault [1977] 1995, 1978).

Conclusion

Education plays a key role in facilitating the instantiation of neo-liberal policies and ideologies (Lipman 2011). The ideologies that schools reproduce, like heteronormative binary gender, further strengthen the neo-liberal social order and its cultural ideals of individualism. As such, transgressing heteronormative binary gender is often seen as the choice of individuals rather than the imposition of structures onto people's expression of gender and sexuality. Heteronormative binary gender is an ideology that structures possibilities for individuals, collectivities, and space in schools, while also contributing to a context in which daily microaggressions are accepted as the norm. The everyday disciplining of gender and sexuality manifests in microaggressions as well as symbolic and physical violence against LGBTQ people.

This work has spatial implications as far as how we understand 'safe space' in schools. Hallways are one of few places for anonymity and animation, but the social interaction that occurs in the unstructured space of the hallway can be invasive and threatening to some students. How can we design schools so that the proxemics and the social interaction that occurs within them are less invasive or violating, that have more space for visually representing all kinds of people, and that are safe for all students to move through and occupy? How can we rethink the spaces of gendered bathrooms and locker rooms and make gender-neutral facilities available for everyone, without social stigma or the marking of difference attached to students' *use* of such spaces? My suggestion is not to abandon safe space discourse altogether, but to examine its limitations and to consider what anti-racist, anti-misogynistic, anti-homophobic, and anti-transphobic work needs to be done to re-examine and refigure what 'safe space' for difference can look like, especially in the current neo-liberal context. Efforts towards constructing safe space for difference in schools need to incorporate an analysis of power and a recognition of the ways all of us can remain complicit and participate in unequal power relations. Discourses of safe space also need to open up room for disagreement, discomfort, painful conversations, and reflection. In the current context of neo-liberalism in which individual and social agency are defined largely through market-driven notions of individualism, competition, and consumption (Giroux 2002), it is more important than ever to have a structural analysis of ideology – the 'common sense' social imaginary – and the ways they structure possibilities for identity and social relations.

Understanding the ways students and teachers read and write gender and sexuality into the world of high school could inform how we work towards the inclusion of difference and diversity in our educational practice. Understanding the mechanism of signification and the ways bodies are read as texts that are gendered and sexualised as well as raced, classed, and (dis)abled can help us to recognise the ways difference is constructed through social interaction and the ways processes of inclusion and exclusion operate. Such inquiry could serve as the basis for thinking through ways of addressing homophobia and transphobia as well as racism, classism, and ableism in schools both proactively and in the moment. My methodology of interpreting the ways gender and sexuality are read and written onto bodies and spaces in school can help us think about how students are signing all the time through various symbol systems. In reading and writing both the word and the world around them (Freire [1970] 2006), students create and contest the dominant ideology of heteronormative binary gender, while also reading and writing other texts. This applies to other domains and sign systems, as developing our attentiveness to seeing the world through a different lens helps to unpack and unfold the deeper practices of inscribing meaning.

The ways in which the ideology of heteronormative binary gender is maintained and challenged can inform how we approach and rethink schooling structures and practices through a different lens. How can we rethink spaces like hallways and bathrooms, the curriculum and pedagogy, and interventions to address homophobic or transphobic language in school? And how can we rethink these things so that they do not reproduce heteronormative binary gender, or so that they build on the challenges teachers and students are already engaged in? Beyond schools, how can this help us to think through ways to address homophobia, transphobia, and other forms of oppression in our society? How can we push back against neo–liberal forces that place the burden of responsibility on the individual and instead centre a structural analysis that accounts for the limitations of 'choice'?

In concluding these thoughts, I wish to extend a call to action to my readers. We need to examine structural violence, equality, and justice in the context of neo-liberal institutions like schools, rather than assume that the discipline, surveillance, and marginalisation experienced by some are the fault of those individuals for crossing the arbitrary boundaries of norms. We must be wary of neo-liberalism's blaming of individuals and rhetoric of choice, freedom, and responsibility, as we have seen the ways heteronormative sexuality and binary gender structure everyday experiences. By examining and targeting interventions at the structural level, we can better understand and change ideologies like heteronormative binary gender and the ways they shape possibilities for identity and social relations.

Lastly, we need to not only identify and name, but also decentre and disrupt heteronormative binary gender. Part of the questions I identified above call on us to rethink schooling so that it does not reproduce the ideology of heteronormative binary gender. We must reframe additive models of diversity or multicultural education so that an analysis of power and intersectionality are centre, or in other words, so that our focus shifts from the individual to the structural level. Moreover, we all need to learn how to identify, call out, and analyse microaggressions so that we better understand their impact on people and contribution to school climate and so that we know how to address and resist such everyday violence. Until we change the ideology of heteronormative binary gender in schools, the climate of daily microaggressions against people of colour, women, LGBTQ people, and others who are marginalised along axes of difference will persist and structure people's experiences and possibilities.

Note

1. All names of places and people have been changed to pseudonyms to protect participants' anonymity.

Acknowledgements

I would like to thank the anonymous reviewers at *Gender and Education* as well as Sarah A. Robert for her careful editing and guidance through the process of writing this article. Earlier versions of this piece, in part, appeared in iterations of various talks I gave between 2012 and 2015. I wish to extend my gratitude to colleagues who provided valuable insight in response to those talks: Patricia Baquedano-López, David Minkus, Deborah Lustig, Christine Trost, Genevieve Negron-Gonzales, Kathryn Zamora Moeller, Becky Alexander, Emily Gleason, Erica Misako Boas, Irenka Dominguez-Pareto, Cecilia Lucas, José Lizárraga, Arturo Cortéz, Usree Bhattacharya, Adam Mendelson, Tadashi Dozono, Jen Collett, Sabina Vaught, Chris Vargas, Greg Youmans, Danny Barreto, Paul Humphrey, Barbara Regenspan, Mark Stern, Navine Murshid, Emma Fuentes, and a special thanks to Monisha Bajaj for encouraging me to consider submitting my work for this issue. The views expressed in this article do not reflect those of the funding agencies, and any errors and shortcomings are my own.

Disclosure statement

No potential conflict of interest was reported by the author.

Funding information

Carving out writing time was made possible by generous funding from a number of sources for which I am deeply grateful: the AAUW American Dissertation Fellowship, the National GLBTQ Youth Foundation Dissertation Grant, the Institute for the Study of Social Change Youth Violence Prevention Graduate Fellowship, the Dean's Normative Time Fellowship, and the Designated Emphasis in Women, Gender, and Sexuality Stipend at University of California, Berkeley.

References

Allen, Q. 2010. "Racial Microaggressions: The Schooling Experiences of Black Middle-class Males in Arizona's Secondary Schools." *Journal of African American Males in Education* 1 (2): 125–143.

Bell, D., and G. Valentine. 1995. *Mapping Desire*. New York: Routledge.

Bogdan, R. C., and S. K. Biklen. 2007. *Qualitative Research for Education: An Introduction to Theories and Methods*. 5th ed. Boston, MA: Pearson.

Bourdieu, P. 1979. "Symbolic Violence." *Critique of Anthropology* 4: 77–85.

Butler, J. [1990] 1999. *Gender Trouble: Feminism and the Subversion of Identity*. New York: Routledge.

Cameron, D., and D. Kulick. 2005. "Identity crisis?" *Language & Communication* 25: 107–125.

Capodilupo, C. M., K. L. Nadal, L. Corman, S. Hamit, O. B. Lyons, and A. Weinberg. 2010. "The Manifestation of Gender Microaggressions." In *Microaggressions and Marginality*, edited by D. W. Sue, 193–216. Hoboken: Wiley.

Center for American Progress and Movement Advancement Project. 2015. "Paying an Unfair Price: The Financial Penalty for Being Transgender in America." http://www.lgbtmap.org/file/paying-an-unfair-price-transgender.pdf.

Collins, P. H. 1986. "Learning from the Outsider Within: The Sociological Significance of Black Feminist Thought." *Social Problems* 33 (6): S14–S32.

Collins, P. H. 2000. *Black Feminist Thought: Knowledge, Consciousness, and the Politics of Empowerment*. New York: Routledge.

Connell, R. W. 1996. "Teaching the Boys: New Research on Masculinity, and Gender Strategies for Schools." *The Teachers College Record* 98 (2): 206–235.

Crenshaw, K. 1991. "Mapping the Margins: Intersectionality, Identity Politics, and Violence Against Women of Color." *Stanford Law Review* 43: 1241–1299.

Fausto-Sterling, A. 1993. "The Five Sexes." *The Sciences* 33 (2): 20–24.

Fausto-Sterling, A. 2000. "The Five Sexes Revisited." *The Sciences* 40 (4): 18–23.

Ferguson, A. A. 2001. *Bad Boys: Public Schools in the Making of Black Masculinity*. Ann Arbor: University of Michigan Press.

Foucault, M. [1977] 1995. *Discipline and Punish: The Birth of the Prison*. Translated and edited by A. Sheridan. New York: Vintage Books.

Foucault, M. 1978. *The History of Sexuality, Vol. 1*. Translated and edited by R. Hurley. New York: Pantheon Books.

Foucault, M. 1980. *Power/Knowledge: Selected Interviews and Other Writings 1972–1977*. Translated and edited by C. Gordon, L. Marshall, J. Mepham, and K. Soper. New York: Pantheon Books.

Freire, P. [1970] 2006. *Pedagogy of the Oppressed*. New York: Continuum.

Giroux, H. 2002. "Neoliberalism, Corporate Culture, and the Promise of Higher Education: The University as a Democratic Public Sphere." *Harvard Educational Review* 72 (4): 425–464.

Giroux, H. A. 2004. *The Terror of Neoliberalism: Authoritarianism and the Eclipse of Democracy*. Herndon: Paradigm.

Goffman, E. 1981. *Forms of Talk*. Philadelphia: University of Pennsylvania Press.

Goodwin, M. H. 2006. *The Hidden Life of Girls*. Malden: Blackwell.

Goodwin, C., and A. Duranti. 1992. "Rethinking Context: An Introduction." In *Rethinking Context: Language as an Interactive Phenomenon*, edited by Alessandro Duranti, and Charles Goodwin, 1–32. Cambridge: Cambridge University Press.

Gramsci, A. [1971] 2012. *Selections from the Prison Notebooks*. New York: International.

Grant, J. M., L. A. Mottet, J. Tanis, J. Harrison, J. L. Herman, and M. Keisling. 2011. "Injustice at Every Turn: A Report of the National Transgender Discrimination Survey." National Center for Transgender Equality and National Gay and Lesbian Task Force. http://www.thetaskforce.org/downloads/reports/reports/ntds_full.pdf.

Hall, E. T., R. L. Birdwhistell, B. Bock, P. Bohannan, A. R. Diebold Jr., M. Durbin, M. S. Edmonson, et al. 1968. "Prosemics [and Comments and Replies]." *Current Anthropology* 9 (2/3): 83–108.

Hammersley, M., and P. Atkinson. 2002. *Ethnography: Principles in Practice*. 2nd ed. London: Routledge.

Hanks, W. F. 1996. *Language and Communicative Practices*. Boulder, CO: Westview.

Hanks, W. F. 2006. "Context, Communicative." In *Encyclopedia of Language and Linguistics. 14*. 2nd ed., edited by Jacob Mey, 115–128. London: Elsevier.

Harvey, D. 2007. *A Brief History of Neoliberalism*. Oxford: Oxford University Press.

Lefebvre, H. 1991. *The Production of Space*. Malden: Blackwell.

Lipman, P. 2004. *High Stakes Education: Inequality, Globalization, and Urban School Reform*. New York: RoutledgeFalmer.

Lipman, P. 2007. "'No Child Left Behind': Globalization, Privatization, and the Politics of Inequality." In *Neoliberalism and Education Reform*, edited by E. Wayne Ross, and Rich Gibson, 35–58. Cresskill: Hampton Press.

Lipman, P. 2011. *The New Political Economy of Urban Education: Neoliberalism, Race, and the Right to the City*. New York: Routledge.

Martin, K. A. 1998. "Becoming a Gendered Body: Practices of Preschools." *American Sociological Review* 63 (4): 494–511.

Massey, D. 1994. *Space, Place, and Gender*. Minneapolis: University of Minnesota Press.

Moerman, M. 1988. *Talking Culture: Ethnography and Conversation Analysis*. Philadelphia: University of Pennsylvania Press.

Nadal, K. L. 2013. *That's So Gay! Microaggressions and the Lesbian, Gay, Bisexual, and Transgender Community*. Washington, DC: American Psychological Association.

Nadal, K. L., Y. Wong, M. Issa, V. Meterko, J. Leon, and M. Wideman. 2011. "Sexual Orientation Microaggressions: Processes and Coping Mechanisms for Lesbian, Gay, and Bisexual Individuals." *Journal of LGBT Issues in Counseling* 5 (1): 21–46.

Ong, A. D., A. L. Burrow, T. E. Fuller-Rowell, N. M. Ja, and D. W. Sue. 2013. "Racial Microaggressions and Daily Well-being Among Asian Americans." *Journal of Counseling Psychology* 60 (2): 188–199.

Rubin, G. [1984] 1993. "Thinking Sex: Notes for a Radical Theory of the Politics of Sexuality." In *The Lesbian and Gay Studies Reader*, edited by Henry Abelove, Michele A. Barale, and David M. Halperin, 3–44. New York: Routledge.

Saussure, de F. [1959] 1998. *Course in General Linguistics*. New York: Philosophical Library.

Schegloff, E. 1987. "Between Macro and Micro: Contexts and Other Connections." In *The Micro-Macro Link*, edited by Jeffrey C. Alexander, Bernhard Giesen, Richard Munch, and Neil Smelser, 207–234. Berkeley: University of California Press.

Scott, J. 1986. "Gender: A Useful Category of Historical Analysis." *The American Historical Review* 91 (5): 1053–1075.

Spade, D. 2011. *Normal Life: Administrative Violence, Critical Trans Politics and the Limits of Law*. Cambridge: South End Press.

Stern, M. 2012. "'We Can't Build Our Dreams On Suspicious Minds': Neoliberalism, Education Policy, and the Feelings Left Over." *Cultural Studies ↔ Critical Methodologies* 12 (5): 387–400.

Stern, M. 2015. "Homonormativity, Charternormativity, and Processes of Legitimation: Exploring the Affective-Spatio-Temporal-Fixed Dimensions of Marriage Equality and Charter Schools." *Berkeley Review of Education* 5 (2): 171–196.

Stryker, S. 2008. *Transgender History*. Berkeley, CA: Seal Press.

Sue, D. W. 2010a. *Microaggressions in Everyday Life: Race, Gender, and Sexual Orientation*. Hoboken: Wiley.

Sue, D. W. 2010b. *Microaggressions and Marginality: Manifestation, Dynamics, and Impact*. Hoboken: Wiley.

Teachers for Social Justice (TSJ). 2004. *No Child Left Behind Talking Points*. Chicago, IL: Teachers for Social Justice. www.teachersforjustice.org.

Thorne, B. 1993. *Gender Play*. New Brunswick, NJ: Rutgers University Press.

Woolley, S. W. 2013. "Speech That Silences, Silences That Speak: 'That's So Gay,' 'That's So Ghetto,' and 'Safe Space' in High School." *Journal of Language and Sexuality* 2 (2): 292–319.

Woolley, S. W. 2015. "'Boys Over Here, Girls Over There': A Critical Literacy of Binary Gender in Schools." *TSQ: Transgender Studies Quarterly* 2 (3): 376–394.

An education in gender and agroecology in Brazil's Landless Rural Workers' Movement

Sônia Fátima Schwendler and Lucia Amaranta Thompson

ABSTRACT
This article explores the implications of a blended agroecology and gender education within *Brazil's Landless Rural Workers' Movement* (MST). The discussion is first situated within MST's struggle for land and for peasant families' livelihoods, generally, and under neoliberalism, specifically. Central to the struggle against neoliberalism have been critical educational models that evolved towards agroecology and a gender-equality-oriented pedagogy. Women have played important roles in the movement's growth, particularly the development of the education sector. Using data from a literature review, observations, and interviews, the article argues that MST's education, focused on agroecology and accompanied by gender-oriented pedagogy, empowers women and men to disrupt the traditional sexual division of labour in rural communities, and within land struggles, more generally.

Introduction

This article explores gender and agroecology education within Brazil's Landless Rural Workers' Movement (MST), Latin America's and Brazil's most prominent agrarian reform movement. We begin with a discussion of the movement's inception and purpose, tracing it from the 1980s to current struggles under hegemonic neoliberal agricultural production. We then explain the emergence of MST's education model rooted in a Gramscian counter-hegemonic education influenced by emancipatory pedagogies (Freire 1973; Pistrak 1981; Makarenko 2005). In response to neoliberalism and women's involvement in the movement, the education model has evolved to emphasise *agroecology*, 'the application of ecological concepts and principles to the design and management of sustainable agricultural ecosystems' (Altieri 2009, 103), and *gender-oriented pedagogy*; a political and pedagogical proposal in which dominant gender ideologies and roles are intentionally and strategically contested within the school environment (Schwendler 2013). Women's roles in the evolution of the movement and the education model are woven into the discussion of how workers' gender relations have been affected by the evolving MST education model.

Data include a literature review, observations, and oral history interviews with students and staff from *Instituto Educar*,[1] a secondary technical school, in an MST settlement. The data illustrate how gender-oriented pedagogy creates an educational environment emphasising egalitarian gender practices. This environment stresses reflection on gender asymmetries, their historic (re)production within cultures, and the possibilities for gender equality. It also translates to a long-term political and educational strategy of deconstructing hegemonic gendered *habitus* in and out of school (Schwendler 2013). We argue that MST's education, focused on agroecology and accompanied by gender-oriented pedagogy, empowers women and men and disrupts the traditional sexual division of labour in rural communities, and within land struggles, more generally.

The context

Peasant social movements, notably the MST, have forced the Brazilian State to address historical inequalities in land ownership (Fernandes 1999; Carter 2009). The occupation of land and the organisation of encampments by the peasant movement led to the creation of over 9070 settlements between 1979 and 2012, on non-productive land of former landed estates as areas of agrarian reform with a social function: to provide livelihoods for landless families. This political strategy of land occupation is based on the 1964 Brazilian Land Statute and 1988 Constitution that states that the government can expropriate land if it is not 'serving its social function' (Wright and Wolford 2003), providing legitimacy to the occupation of non-productive lands. The Brazilian Government responded by converting the settled estates into peasant territories, populated by 933,836 families (NERA 2013).

As landless workers settled their families education was needed for children and to reduce high rates of illiteracy among adults. Although a public education is provided by municipalities and the State, it has usually been disengaged from the land struggle. Additionally, children from encampments and settlements faced discrimination in urban public schools (Camini 2009). Thus since MST's inception in 1984, education has been central to the broader struggle for land.

MST's education evolved from a Gramscian *counter-hegemonic model* emphasising a resistance against dominance over forms of knowledge and power of one group over another. The MST model also draws from emancipatory pedagogies including Pistrak (1981), Makarenko (2005), and Freire (1973). Freire's *Pedagogy of the Oppressed* has become an instrument within the curriculum, encouraging students ' ... to perceive social, political, and economic contradictions, and to take action against the oppressive elements of reality' (Freire 1973, 17). The model and pedagogy root landless workers in a collective, dynamic social struggle that shapes knowledge and develops a culture of participation (Caldart 2000). Women have played a major role within MST's education sector, officially created in 1987. Paradoxically, by occupying traditional feminine spaces such as schools, women have accessed higher education and increased their participation and leadership in different areas of the social movement such as agricultural production (Schwendler 2013).

This article is based on a case study of Educar, an agroecological secondary-level technical school[2] founded in 2005 by the MST, in collaboration with the Federal Institute of Education, Science and Technology of Rio Grande do Sul, Sertão and the National Programme of Education in Agrarian Reform Areas – *PRONERA*. The latter was founded in 1998, as a response to demands by the Brazilian peasant movement, which has been key in addressing illiteracy in the agrarian reform settlements and has provided access to technical and higher education for the landless youth. It gives financial support for institutional partnerships between agrarian social movements and educational institutions (Molina 2003).

Educar is located in the *Assentamento Nossa Senhora Aparecida*, on the former *Latifundium do Annoni* (Annoni landed estate) and situated in the municipality of Pontão. The Annoni, located in the southern state of *Rio Grande do Sul*, was the first mass-land occupation undertaken by the MST and is considered a symbol of resistance. 'Annoni provided the sustenance and strength that the movement needed in order to become constituted as an entity' (J. P. MST's former national leader, Annoni settler, interview 2011[3]).

The search for alternatives: resisting the neoliberal model of production

The MST emerged in response to early iterations of neoliberalism in commodity production that began during the military dictatorship (1964–1985). These included the increasing concentration of land and mechanisation of agriculture which made countless landless peasants redundant, resulting in forced migration to urban areas to seek a living. For those landless workers that remained their only choice was to occupy unproductive landed estates, many of them acquired by landowners through the historical practice of *grillagem*[4] (Stedile and Fernandes 1999).

Still at its inception, the MST created cooperatives that adopted capitalist modes of production including large-scale production techniques (MST 1991). The rationale was that by working collectively to increase production, the families would be able to increase competitiveness. Some cooperatives were successful, such as the COOPTAR (*Cooperativa de Produção Agropecuaria Cascata Ltda*), located in the Annoni. The majority failed. Neoliberal approaches to commodity production based on limited state intervention in the market further exacerbated MST members' struggles. For MST member farms, this translated to reduced State support which in turn meant reduced ability to compete against large agribusiness. Alternatives had to be found to resist neoliberalism.

The MST has challenged neoliberal structures of inequality through the experience of collectivisation. By sharing resources and working as a community, the MST has rejected neoliberal notions of individualisation and market forces that presumably bring about a 'natural' balance where those who simply 'work hard' succeed. It has also challenged the concentration of power and resources, ideally distributing both equally to all sectors of the movement.

Nevertheless, as part of the patriarchal culture strongly ingrained in the countryside, men were in the great majority of encampments and settlements' general coordination when the Annoni was first occupied.

> The women were the ones who most participated in the encampment (in) education, health, nutrition and the distribution of clothing … Women have always participated. The only difference was that when the direction recruited members, it was the men that applied … The men themselves said that, when it came to the political roles it had to be a man, not a woman. (I. V., Educar staff and regional leader)

The MST changed its organisational structure in 2000 to create more space for political participation. During this (re)organisation, women challenged the movement to address persistent gender constraints within the land struggle. This led to an increase in women's participation in different sectors and levels of organisation. This is elaborated later in the article.

Contrary to the neoliberal agricultural emphasis on food as commodity, MST adopted a food sovereignty model (Tardin and Kenfield 2009), which emphasises food production for local consumption and a critique of 'what food is produced, where it is produced, how it is produced and at what scale' (Desmarais 2003, 142). In 2000, the MST also adopted agroecology to orient production to resist neoliberalism in addition to food sovereignty. Altieri (2009) argues that the combination of modern agroecological science and indigenous knowledge systems developed by farmers, NGOs, and some government and academic institutions has been shown to improve food security whilst preserving natural resources, biodiversity, soil, and water. M. S. C., (Settler and Educar teacher) highlights the need for agroecology explicitly and food sovereignty implicitly:

> ... to re-assess the issue of smallholder agriculture and if we want to save the planet, be healthy, we have to develop ... technology in this area. There are no studies or research because everything is focused on/aimed at the large agricultural businesses rather than agroecology that focuses on life. You have to invest in order to make it feasible for people to live in the countryside ...

Agroecological education against neoliberalism

Since 2000, the MST in conjunction with other rural social movements, have institutionalised agroecological education. Schools, such as Educar, with a focus on agroecology have provided a younger generation of landless settlers and small farmers. The programme of study 'articulates practice and theory into a praxis, and finds expression in times and spaces that alternate between the school and property, community, settlement, camp or social movement to which the student is linked' (Ribeiro 2008, 3). Through an alternating pedagogy, students spend three months at school (*tempo escola*) followed by three months at home, referred to as community time (*tempo comunidade*) over three years. During school time, students develop their theoretical and practical knowledge visiting agroecology projects across the state.

> The state educational institutions take the students on 3 or 4 field trips throughout the whole three years of the course and we do three field trips every phase (year). We take them so that they can see the viability of being a smallholder. We take them to see everything that there is in the state related to agroecology. (M. S. C., Educar staff, interview 2015)

Community time encourages students to maintain local relationships, a pedagogic space to engage in local discussions related to their settlement. Students also obtain practical experience supervised by a community leader, which can be brought back to school as hybrid scientific and peasant social knowledge. The programme is based on Freire's statement that '[i]f education alone cannot transform society, without it society cannot change either' (2000, 67). The MST advocates that the school must be involved in the transformation of the countryside. Thus school curriculum has been developed to intentionally contribute towards the political and ideological development of its students (MST 1996), encouraging them to contest material realities and capitalist relations of production.

By focusing on agroecological education, the MST aims to transform students into organic intellectuals, capable of 'influencing agricultural production by advancing counter-hegemonic agricultural practices' (Meek 2015, 1180). According to Gramsci, every social group creates 'one or more strata of intellectuals which give it homogeneity and awareness of its own function not only in the economic but also in the social and political fields' (1971, 5). Students remain in the countryside as MST activists devoted to improving the quality of life in their communities through an alternative matrix of production.

While the two-pronged education model seems a strong fit to counter neoliberalism, C.R., an alumni and current staff member of Educar, explains the difficulty of implementing food sovereignty blended with agroecology in the settlements.

> For me, agroecology is fundamental, because it is life that is in play … It is difficult because people here have the concept of agriculture for export. 'I go there, I farm, I place the poison and then I harvest' … the less they need to do the better … Today, people are not paying attention to the importance of having a healthy diet, or the equilibrium in nature.

Opposition to the implementation of agroecology is mainly based on the assumption that the new model places heavier demands on the farmers. Additionally, it is also related to the community's exposure to the concept of production and food as commodities. Government agroecological projects and assistance might ease the insertion of new ideas and lead to a questioning of the hegemonic norms of production by the community.

> Where there is already organic production, agroecological projects or even the Food Acquisition Programme[5] or the National School Meals Programme (that are government programmes), the young find it easier to develop projects related to the field of the course. But where there is a predominance of monoculture the conflict arises. (M.S.C., Educar staff, interview, 2015)

Despite the difficulties faced by the new generations when introducing alternative economic practices in their communities, agroecological education has become an important tool, not only to dispute the hegemonic agricultural and developmental model but also to empower women to challenge the patriarchal gender regimes in the countryside.

Women's struggle to contest hegemonic norms

Women's work continues to be invisible, undervalued, and accepted simply as a 'helping hand', despite the fact that, historically, women's agricultural activities have played a major role within peasant economies, ensuring food sovereignty and biodiversity (Faria 2009). Activities carried out by women were seen as an extension of their domestic work, with the home institutionalised as the 'women's natural place' (Alvarez 1990; Silva and Portella 2006; Jacobs 2010). As a consequence a wide range of unpaid labour that generates goods and services for family consumption have been disregarded (Schwendler 2013).

The family was seen by the social movement and government development policy as a unit and a site in which all members benefit equally from any resources received, leading to policy blindness and exacerbating patriarchy within family structures (Deere 2003). Implicit patriarchal gender regimes within the social constructs of the movement meant that men were not only considered the head of the household, but also the main agricultural worker and, therefore, the rightful land-title holder.

Family structure had a significant impact on policy development, household decision-making, and the organisation of the social movement. Silva and Portella (2006) demonstrate that women's position as 'helper' does not give them the same legitimate place and experience to make decisions on agricultural issues as men. Elson and Pearson (2011) also show that women have not been full members of society, thus making it even more difficult to access resources that increase social and economic power and independence. One example is women's land rights in the agrarian reform programme. The 1964 Land Statute supported the redistribution of land towards the family unit:

> At the time even we, as women, did not think that a piece of land would be put under both our names ... That was never even discussed. To the point that in our encampment [the Encruzil-hada Natalino, in 1981] there were no young people or women registered [to get access to land titles], only men ... (M.S.C., Educar staff)

As a consequence of women's organisation at the Annoni settlement, the 1988 Brazilian Federal Constitution established that for land distributed via agrarian reform 'titles of ownership and use rights should be granted in the name of men, women, or both, independently of their marital status.' M.D., a leader in the Annoni settlement, explains:

> There was an organised movement in the Annoni for single women to be recognised as citizens with the same rights and duties of men ... It was the MST, the struggle of women who ended up raising a conscience.

Up until the legislation for women's land rights became compulsory in 2003 (Ordinance 981/2003), only 13% of land beneficiaries were women (Butto and Hora 2010).

Whilst, the changes in gender policy have led to an increase of women taking part in the MST's production sector, women still face enormous barriers and struggle to position themselves as subjects with the power to put forward their ideas and make decisions (Schwendler 2013). This is clearly described by I.M.L., (Educar staff, Annoni settler):

> In terms of finance [and] production, we have many women that are reluctant to enter these spheres ... Even men resist women's entrance because it is a sphere that they control ... Women really need to be educated and trained within this area.

Women's empowerment and agroecology education

Education has empowered young women within their communities and within the social movement itself. Empowerment is defined in this paper as a process that requires challenging the ideologies that validate social inequality, the patterns of access to and control over economic, natural, and intellectual resources, and the institutions and structures that (re)produce existing power relations (Batliwala 1997).

This is important, not only because of women's historically unequal access to productive resources, services and knowledge in comparison to men, but also because of the impact that neoliberal agricultural policies have had on women's livelihood and culture. E.P., (PRONERA agronomy graduate, MST leader) expresses how important education has been for her to access MST's productive sector: 'If I did not have this knowledge I would struggle to find the space to participate'. This is also emphasised by I.M.L. (Educar staff).

> We have many women in the movement that have technical education that they master very well and then they take up the challenge of entering this space … The rest of the militant women, me included, do not go there a lot, which is due to limitations in our own education … The movement has sought to create more formal [technical] courses. Where … there are many women participating.

These personal experiences demonstrate that access to formal education, particularly agroecology and politics, is crucial to the transformation of gender relations. Around 20–25% of Educar students are women. Despite the small percentage of female participation, these women have gone on to occupy important positions within sectors of the movement that had historically been dominated by men in both the encampments and settlements. Women's involvement in the educational field, as teachers, and their access to higher education has also enabled them to take part in the MST's national leadership. These women have also been empowered by their participation in MST gatherings, such as the *Jornada da Agroecologia* (carried out to promote alternative economic practices), as well as in the peasant women's resistance movement against monoculture known as the *Jornada de Luta Contra o Agronegócio* (which takes places on International Women's Day).

Landless women also increased their gender awareness through contact with feminist concepts of gender equality and rights, as well as their participation in the autonomous Rural Women Workers' Movement or within the MST's structure.

> We are trying to construct a more revolutionary feminism, to get both men and women involved in the debate. We are increasing the level of women's participation by ensuring that in the organisational structure there is one woman and one man [at each level]. […] she will be able to participate in various activities, not just meetings, but also studies and analyses of the crises, which are moments in the struggle that politicise the landless workers. So it is one more [woman] that is managing to convey her opinion, make an analysis to be able to come back into the community and talk [with authority]. (J.S., Educar staff)

Women's participation in the transnational peasant movement, the Latin American Coordination of Rural Organisation (CLOC) and *Via Campesina*,[6] has empowered them to demand the adoption of feminism within the land struggle. This is significant considering that in the 1980s and early 1990s, feminism was taboo, identified as a *petit bourgeois* ideology and synonymous with machismo, particularly in communities where the church had a strong influence.

Since the late 2000s, participants of women's' peasant movements at a national and international level started to advocate peasant and popular feminism based on the Pedagogy of the Oppressed ingrained within the peasant culture (Schwendler 2014). They demanded a gender-oriented MST struggle and agroecological education. 'In my opinion, agroecology is about more than the production of food. It is a way of life and it is why the issue of gender has everything to do with agroecology, as well as social justice and socialism' (M.S.C., Educar staff, interview 2015). This engagement with and in feminism led to the adoption of gender parity in 2000, which stipulated that every *base-nucleus* (a small group of families) in encampments and settlements must be coordinated by one man and one woman. Later, this norm was also adopted in MST's entire organisational structure. However, the women's movement within the MST had struggled many years for the establishment of gender parity at the national level.

These changes are not uniform and do not affect all landless women in the same way. Still gender education has been viewed as essential to overcoming the persistence of countryside patriarchal structures. Rural women are affected differently depending on the gender regime they have been exposed to and the opportunities they have had to challenge them (Walby 1997). The next section will explore how formal educational offerings, including the Educar Institute, are seen and used by the MST's feminist activists as a forum through which gender inequalities can be taken into consideration and addressed.

Challenging existing gender discourse through education

This section analyses how the MST's pedagogical approach supports gender parity and women's empowerment. There are three main reasons why the MST's gender-oriented pedagogy at Educar supports gender equity in the broader movement discussed in the pages that follow. First, debates and discussions about gender relations are intentionally incorporated into the school curriculum. Second, women and men are involved in the same work practices, challenging the sexual division of labour. Third, women learn the technical knowledge needed to participate in agroecological production.

Gender-oriented curriculum

A gender-oriented pedagogy is shaped by and shapes the environment in which it is located. In the MST's case it is grounded in feminist theory, alongside Marxist theory and critical pedagogy. It aims to simultaneously contest the hegemonic mode of production and patriarchal culture through a counter-hegemonic education based on the Pedagogy of the Oppressed. An important instance of education is the intentional production of counter-cultures, connected to ideologies that contest oppressive capitalist and gender relations. For instance, in MST schools, everyday lessons are preceded by a *mística*, which is a performance through words, art, symbolism, and music that portrays the struggles and reality of the movement, serving as 'pedagogy of empowerment' (Issa 2007, 126). Gender awareness and the production of a counter-hegemonic culture is also developed through this performative instance of education.

Additionally, Educar intentionally introduced into the curriculum discussions about the historic (re)production of gender asymmetries within society in general and peasant culture in particular. Debates probe the possibilities to overcome the sexual division of labour and persistent gender hierarchies in the countryside.

> Gender issues are debated in the day to day political education of the school; in seminars, readings and debates in many classes such as: Portuguese language, art, history, geography, sociology, philosophy in the technical course. In the agronomy course it is also worked on every day, in their political education, in the boarding school and in the module: Introduction to Social Thinking, in seminars, reading, debates and other activities in the course. (M.S.C., Educar staff, interview 2015)

Educar understands the importance of raising gender awareness through different strategies, which includes both theoretical analysis and practical experiences, in which students are challenged to undertake gender-oriented collaborative work and attitudes.

The MST's educational project rejects the separation between intellectual and manual labour. Inspired by Pistrak (1981), the movement takes education for work and through work as essential to its pedagogical proposal (MST 1996). For instance, all manual tasks necessary for a school to function are considered key mechanisms of the learning process. Students are responsible for daily tasks ranging from, managing the class schedule and facilitating classroom discussions to cleaning up the entire school and managing disciplinary issues. In addition, they are responsible for the cultivation of food and rearing of animals for consumption within the school, which also becomes part of the practical understanding of agroecology. 'Rather than schools simply being "ideological apparatuses," as in Althusser's conception, MST schools are also spaces of work that allow for alternative social relations of production to develop' (Tarlau 2013, 12), which also includes gender relations.

Challenging the sexual division of labour

Another critical pedagogic principle adopted by Educar is educating students as members of a collective, with the collective co-responsible for educating the collective (Caldart 2004). Inspired by Makarenko's perspective of education (2005), the MST organises its schools through *base nuclei*. These are small student collectives that are the organisational base of Educar. Through them, students organise their activities, develop their tasks, and produce collective studies. All issues are discussed and resolved within them. Base nuclei contest individualism and create a culture of cooperation (MST 1996). What is important from a gender perspective is that through this collective organisation the school challenges the sexual division of labour as all members carry out all activities.

> We have an organisation where the work is distributed amongst the girls and boys who are then collectively responsible for these chores. Each group rotates between chores during each phase of the course, that way they all get to experience all areas of work. (M.S.C., Educar staff, interview 2015)

The school has also developed discussions on gender issues to guide students in facing their gendered habitus. The school's egalitarian structures attempt to introduce new structures and ways of working to the students. M. P. (Educar student), states that 'At school there is a strong focus [on gender issues]. We are organised in groups, there is always one woman and one man, in terms of work outside (production) without having any kind of differentiation.' There is also an attempt to challenge assumptions that students have of women's and men's work, and to teach that gender roles are constructed socially and culturally, which means that they can be deconstructed. However, for some students, especially boys, who have been raised within conservative peasant culture, it can be a shock to work within these more gender egalitarian structures.

> It is a huge shock, the youth are brought up within very conservative peasant families, where there always existed a division between a woman's and man's place. (M.P., Educar student)

The nature of the school and studies mean that both men and women are included within this feminist education. As the imposition of power is based on the domain of knowledge and experience, the school teaches students how to contribute within and outside the agricultural home regardless of gender.

> One of the things that helps people develop here at the school is making everyone learn how to do everything. Whoever comes here leaves a completely different person... (T.S., Staff and former Educar student)

Although more egalitarian gendered authority patterns emerge from the MST's formal education, this has to work alongside the continuous reproduction of a hegemonic and patriarchal sexual divisions of labour, particularly within the organisation of the student's family. C. R., staff member and former student at Educar, discusses the difficulties in challenging hegemonic patterns of gender in the family:

> We hardly learn anything at home, all my knowledge about gender was learned here [in school]. Here we are divided into base nuclei and we all have to do something, does not matter whether we are men or women... Within the family unit, if you are a boy, you are not going to wash the dishes for your mum... In here it is easy because everybody contributes, but when you go back into the community, people ask what us students do ... and then they kind of mock you, 'oh so you guys are washing pans'.

In social struggles, mobilisations, marches, mass demonstrations, and informal education or other spaces of formation, women and men share different tasks more easily, but when they go back to their local spaces (the community and the family) it is more difficult for them to continue with this dynamic (Schwendler 2013). The student expresses his awareness:

> We work on this in school, and we incorporate this ideologically, it is important to not have gender inequality, and you realise that sometimes you find it hard to change, you reproduce. The idea is to maintain that equality present, even in the family, otherwise you will just fall back into the daily routine and forget. (M. P. Educar student)

M.S.C. (Educar staff), emphasises that students are changing their assumptions and attitudes due to the gender education developed by Educar. Nevertheless, 'it does not mean that after a few debates, studies and assignments ... the problem has been solved. Gender issues have to be experienced and confronted in the day to day'. Therefore, the Educar's alternating methodology is crucial, as students need to confront the principles of a gender education not only during the school time but also during the community time.

The transformation of gender relations, within this context, has to include the participation of male students as they are part of patriarchal social dynamics in the countryside. Additionally, many men/boys are open to challenges to ingrained assumptions about gender. Following is an example of how Male *Educar* students showed awareness in interviews of gendered dynamics by discussing the unequal division of work within the household and the devaluation of their own mothers work.

> I am not as self-conscious as I used to be... I used to sweep the floor at home and then somebody would arrive, a colleague, another women, I used to sort of hide in order to not be seen doing [housework], because I was convinced that that work just was not for me. Later on [after starting school], people would arrive and I would just continue [with the housework]... I help my mother do her chores ... she is on her own, even today I help her when I go back home... (C. R., Alumni and Current Educar Staff)

Despite gender awareness of more equal relations, there is a discourse that still reproduces traditional gender patterns, in which domestic chores taken on by men are usually judged as help, as they are considered women's responsibilities, with less social value. Similarly, as discussed previously, women's agricultural work is still regarded as help, as it is considered a male territory.

C.C.S. (Educar Student) discusses how the gender pedagogy at Educar has changed his own attitudes towards housework. Additionally, he expresses how he is able to communicate these ideas back into the community, which in turn has led to other males attempting to change dynamics within their homes as well.

> I have a friend who, once, when I was cleaning my house, asked, '...and your sister, what is she doing?'... [I responded] 'I am cleaning the house and she is doing other chores: her schoolwork'... then we had a conversation and he would say 'the women must do this and the man that' we continued to talk and he was kind of [thinking about it]. The next day I went to his house and he was washing the dishes.

Challenging gender roles through agroecological education

The school seeks to challenge these structures of rigid sexual divisions of labour that historically have relegated women to a secondary role in work, political activities, and community organisations, making them 'naturally' responsible for the domestic and care work (Schwendler 2003).

> In the beginning, I thought that the course was just for men ... most classes have a majority of men. Sometimes, women stop themselves [from doing things] 'ah, let's leave the men to do this.' (the heavy work for the men and the lighter for the women).... Everyone has the same ability. (C.R., Alumni and Current Educar staff)

This notion of 'heavy'/men's and 'light'/women's work is a cultural construction, in which the type of work is identified by the gender of the person who does it. Agricultural labour performed by women is usually considered 'lighter' than the 'heavier' productive work performed by men, even though it involves the same amount of time and effort (Paulilo 1987). The way in which the value of labour is gendered is also influenced by the use of technologies. For instance, the shift of production from family consumption to production for the market implies the use of more advanced agricultural technologies, such as the tractor, which has been associated to 'male's farm identity and power' (Brandth 1995, 113).

'The issue is that the boys come with some practical experience [of agricultural technologies], whereas the girls learn here' (J.S., Educar staff). J. S., Educar staff, states that despite some limits that girls face in the agroecological school, the major problems occur when they go back to the communities 'The issues arise when back in the settlement, where they do not trust women... or believe that they are capable.'

Patriarchal culture still resists shifts in the sexual division of labour in local communities and families. T.C. (Educar student) also reports how difficult it is for young women to teach agroecology in the community.

> Well, I work with men and women. But because I am a woman and young, the men do not have a lot of faith in me. I could even be very knowledgeable, but they prefer men. We know, and try to communicate firmly, but for them, we do not really know what we are doing.

The MST had the intention of bringing forward the gender debate due to the evident need within the settlements.

It was evident that in our territories *machista* attitudes and ideas are prevalent, as well as the oppression of women. The value of this is that our movement is dedicated to addressing this debate, confronting the situation of the existing internal issues, which allows progression in term of our gender awareness… (M.S.C., Educar staff, interview 2015)

Despite its limits, education has been seen by the MST activists as an important space for the new generation of landless workers to develop skills and acquire the knowledge necessary to produce a counter-hegemonic culture based on gender equality and sustainable peasant agriculture.

The pedagogic method in the school is an instrument that facilitates criticism and the ability to confront our own limitations with confidence and resolve. Psychoanalysis also helps us to recognise human richness as well as limitations and therefore deconstruct ideas, especially those of oppression and *machismo*. (M.S.C., Educar staff, interview 2015)

Regardless of the gender of the student, challenges will surface when entering back into the community. Being able to re-enter the school environment, discuss these issues and get feedback on how to address and confront these challenges means that the ability to question gender relations is continuously reinforced in the student.

Conclusion

This article argued that MST's education, focused on agroecology and accompanied by gender-oriented pedagogy, empowers women and men and disrupts the traditional sexual division of labour in rural communities, and within land struggles, more generally.

MST's principle objectives are to counteract neoliberal economic and political models that threaten rural livelihoods, forcing peasant communities to leave their territories. The MST struggle was for land redistribution and the transformation of the agrarian system. It initially attempted to resist neoliberalism by forming cooperatives and applying capitalist modes of production. However, they found that it was very difficult to compete with large agribusiness. For this reason, the MST sought alternatives to subsist 'outside' of the hegemonic agricultural market. The only way to do so was to seek more sustainable and independent forms of production including food sovereignty and agroecology.

Education, while a foundational element of the movement, is crucial to the dissemination of these alternative practices to a new generation. The MST formed technical schools that provided students with the skills to carry out agroecology and opportunities to go back to their communities and implement alternative projects, which have not always been accepted. The alternating pedagogy allows the school to participate, guiding the students in the whole process of implementation of agroecology projects in the community. Permitting the school to provide feedback and help students overcome hurdles to the gender-oriented pedagogies learned and practiced at school. This not only serves as a learning process for the students but also for the school, which is able to refine the ways in which it is able to support students.

As women struggles for equal status, they used the spaces that were available within the movement to open up other spaces in which they could further a women's equality agenda and introduce a feminist discourse. Women's input has been crucial to the development of MST's education, agroecology, and the introduction of food sovereignty. Additionally, women have challenged entrenched gender norms through MST education.

A gender-oriented pedagogy creates a space to empower the younger generations to address systemic inequalities. It includes discussion and practical implementations of gender equal practices designed to challenge students' conceptions of gender. Moreover, it has provided students with the tools to build new relationships and critically evaluate structures that may subordinate certain social groups. The last section has shown how, being able to spend periods of time in school and community, leads to student reflections and discussions around gender practices they are able to observe within their own communities. This allows the school to offer solutions and techniques that can help students maintain gender egalitarian practices and, in this way, continue to confront entrenched patriarchal dynamics within the community.

Cooperative pedagogies, that support collective and sustainable work practices, whilst incorporating gender discussions, are critical for disrupting gender relations because they challenge notions of the public-male and private-female separation of spaces so entrenched in many rural communities. The strength of this education is that it is relevant to everyday lives. Teaching young women to carry out 'male tasks' and vice versa creates a change in behaviour as well as thinking, an embodiment of discourse by students who then take these ideas and practices back into their communities.

Providing young women with agroecological knowledge has also been critical to their empowerment within communities and the social movement. This has, at the very least, allowed them to enter traditional male spaces with more autonomy and self-confidence.

Accessing education and raising gender consciousness is crucial to contest traditional gender roles, but these measures are insufficient unless it also involves the transformation of economic relations of production, and women's access to land, financial support, and technologies.

Funding

This research was supported by the University of London (Convocation Trust Appeal Fund for the Central Research Fund) and the CAPES Foundation, Ministry of Higher Education, Brazil.

Notes

1. *Instituto Educar* is referred to simply as Educar in the rest of the article, reflecting the colloquial name for the institute.
2. In addition to secondary-level education in 2014 Educar began an undergraduate agronomy course with the Federal University of Fronteira Sul, Erechim.
3. The interviewees are referred to by initials. All interviews were completed by Schwendler in 2011 unless specified otherwise.
4. The falsification of land titles.
5. This programme involves the purchase of organic food, seeds, milk by the government from the smallholders to be distributed for free to hospitals, community restaurants, etc.
6. Via Campesina is an international movement which joins peasants, small and medium-size farmers, landless people, women farmers, indigenous people, migrants, and agricultural workers from around the world (VIA Campesina 2011).

Disclosure statement

No potential conflict of interest was reported by the authors.

References

Altieri, M. A. 2009. "Agroecology, Small Farms, and Food Sovereignty." *Monthly Review: An Independent Socialist Magazine* 61 (3): 102–113.

Alvarez, S. 1990. *Engendering Democracy in Brazil: Women's Movements in Transition Politics.* Princeton, NJ: Princeton University Press.

Batliwala, Srilatha. 1997. "El Significado del empoderamiento de las mujeres: nuevos conceptos desde la acción." En León, Magdalena. *Poder y empoderamiento de las mujeres,* 187–211. T/M Editores, Santa Fe de Bogotá.

Brandth, B. 1995. "Rural Masculinity in Transition: Gender Images in Tractor Advertisement." *Journal of Rural Studies* 11 (2): 123–133.

Butto, A., and K. E. R. Hora. 2010. "Mulheres e reforma agrária no Brasil." In *Mulheres na reforma agrária: a experiência recente no Brasil,* edited by A. Lopes and A. Butto, 19–37. Brasília: MDA.

Caldart, R. 2000. *Pedagogia do Movimento Sem Terra: escola é mais do queescola.* Petrópolis, RJ: Vozes.

Caldart, R. 2004. "Por uma Educação do Campo: traços de uma identidade em construção." In *Por uma Educação do Campo,* edited by M. G. Arroyo, R. S. Caldart, and M. C. Molina, 147–158. Petrópolis, RJ: Editor Vozes.

Camini, Isabela. 2009. *Escola Itinerante: na fronteira de uma nova escola.* São Paulo: Expressão Popular.

Carter, M. 2009. "The Landless Rural Workers' Movement and the Struggle for Social Justice in Brazil." In *Rural Social Movements in Latin America: Organising for Sustainable Livelihoods,* edited by C. D. Deere and F. S. Royce, 87–114. University Press of Florida.

Deere, Carmen Diana. 2003. "Women's Land Rights and Rural Social Movements in the Brazilian Agrarian Reform." *Journal of Agrarian Change* 3: 257–288.

Desmarais, A. A. 2003. "The Via Campesina: Peasant Women on the Frontiers of Food Sovereignty." *Canadian Woman Studies/les cahiers de la femme* 23 (1): 140–145.

Elson, D., and R. Pearson. 2011. "The Subordination of Women and the Internationalisation of Factory Production." In *The Women Gender & Development Reader,* edited by N. Visvanathan (coord.), 212–224. London: Zed Books.

Faria, N. 2009. "Economia feminista e agenda de luta das mulheres no meio rural." In *Estatísticas rurais e a economia feminista: um olhar sobre o trabalho das mulheres,* edited by A. Butto, 11–28. Brasília: NEAD.

Fernandes, B. M. 1999. *Brasil: '500 anos de luta pela terra'. Revista de Cultura Vozes, 2.* Accessed July 6, 2014. http://www.culturavozes.com.br/revistas/0293.html.

Freire, P. 1973. *Pedagogy of the Oppressed.* New York: Continuum Publishing Company.

Freire, P. 2000. *Pedagogia da Indignação: cartas pedagógicas e outros escritos.* São Paulo: UNESP.

Gramsci, A.1971. *Selections from the Prison Notebooks.* London: Lawrence and Wishart.

Issa, D. 2007. "Praxis of Empowerment: Mística and Mobilisation in Brazil's Landless Rural Workers' Movement." *Latin American Perspectives* 34 (2): 124–138.

Jacobs, Susie. 2010. *Gender and Agrarian Reform.* New York: Routledge.

Makarenko, A. 2005. Poema pedagógico, Tradução de Tatiana Belinky, São Paulo, Editora 34.

Meek, D. 2015. "Learning as Territoriality: The Political Ecology of Education in the Brazilian Landless Workers' Movement." *The Journal of Peasant Studies* 42 (6): 1179–1200.

Molina, M. 2003. "A Contribuição do Pronera na construção de políticas públicas de educação do campo e desenvolvimento sustentável." PhD diss., Centro de Desenvolvimento Sustentável. Brasília, Universidade de Brasília.

MST. 1991. "A experiência do MST na cooperação agrícola." In *Assentamentos: A resposta econômica da reforma agrária,* edited by F. S. A. Görgen and J. P. Stedile, 134–179. Petrópolis: Vozes.

MST. 1996. "Princípios da educação no MST." (Caderno de Educação nº 08). São Paulo.

NERA (Núcleo de Estudos, Pesquisas e Projetos de Reforma Agrária). 2013. *Relatório DATALUTA – Banco de Dados da Luta pela Terra – 2012.* Presidente Prudente: NERA.

Paulilo, M. I. 1987. "O peso do trabalho leve." *Revista Ciência Hoje* 28: 64–70.

Pistrak, M. 1981. *Os Fundamentos da Escola do Trabalho.* São Paulo: Brasiliense.

Ribeiro, M. 2008. "Pedagogia da alternância na educação rural/do campo: projetos em disputa." *Educação e Pesquisa* 34 (1): 27–45.

Schwendler, S. F. 2003. "The Construction of the Feminine in the Struggle for Land and in the Social Re-creation of the Settlement." In *The Sights and Voices of Dispossession: The Fight for the Land and the Emerging Culture of the MST*, edited by E. R. P. Vieira. Nottingham: University of Nottingham. Accessed 5 May 2015. http://www.landless-voices.org/vieira/archive-05.php?rd=CONSTRUC567&ng=e&sc=3&th=42&se=0

Schwendler, S. F. 2013. "Women's Emancipation through Participation in Land Struggle." PhD diss., University of London, London.

Schwendler, S. F. 2014. "International Women's Day in the Brazilian Countryside: New Forms of Political Protest and Resistance." *History of Women in the Americas* 2: 1–24.

Silva, C., and A. P. Portella. 2006. "Divisão sexual do trabalho em áreas rurais no nordeste brasileiro." In *Agricultura familiar e gênero: práticas, movimentos e políticas públicas*, edited by P. Scott and R. Cordeiro, 127–144. Recife: Ed. da UFPE.

Stedile, J. P., and B. M. Fernandes. 1999. *Brava gente: a trajetória do MST e a luta pela terra no Brasil*. São Paulo: Fundação Perseu Abramo.

Tardin, J. M. and I. Kenfield. 2009. "The MST and Agroecology." In *Food Rebellions! Crisis and the Hunger for Justice*, edited by E. Holt-Giménez and R. Patel, 104–106. Cape Town: Pambazuka Press.

Tarlau, R. 2013. "The Social(ist) Pedagogies of the MST: Towards New Relations of Production in the Brazilian Countryside." *Education Policy Analysis Archives* 21:1–23.

VIA Campesina. 2011. The international Peasant's voice. Accessed May 4. http://viacampesina.org/en/index.php/organisation-mainmenu-44.

Walby, S. 1997. *Gender Transformations*. Routledge: London.

Wright, A., and W. Wolford. 2003. *To Inherit the Earth: The Landless Movement and the Struggle for a new Brazil*. Oakland, CA: Food First Books.

Aligning the market and affective self: care and student resistance to entrepreneurial subjectivities

Luciana Lolich and Kathleen Lynch

ABSTRACT

The paper examines the ways in which higher education students negotiate contemporary global transitions premised on improving competitiveness and opportunity in a system driven by the ideology of the market-led, knowledge-based economy (HEA. 2011. *National Strategy for Higher Education to 2030*. Dublin: Department of Education and Skills; OECD 2004. *Review of National Policies for Education in Ireland*. Paris: OECD; 2006. *Higher Education in Ireland*. Paris: OECD; 2013. "Education at a Glance 2013: OECD Indicators." Accessed March 15, 2014. doi:10.1787/eag-2013-en). Using data from a large cohort of students (4265) in three very different types of higher education institutions (Public University, Public Institute of Technology and a private for-profit College), and through the analysis of recent policy developments, the paper shows that there is an explicit requirement on colleges to create entrepreneurial students in Irish higher education. However, the paper also demonstrates how this narrative is mediated and resisted by the students' own educational and care imaginaries: they are expecting to be better cared for in colleges than they are currently; and their presumed future, and for some, current lives are not only defined in terms of occupational goals but in terms of care and nurturing (affective) relations. The data suggest that the affective domain of care or social reproductive relations (Federici 2012. *Revolution at Point Zero: Housework, Reproduction and Feminist Struggle*. PM Press/Common Notions/Autonomedia) may constitute an emerging site of gendered resistance to the globalised commercialisation of higher education.

Introduction

Teaching has long been considered a 'caring profession' (O'Connor 2006); however, 'care' is not a dominant narrative in higher education (HE) given its focus on educating an autonomous, rational person, *homo sapiens*, whose relationality is peripheral to her or his being (Lynch 2010; Moreau and Kerner 2015). This indifference to the caring subject within HE has intensified in the past decade with the rise of the ideology of the knowledge-based economy (KBE)[1] and its influence on HE's role and mission (Bano and Taylor 2015). The focus is on educating the citizen to achieve her or his potential in the public sphere of life, developing an entrepreneurial self (Peters 2005) while largely ignoring the relational caring self both as learners (Lynch, Lyons, and Cantillon 2007) and as educators (Lynch, Baker, and Lyons 2009).

Feminist scholarship has demonstrated clearly, however, that all human beings have both a need and a capacity for intimacy, attachment and caring relationships (Tronto 1993, 2013; Nussbaum 1995; Kittay 1999; Held 2006). Because human beings live in affective relational realities,[2] they have emotional ties and bonds that compel them to act as moral agents, to act 'other-wise' rather than 'self-wise' (Tronto 2013). Their lives are not only lived out in terms of interests in class, status and power, in the classic Marxist-Weberian sense of these terms, they are also lived out in terms of their affective (care) histories and their affective futures. People generally value the various forms of social engagement that emanate from such relations and define themselves in terms of them (Lynch, Baker, and Lyons 2009). While care relations are classed, gendered, aged, raced and function within given power and status relations (Gutierrez-Rodriguez 2014), they also operate as a discrete affective system, involving primary, secondary and tertiary circles of care (Lynch, Lyons, and Cantillon 2007) with unique forms of care consciousness (Crean 2016).

Despite the centrality of love and care in everyday life, and the growing evidence that care matters for young people at home and in school (Luttrell 2013; Feeley 2014; McGovern and Devine 2016), there is little research on care in HE (Mariskind 2014). While there has been some research on teachers and managers (O'Connor 2006; Lynch, Baker, and Lyons 2009; O'Brien 2010; Robert 2014), there is very little on students' needs to care and be cared for (Bandura and Lyons 2012). Given the moral imperative on women to do care work (O'Brien 2007) and on men to be care-less (Hanlon 2012), the institutional denial of the realities of care work and care relations in student lives has highly gendered outcomes. Implicitly, if not explicitly:

> The ideal learner continues to be based on masculinist conceptions of the individual, with this learner constructed as male, white, middle class and able-bodied … an autonomous individual unencumbered by domestic responsibilities, poverty or self-doubt. Such conceptualizations are not only gendered, but also rooted in white Western cultural constructions of an independent self. (Leathwood and O'Connell 2003, 599)

Moreover, the visualisation of women as passive subjects persists in the public relations imaginary of higher educational institutions themselves (Leathwood 2013).

This article analyses the ways in which HE students in Ireland negotiate contemporary global transitions premised on improving their store of human capital and their competitiveness in a knowledge-based capitalist economy (Bathmaker, Ingram, and Waller 2013; Seddon, Ozga, and Levin 2013; Robert 2014) in gendered ways. The paper focuses in particular on questions about the significance of affective relations (Lynch, Baker, and Lyons 2009) for students both within HE and in their future life in the context of an increasingly market-led HE regime.

Neoliberalism and HE

Neoliberalism is the primary producer of cultural logic and value in HE in Ireland (Lynch 2006; Lynch, Grummell, and Devine 2012).The goal is to create an enterprise-led university, one in which the values of a consumer society are embedded in educational relationships (Morley 2001). HE is increasingly portrayed as meeting highly individualistic goals and granting a number of extrinsic benefits in which students are consumers of an educational product (Astin 1991; Delucchi and Korgen 2002; Saunders 2007). At a macro level, and arising from the financial crisis in particular, HE has also been framed as a key player in determining the future economic security of the Irish nation (Higher Education Authority [HEA] 2011; OECD 2006, 2013; Loxley, Seery, and Walsh 2014). The 'knowledge economy' is about servicing business rather than society. As clearly explained by the Department of Education and Skills: 'Higher education is the key to economic recovery in the short term and to longer-term prosperity' (HEA 2011, 29).

While nation states do make strategic HE and policy decisions within their borders, the globalisation of trade, and the ideology of globalisation itself, has meant that governments can and do use 'globalisation' as an operational device that absolves them of responsibility for the implementation of neoliberal reforms. The narrative is created that in order to 'survive' as an independent country, it is imperative to follow the market path and invest in HE for industries that have global market potential, namely the business-relevant areas of the STEM subjects, Science, Technology, Engineering and Mathematics (Government of Ireland 2008).[3]

Ireland is presented as being 'under threat' from low-cost countries and therefore must provide services that are cost-sensitive, but require ingenuity and creativity. This is the imaginary space for enabling the creation of the marketised neoliberal self: it includes imagining and inserting oneself into a globalised entrepreneurial student body where one can become a successful global competitor (Hay and Kaptizke 2009).[4] The narrative emerged originally in the Government's *Investment in Education* Report 1962 (O'Sullivan 2005) but found far more focused expression 50 years later in the *National Strategy for Higher Education to 2030* (HEA 2011). The shift to the marketable student is represented as inevitable, arising not so much as the choices of government but from the inexorable demands of living in a globalised world (Loxley, Seery, and Walsh 2014; Clancy 2015).

Within this paradigm, HE is hailed as a form of insurance against the risk of unemployment, under-employment and/or poverty. Internal to this is a conception of society that, when deployed as a form of governmentality (Gordon 1991; Dean 1999), creates new citizen-subjects and disseminates market values to all institutions and social actions, including education. HE is tasked with creating new student subjectivities through regimes of practices and technologies of government that are market-led.

Production metaphors, borrowed from industry, are central to the new discourse: students are presented as produced subjects with measurable attributes and marketable skills.[5] It the neoliberal system, social class advantage is increasingly sought through acquiring credits outside of academic achievements, including prestigious internships and cultural and social capital-enhancing extracurricular activities (Bathmaker, Ingram, and Waller 2013). The enterprise university model and the managerialistic discourses also impact on academics' time and energy for caring, including caring for themselves (O'Connor 2006; Walker, Gleaves, and Grey 2006; Gill 2010: Devine, Grummell, and Lynch 2011), often in ways that are highly gendered (Morley 2007).

Because managerial principles originated in a commercial context where process is subordinate to output and profit, managerialistic values manifest themselves in education through the promotion of forms of governance (i.e. measurement, surveillance, control and regulation) that are often antithetical to the caring that is at the heart of good education (Noddings 2005; Lynch 2013b; Ball and Olmedo 2013). A focus on measurability and accountability re-orients pedagogical and scholarly activities towards those ends that are likely to have a positive impact on measurable performance outcomes and deflect attention away from aspects of social, emotional or moral development that have no immediate measurable performative value (Ball 2012; Lolich and Lynch 2014). It ignores the emotional aspect of teaching, consistent with a masculine cultural project (Davies 1996); it presents the affective labour that goes into teaching relationships as a natural female trait and therefore immaterial, unproductive and unskilled. However, as Bolton (2009) has demonstrated, 'affective labour' has material outcomes that directly affect students' performance and productivity, even if gains are generally not measurable in a narrowly specifiable time frame (Lynch 2013b).

When universities foster individualism and competition between staff, it can be difficult for a caring community to thrive (Harkavy 2006). While educators do resist the undermining of their ethical dispositions and their caring work, the resistance is often at an individual level (Ball and Olmedo 2013). The ethics of competition and performance persist, and are very different from the older ethics of professional judgement and cooperation (Ball 2003; Walker, Gleaves, and Grey 2006). Accountability as an ideology gives priority to the individual pursuing his or her self-interest over considerations of the collective or common good (Lingard 2014). Academics have no real incentive to share best practices unless this sharing can be measured and rewarded. Instead, they are compelled to invest in themselves, to become unique and clearly differentiate themselves from their peers (Slaughter and Leslie 1997).

The changes in the management and purpose of HEIs have also led to the reconceptualisation of the student (Delucchi and Korgen 2002; Leathwood and O'Connell 2003; Naidoo and Jamieson 2005; Saunders 2007). Focusing on measured performance promotes self-interest and credential acquisition among students (Lolich 2011). It encourages them to focus on education's instrumental value and to ignore its academic meaning or moral character (Arum and Roksa 2011). Competitive individualism is no longer seen as an amoral necessity but rather as a desirable and necessary attribute for a constantly reinventing entrepreneur (Ball 2003; Apple 2004). As such, it carries a deep indifference to the inevitable dependencies and interdependencies that are endemic to the human condition (Gilligan 1995). It is disregarding of the role that emotions play in relationships and learning, and correlatively indifferent to the central role of care and love relations in defining who we are (Lynch 2006).

The gendered narrative of carelessness that is implicit in the organisation of HE (Lynch 2010) manifests itself in two ways. It is evident in the narrative of students as care-free individuals, sole traders, young (*sic*) people encouraged to think only about themselves and their academic work. Second, it is part of the doxa of the university that educational nurturing is a cerebral activity, devoid of emotional substance in the relational sense. It devalues the importance of emotions in HE not only the 'affective labour' that students, especially women do outside college, but also the care that students need from teachers and institutions.

The indifference to affective relations does not mean that emotions are not managed or recognised. With the move from manufacturing to services, a focus on the creation of emotional ecologies has developed in the global market and, with it, the idea that emotions can be made to work to produce things like laughter and well-being that are of market value (Bolton 2009, 2). Hochschild (1983, 2011) has explored how our feelings are many times appropriated by diverse work organisations with a definite aim in mind, to benefit capital. While HE institutions do not focus on the affective lives of students, ironically, it is students' own recognition of their affective relations, especially in the future, that pushes many of them to become successful in the enterprise of the self, although this happens in gendered ways as discussed below.

As noted by Saunders (2007), there is a need for empirical research on the new types of subjectivities being created in HE that moves away from the simple concept of student consumerism and instead connects these changes in the personhood of students to broader macro and institutional forces. There is a need to take an affective perspective regarding the operationalisation of neoliberalism for HE students.

The study

The study addressed calls for research on the purpose and role of HE for students attending college, from a student perspective (Hay and Kaptizke 2009; Guerin, Jayatilaka, and Ranasinghe 2015). It examines the ways in which HE students negotiate contemporary global transitions premised on improving their competitiveness and opportunities within an era of neoliberalism and risk (Seddon, Ozga, and Levin 2013; Robert 2014). The paper focuses in particular on the role of affective relations and 'affective labour' in the lives of students in HE.

Methodology

To elicit student experiences of HE, an online questionnaire was developed using the online Survey-Monkey software. The survey was live from September 2010 to May 2011. Questionnaire items were modelled primarily on two national student surveys examining students' experience and reasons for undertaking HE: the UK's Higher Education Careers Service Unit (HECSU) research on higher education in 2010 and the US Cooperative Institutional Research Program (CIRP) research on third-level students.[6] This resulted in a questionnaire with a set of 29 close-ended questions and 1 open-ended question.[7]

This study was cross-sectional rather than longitudinal like the HECSU and CIRP; therefore, while the questionnaire drew on these survey instruments, it comprised a once-off survey rather than capturing how the experience changed over time. This paper examines the findings of one section that focused on how important seven different goals were for students. The goals ranged from individualistic goals like expertise and financial, to more relational goals like family and helping others, and, finally, broader goals like politics and the environment. The objective was to explore to what extent smart economy discourses affect students goals and aspirations. The study was not originally designed to examine care in HE; however, the need to care and be cared for came up very strongly in students' accounts of their HE experience. This paper relies on students' narratives from the open-ended question to consider how care is constructed and gendered in the stories they tell.

Three third-level institutions were involved, a university, an institute of technology and a private college, all based in Dublin. The colleges were strategically selected to study students' attitudes in the three major sectors of Irish HE (HEA 2011). After approval by the Research Ethics Committee at each institution, the questionnaire was distributed to the whole student populations. Questionnaires were completed by 4265 individuals.

The last question asked students if they had any further comments they wished to make about their experiences of HE and the smart economy. This was a free-text question and there was no limit as to how little or how much students could write. Overall, 744 students (17.4%) commented on this. The comments were a really valuable resource, adding texture and depth to the quantitative findings and the theme of care and affective relations was dominant within them.

Response rates by individual HE institutions participating in the study are presented in Table 1. The average response rate was 8.5%. This compares well with other blanket surveys in HE Ireland with overall response rates of 8.0%[8] and 7.5%.[9] Population figures for the three institutions are not provided in order to preserve the anonymity of respondents. While female students were over-represented in the responses (62.1%), just 50% of all Irish higher education students are women.[10] About 53.5% of respondents had an age that ranged from 18 to 21 years, which is quite typical of Irish students. Given that the study was concentrated in Dublin Colleges, that are more middle class in intake than regional colleges, it is not surprising that both middle and upper classes (professional and managerial) are significantly over-represented (by 23.8%), while working-class (semi-skilled and unskilled manual) students are significantly under-represented (by 20.6%).

Findings and discussion

The research findings point to a very diverse set of goals and experiences among HE students. While many of them want to do well in the labour market, economic goals can conceal other motives that are centred on students' relationality and affective relationships. It was through the students' comments that it became clear that students negotiate a global economic imperative to succeed in the labour market with what matters to them at a local and personal level. Their affective selves are constantly being aligned with their market selves. The need to care and to be cared for emerged as a dominant theme in this study, within a frame of struggle and stress.

Students were asked to express the level of importance attributed to particular goals and values on a series of statements used in other international student surveys. Values ranged from 1 to 7, with 1 being 'extremely important' and 7 being 'not at all important'. The three most important factors as rated by students were 'Becoming an expert in my field' ($n = 3825$ $M = 2.35$), 'Helping others who are in difficulty' ($n = 3812$ $M = 2.60$), and 'Raising a family' ($n = 3809$ $M = 2.80$).

As can be seen from Table 2, factors that related to improving the wider environment, and political issues were considered to be least important. Twenty years previously, Astin (1991) observed a declining interest in altruism and social problems between the 1960s

Table 1. Response rate to the questionnaire based on total population.

Third-level institution	Response rate %
Total university	11.3
Total IoT	4.6
Total private college	9.7
Overall total	8.5

Note: IoT, institute of technology.

Table 2. Importance of personal values and goals – all students (values ranged from 1–7**).

	N	Overall mean (M)
Becoming an expert in my field	3825	2.35
Helping others who are in difficulty	3812	2.60
Raising a family	3809	2.80
Being very well off financially	3813	2.84
Influencing social values	3805	3.78
Becoming involved in programmes to clean up the environment	3806	4.06
Influencing the political structure of Irish society	3815	4.49

** the lower the score, the higher the importance of these factors.

and 1980s among young traditional students in America. A more recent report (Pryor et al. 2010) confirms this trend with a low percentage of American students claiming an interest in influencing social values, politics or improving the environment.

The enterprise of affect

Expertise was the most important goal for students with 67.2% considering this factor as extremely or very important. However, it was through the extensive analysis of the 744 comments, that the overlapping of different goals became apparent. Most students listed a range of goals along with expertise; the desire to develop a secured economic future with solid affective relationships, emerged time and time again in students' open-ended comments. Edward explained how he wanted to do good and do well, while Robert, spoke about doing good and having a good relational life.

> I wish to become an expert in my field and then hope to go further than that still, to become an important figure in an important company, so I can affect the social community in a good way. Also it would mean I have done something in life for myself and the community. (Edward, male, undergraduate, Business & Law, University)
> I wanted to study in College in order to widen my field of expertise. But, my real purpose in life is to have my own family, a strong network (friends, co-workers, etc) and to be working on something I enjoy, so that I could be more effective every day. (Robert, male, undergraduate Business & Law, Private College)

Despite the fact that the ideal student is increasingly defined as a self-sufficient and rational citizen (Masschelein and Simons 2002; Peters 2005; Lynch, Lyons, and Cantillon 2007; Bandura and Lyons 2012), students feel a strong commitment to a relational life as interdependent, caring and other-centred human beings (Lynch, Baker, and Lyons 2009). For many students, expertise and success were important but so was the feeling of belonging, being part of a group: family, work and community. The entrepreneurial self is negotiated in the local space of the enterprise university. Students like Robert and Edward mediate the idea of the independent neoliberal subject by demonstrating how important their personal and local ties are to them (Black 2014).

Given the relationality expressed by students, it is not surprising that the second most important goal for over half of all students (57.9%) was 'helping others who are in difficulty'. Responses varied by gender in this regard. While female students ($M = 2.36$) consider this factor as significantly more important than male students ($M = 2.90$) as their mean scores show (Table 3), nonetheless, male students also rated helping others as very important.

NEOLIBERALISM, GENDER AND EDUCATION WORK

Table 3. Results of *t*-test and Descriptive Statistics for 'Helping others who are in difficulty' by gender.

	Gender								
	Male			Female			95% CI for mean difference	Sig.	df
	M	SD	*n*	*M*	SD	*n*			
Helping others who are in difficulty	2.90	1.68	1246	2.36	1.52	2060	−.654, −.426	.000*	2421.66

*p < .05.

For Julia, losing her job acted as a trigger to go back to college; however, while financial stability was important, having meaningful work that involved helping others also mattered. Sadhbh describes her desire to 'help others as a reason for choosing law as a career.

> We are a one-income family with three kids and when I was let go in my part-time job it finally helped me make the decision to go to college. [...] My partner would say at the end of this, me having a competitive wage is important but to me it is about the job. I would like to wake up every morning and be looking forward to going to work and hopefully help people in either a small or large way. (Julia, female, undergraduate, Arts & Education, Private College)
> [...] My ultimate aim is to help people. I chose law from an idealistic viewpoint and I figured that it would be interesting and enable me to help others. (Sadhbh, female, undergraduate, Law & Business, University)

On a related item, 57.5% of students reported 'Raising a family' as extremely or very important. Again, mean scores on this item show that this goal was significantly more important for female (*M* = 2.70) than male students (*M* = 2.92) (Table 4).

Relationship goals are sometimes hidden behind other goals, with 'Being very well-off financially' acting as a facilitator to build and sustain relationships.

> I hope that when I finish my degree I will be able to get a good job in management and hopefully have enough money to start a family. (Maria, female, undergraduate, Business & Law, Private College)
> [...] I find college a method in which I can hopefully improve my life and the life of my family. A better chance of a better life is the main reason why I decided to go to college [...]. (John, male, undergraduate, Technology, IoT)

Smart-economy discourses purport to equalise market opportunities for everybody though education. However, many students embrace this imperative to up-skill, not only for employment reasons but also to safeguard what matters to them in terms of their relational identities both in the community and in the family. Students mediate the KBE demands for entrepreneurial selves – making them more unique and competitive for the labour market – in order to build and maintain their affective selves. How care is approached is gendered in that women talk about wanting to be able to take time out of their careers to care for children whilst males seem to focus more on wanting to

Table 4. Results of *t*-test and Descriptive Statistics for 'Raising a family' by gender.

	Gender								
	Male			Female			95% CI for mean difference	Sig.	df
	M	SD	*n*	*M*	SD	*n*			
Raising a family	2.92	1.99	1249	2.70	1.93	2056	−.352, −.077	.002*	3303

*p < .05.

have a good career in order to be able to support dependents; the breadwinner model of caring is still the male-defined way to care and love.

> ... I should have been promoted to director level by the time I finish my course and therefore I should have enough work experience to move into a managerial role in another company. The sky is the limit salary wise and once you have made a name for yourself there will be a lot of support when taking time when having a family which is important to me. (Leona, female, undergraduate, Business & Law, Private College)
> [...] I have ambitions professionally and creatively which I want to fulfil but ultimately my personal happiness is of paramount importance and therefore I want to have time to raise a family. (Sadhbh, female, undergraduate, Business & Law, University)
> My primary motivation to study now is to ensure the economic survival of my family which is in doubt due to unemployment, pay cuts, a massive mortgage and no development prospects in my current career. What should have been an enjoyable process, higher education has now evolved in to a desperate struggle for financial survival. (Andrew, male, undergraduates, Arts & Education, Private College)

The global demands of the KBE are endorsed by students, not least because their future welfare and security is increasingly dependent on their individualised efforts in light of the State's gendered retreat from social service provision (Ouellette and Wilson 2011; Dukelow and Considine 2014). But their responses to entrepreneurialism are mediated through the lens of their affective labours and identities. While students realise that without economic security affective relations are threatened, the development of a marketable self is neither the only nor ultimate objective of pursing HE. Students attribute significant value to their relational lives; developing the marketable self is a means to protecting affective relations, albeit in highly gendered ways.

A very lonely place

It was clear as well through the 744 comments that students were not only concerned about caring for others but also they wanted to be cared for while in college. Although many students spoke very positively about their third-level experiences, and most were very pleased that they had decided to go to college, for many, the experience was one of struggling against the odds. 'Struggle' was a constant theme in the qualitative data. While financial worries were a huge source of stress for students, other factors such as lack of confidence in one's ability and a lack of care from academics and institutions were mentioned time and time again in students' accounts (Leathwood and O'Connell 2003).

Considering that the self-sufficient and independent student is at the apex of the literature of the KBE, it is remarkable how many students struggle with lack of confidence in their abilities or performance.

> There is information overload. I was expecting something different, now I have just 3 weeks left to my exams and I am not sure I [will] pass them because of lack of time. We should get more time to prepare. (Jacqueline Female, Undergraduate, Arts & Education, IoT)
> [...] I feel overwhelmed with my workload and find myself constantly worrying that I will fail and wondering how I afford to pay for repeats. The jump from 2nd to 3rd level education is huge and I feel I was poorly prepared by my 2nd level education even though I did quite well in my Leaving Certificate. (Sandra, female, Undergraduate, Arts & Education, IoT)

Working-class students and those from a disadvantaged socio-economic background expressed feelings of not being welcome or being 'looked down upon' by lecturers and other students. The three students below came from a semi-skilled and non-skilled manual background.

> [I] had done my undergraduate at [name of institution] where I was encouraged and praised for my work. Lecturers were very approachable and always willing to assist you with any problems or questions you may have. Having successfully obtained a place for my masters at [name of institution] I was very disappointed with the formalities and snobbery from both students and lecturers. I understand I am at a different level but I feel very isolated which has, in turn, knocked my confidence in my abilities. (Alice, female, Postgraduate, Business & Law, University)
> The experience was made very difficult by my background, coming from the bottom of the socio-economic ladder, only having primary school education, and a number of other personal difficulties arising as a result of my background. (Nicholas, male, postgraduate, Business & Law, University)
> My college career has been severely hampered by [class-based] 'discrimination shown by course tutors and then held up by the college'. (Rose, female, undergraduate, Arts & Education, IoT)

Some mature students felt that they lacked the support that matched their needs, as they had been out of education for a while. Walter, Cynthia and Enda below are all over 30 years of age.

> Third-level education is very challenging for me as I am a mature student who lacks confidence. I hope I have made the right choice in taking on this course, am very conscious about what it will lead to. If I am only scraping through I will then begin to think it was a waste of time. Life is difficult for me personally and [I] find it hard to concentrate fully on the task in hand.[...] The supports are there but [I] feel embarrassed to use them. (Walter, male, undergraduate, Arts & Education, University)
> [We need] some additional help for mature students who have been out of academia for many years. (Cynthia, female, Postgraduate, Arts & Education, University)
> Higher education is hard work, especially if you are a mature student. The maintenance grant doesn't cover much you are living from week to week, some weeks you don't even have the bus fare home. Re the smart economy how is that going to get up and running when the government is cutting before them and behind them. They should be investing in education and not cutting the funding. Smart economy my arse. (Enda, male, undergraduate, Business & Law, IoT)

Many of those who acknowledged that they were struggling academically felt that this was compounded by a lack of support from the university or college attended. In line with findings in other studies (Leathwood and O'Connell 2003; Arum and Roksa 2011; Bandura and Lyons 2012), a dominant theme that emerged was the desire on the part of the vast majority of students for a greater degree of contact with, and support from teaching staff. Students commented about feeling lonely and isolated; overall, HE was a very difficult experience for many:

> The problem I find that has hindered my education most at [name of institution] is the fact that it is a massive vacuum where students and their concerns can easily be swallowed up. It's scary. We need more student support, and to have someone to account for us. Not that I want to be 'mummied' or anything, but it would be nice for someone to be accountable to. (Phyllis, female, undergraduate, Arts & Education, University)
> I just joined higher education and dislike it very much. It is a lonely broad place, and I shall be leaving after this year. (Brid, female, undergraduate, Arts & Education, University)

> I find in general that [name of institution] is such a big place that it can be incredibly isolating and lonely, very tough dynamic for mature students parenting alone. (Brian, male, postgraduate, Arts & Education, University)

It is clear that some students need more support in HE; yet, the amount of time faculty members spend engaging with students outside class, for example, in an advisory capacity, has declined over the years (Massy and Zemsky 1994; Arum and Roksa 2011). This had to do with a range of factors, including an increased managerial culture where 'care' for the students is not recognised as an important key performance indicator (and arguably, it cannot be measured) and the significant cuts in resources to HE in countries like Ireland, particularly since the financial crisis.[11] Moreover, measures of teaching standards and performance do not acknowledge affective labour's materiality (O'Connor 2006) and overlook the fact that it is hard and productive work (Lyon and Glucksmann 2008). Also, the focus, especially in major universities, on research, and the increased amount of administration duties that teaching faculty need to undertake, leaves little time for care. Providing extra guidance and support not only becomes increasingly difficult but also is not generally perceived as being significantly rewarded (Arum and Roksa 2011). In this transactional model of education, the care for the student is pushed outside of the educational agenda (Lynch 2010). The result is that many of the students felt that they had been expected to be 'independent' too early in their studies.

Student parents were especially concerned about the lack of supports (Leathwood and O'Connell 2003), and these were mostly mothers:

> The college forgets about students with families to raise, who also work to support said families once they have enticed them to enrol and pay the enormous fees! (Lori, Female, undergraduate, Business & Law, University)
> Trying to balance home and children with college is very hard. (Lila, female, Arts & Education, undergraduate, Private College)
> It is the fourth and final year of my degree. I find attending college two nights a week, along with full time work and a young daughter a struggle. (Susan, female, Undergraduate, Arts & Education Private College)

It is clear that students are not only under pressure in terms of balancing work, study and a personal life, but also struggle with feelings of low confidence and loneliness. Non-traditional students were especially vocal about the barriers and challenges they faced and the lack of specialist services and supports. In their view, there was insufficient recognition that the student in HE today is very different from the elite students of the universities of the past.

Conclusions

This study revealed that many students want more care in HE, challenging the idealised myth of the self-sufficient independent adult learner. They also want to be carers/cared-for persons in their future adult lives. Their identities are relational, connected and care-led (Gilligan 1995) in a way that purveyors of market logic do not expect or plan for in an era of entrepreneurial HE. While the care focus of students is gendered in some ways, care concerns seem to move beyond current gendered and binary thinking (Mariskind 2014).

The paper has shown that, while the feminised discourse of loving and caring is not a legitimate part of the public narrative within HE, except and insofar as it facilitates productivity and high performances, many students are dissenting from market entrepreneurialism; they are not simply fodder for a 'smart economy' but affective actors in the management of their daily lives and assumed futures (Lolich and Lynch 2015). Students are agentic, 'resisting', 'redrawing', 'redefining', 'reframing' and 'renewing' the boundaries, not only of their neoliberal subjectivity, but of the local and global agendas of a smart economy that play themselves out within it (Black 2014, 2). Similar to Reay, Crozier, and Clayton's (2009) findings in their study of working-class students in elite universities, students are capable of 'redefining' external pressures/expectations in order to achieve what matters to them. While they are incorporated into the KBE out of economic necessity, they are also reframing it as they engage with it. The desire to carve out an affective space for themselves within a strong economic imperative, might not transform education policy and hegemonic ideas about the official role and purpose of HE in the short term (Braun 2011; Robert 2014), but it is an attempt by students to exercise agency. It is an attempt to resist and carve out a narrative for themselves about their own life that is deeply ethical in the sense that it is tied to their anticipated (and current) relational selves, the requirement that one lives 'other-wise' and not simply 'self-wise' (Tronto 2013). And while it is a highly gendered narrative, reflecting how 'self-work is crucial to contemporary discourses of post-welfare citizenship' especially in the affective domain (Ouellette and Wilson 2011, 556), it is a signal by students that they are not simply units of human capital servicing the economy but people living in profound states of interdependency.

Given how silenced the care narrative is in HE, the students' accounts read like a form of individualised resistance, not unlike that noted among academic staff (Ball and Olmedo 2013). But it is also more than that. It is a claim to another life lived alongside and within the realms of the so-called 'smart economy'.

Many of the students spoke very positively about their courses and how they benefited from their education. However, learning as a pleasurable and fulfilling experience was countered by the constant struggle, which many articulated. Within the enterprise university, there is a demand for more care (including a recognition of the different classed, gendered and care positioning of students) for more investment in affective labour, an expectation that lecturers and tutors do caring; yet, this expectation is not articulated or enabled (Devine, Grummell, and Lynch 2011).

The new subjectivity created under neoliberalism is classed and gendered because the possibility of being productive and unencumbered by the need or the responsibility of care, are not available to all. Not every student has the resources to be a scholar and nothing else while in HE. Some need to work, others have care commitments.[12] Even among those students who are not bound by cash or care issues in HE, an appreciation of how care and affective relations mediate the experience of HE is necessary to understand the new gendered resistance to globalised commercialisation in HE.

Notes

1. The concept of the knowledge economy implies that the generation and the exploitation of knowledge *per se* are central to the creation of wealth. 'A number of separate discourses from economics, management theory, futurology and sociology can be identified as having

contributed to shaping the present policy narrative of the 'knowledge economy' (Peters 2001, 4) all of which centre on the idea that knowledge and technical skills (advanced human capital) will be the drivers of economic advantage globally. Unfortunately, policy usage of the concept does not distinguish generally between knowledge and information or between the knowledge society (which would impute rights to advanced education as essential for all) and the knowledge economy (Peters 2001). The latter term is frequently used to refer primarily to those forms of knowledge that service multinationals. This is especially true in Ireland where the focus is on STEM (Science, Technology, Engineering and Mathematics) subjects (HEA 2011) for the development of the economy.

2. Nurturing relations constitute a discrete site of social practice within and through which human beings are created as social persons. Primary, secondary and tertiary care relations operate as intersecting circles of care (or in the case of their absence, as systems of neglect or abuse) moving from the intimate to the institutional to the political. We have termed these the affective relations of love, care and solidarity, respectively (Baker et al. 2004; Lynch, Lyons, and Cantillon 2007; Lynch, Baker, and Lyons 2009). The affective world operates as a discrete system and is therefore a site of political import that needs to be examined in its own right while recognising its inter-relatedness with economic, political and cultural systems (Lynch 2013a).

3. As stated in Building Ireland's Smart Economy (Government of Ireland 2008, 36): "a reliance on traditional manufacturing and low-skilled services will not be sufficient to allow developed countries like Ireland to remain at the forefront of economic and technologies curves".

4. The Hunt report on the future of higher education clearly articulates that:

> The educational level of the Irish population has to be raised. We need more graduates at every level. People who are already employed need to raise their level of qualification and broaden their educational base. Unemployed people need new educational opportunities that are attuned to the demands of the new economy and significant research effort has to be expended on priority areas where we, as a country, have the talent, experience and resources that will enable us to succeed on a global scale. (HEA 2011, 29)

5. The purposes of all forms of education are increasingly construed in market terms at national level as education is linked to skills' needs within the economy (Expert Group on Skills Needs, 2015 *Monitoring Ireland's Skills Supply: Trends in Education and Training Outputs*. Dublin Department of Education and Skills.

6. *HECSU* In 2005, HECSU launched a major longitudinal study, named *Futuretrack*, of all applicants to full-time UK higher education courses who applied through the Universities and Colleges Admissions service (UCAS) in 2006. The programme of research was designed to explore the process of entry into and through higher education. Due to the longitudinal aspect of this research, five different questionnaires were designed to capture different stages in the educational journey of learners. *CIRP*: The CIRP is a national longitudinal study of the American higher education system. Established in 1966 at the American Council on Education, the CIRP is now the nation's largest and oldest empirical study of higher education, involving data on some 1900 institutions, over 15 million students, and more than 300,000 faculties. CIRP surveys have been administered by the Higher Education Research Institute since 1973. The CIRP longitudinal programme consists of the four surveys: freshman survey, first college year survey, diverse learning environment survey and the college senior survey. The Higher Education Research Institute (HERI) is housed in the Graduate School of Education & Information Studies (GSE&IS) at the University of California, Los Angeles (UCLA).

7. The questionnaire was designed to measure students' goals and ambitions in higher education generally and was limited by the closed-end nature of the questions asked. This did not allow to focus in depth on students' affective labour and the relationship between their current, and assumed care lives in the future. We relied heavily on the qualitative comments volunteered by students on this subject. It would be important to do further research examining to what extent students' goals and choices in higher education are mediated by the

need to engage in affective labour, and how gendered these decisions are. Second, it would be important to explore students' need for care in higher education.

8. EUROSTUDENTSURVEY III Report on the Social and Living Conditions of Higher Education Students in Ireland 2006/2007.
9. EUROSTUDENT SURVEY IV Report on the Social and Living Conditions of Higher Education Students in Ireland 2009/2010.
10. HEA statistics 2004/2015 http://www.hea.ie/node/1557 (retrieved 25 August 2015).
11. Public funding accounted for around 80% of the Irish higher education sector's core income in 2008; in 2015, the government contribution was reduced to 65% of higher education funding. Ireland is now out of line with most of its EU partners: 79% of funding in the original EU21 countries comes from public sources (OECD *Education at a Glance* 2013, Table B3.2.c).
12. This study found that that 41.6% of full-time students are working between 9 and 16 hours per week and a further 19.7% are working between 17 and 24 hours per week. On the other hand, 16.6% of part-time students are working between 25 and 35 hours and 71.8% are working more than 35 hours each week. Just 4% of full-time students worked more than 35 hours per week.

Acknowledgements

The authors would like to thank two anonymous reviewers who provided valuable feedback to improve this article.

Disclosure statement

No potential conflict of interest was reported by the authors.

References

Apple, M. 2004. "Creating Difference: Neo-liberalism, Neo-Conservatism and the Politics of Educational Reform." *Educational Policy* 18 (12): 12–44.

Arum, R., and J. Roksa. 2011. *Academically Adrift*. Chicago, IL: The University of Chicago Press.

Astin, A. 1991. "The Changing American College Student: Implications for Educational Policy and Practice." *Higher Education* 22 (2): 129–143.

Baker, J., K. Lynch, S. Cantillon, and J. Walsh. 2004. *Equality: From Theory to Action*. Hampshire: Palgrave Macmillan.

Ball, S. 2003. "The Teacher's Soul and the Terrors of Performativity." *Journal of Education Policy* 18 (2): 215–228.

Ball, S. 2012. "Performativity, Commodification and Commitment: An I-Spy Guide of the Neoliberal University." *British Journal of Educational Studies* 60 (1): 17–28.

Ball, S. J., and A. Olmedo. 2013. "Care of the Self, Resistance and Subjectivity under Neoliberal Governmentalities." *Critical Studies in Education* 54 (1): 85–96.

Bandura, R., and P. Lyons. 2012. "Instructor Care and Consideration Toward Students—What Accounting Students Report: A Research Note." *Accounting Education: An International Journal* 21 (5): 515–527.

Bano, S., and J. Taylor. 2015. "Universities and the Knowledge-Based Economy: Perceptions from a Developing Country." *Higher Education Research & Development* 34 (2): 242–255.

Bathmaker, A., N. Ingram, and R. Waller. 2013. "Higher Education, Social Class and the Mobilisation of Capitals: Recognising and Playing the Game." *British Journal of Sociology of Education* 34 (5–6): 723–743.

Black, R. 2014. "Educators, Professionalism and Politics: Global Transitions, National Spaces and Professional Projects." World Yearbook of Education 2013. *Globalisation, Societies and Education*.

Bolton, S. 2009. "The Lady Vanishes: Women's Work and Affective Labour." *International Journal Work Organisation and Emotion*. Accessed August 17, 2015. http://www.researchgate.net/publication/247834788.

Braun, A. 2011. "'Walking Yourself Around as a Teacher': Gender and Embodiment in Student Teachers' Working Lives." *British Journal of Sociology of Education* 32 (2): 275–291.

Clancy, P. 2015. *Irish Higher Education: A Comparative Perspective*. Dublin: Institute of Public Administration.

Crean, Mags. 2016. "Care Consciousness: Classed Care and Affective Equality." Unpublished PhD School of Social Justice, University College Dublin.

Davies, C. 1996. "The Sociology of the Professions and the Profession of Gender." *Sociology* 30 (4): 661–678.

Dean, M. 1999. *Governmentality: Power and Rule in Modern Society*. London: Sage.

Delucchi, M., and K. Korgen. 2002. "We're the Customer – We Pay the Tuition: Student Consumerism among Undergraduates Sociology Majors." *Teaching Sociology* 30 (1): 100–107.

Devine, D., B. Grummell, and K. Lynch. 2011. "Crafting the Elastic Self? Gender and Identities in Senior Management in Irish Education." *Gender, Work and Organization* 18 (6): 631–649.

Dukelow, F., and M. Considine. 2014. "Between Retrenchment and Recalibration: The Impact of Austerity on the Irish Social Protection System." *Journal of Sociology & Social Welfare* XLI (2): 55–72.

Feeley, M. 2014. *Learning Care Lessons: Literacy, Love, Care and Solidarity*. London: Tuftnell Press.

Federici, S. 2012. *Revolution at Point Zero: Housework, Reproduction and Feminist Struggle*. Oakland, CA: PM Press/Common Notions/Autonomedia.

Gill, R. 2010. "Breaking the Silence: The Hidden Injuries of the Neoliberal University." In *Secrecy and Silence in the Research Process: Feminist Reflections*, edited by R. Ryan-Flood, and R. Gill, 228–244. London: Routledge.

Gilligan, C. 1995. *In a Different Voice*. Cambridge: Harvard University Press.

Gordon, C. 1991. "Governmentality Rationality: An Introduction." In *The Foucault Effect: Studies in Governmentality*, edited by G. Burchell, C. Gordon, and P. Miller, 1–51. London: Harvester Wheatsheaf.

Government of Ireland. 2008. *Building Ireland's Smart Economy, A Framework for Sustainable Economic Renewal*. Dublin: Department of the Taoiseach.

Guerin, C., A. Jayatilaka, and D. Ranasinghe. 2015. "Why Start a Higher Degree by Research? An Exploratory Factor Analysis of Motivations to Undertake Doctoral Studies." *Higher Education Research & Development* 34 (1): 89–104.

Gutierrez-Rodriguez, E. 2014. "Domestic Work–Affective Labor: On Feminization and the Coloniality of Labor." *Women's Studies International Forum* 46: 45–53.

Hanlon, N. 2012. *Masculinities, Care and Equality – Identity and Nurture in Men's Lives*. London: Palgrave Macmillan.

Harkavy, I. 2006. "The Role of the Universities in Advancing Citizenship and Social Justice in the 21st Century." *Education, Citizenship and Social Justice* 1 (1): 5–37.

Hay, S., and C. Kaptizke. 2009. "'Smart' State for a Knowledge Economy: Reconstituting Creativity Through Student Subjectivity." *British Journal of Sociology of Education* 30 (2): 151–164.

Held, Virginia. 2006. *The Ethics of Care: Personal, Political and Global*. Oxford: Oxford University Press.

Higher Education Authority (HEA). 2011. *National Strategy for Higher Education to 2030*. Dublin: Department of Education and Skills.

Hochschild, A. R. 1983. *The Managed Heart, Commercialization of Human Feeling*. Berkeley: University of California Press.

Hochschild, A. R. 2011. "Emotional Life on the Market Frontier." *Annual Review of Sociology* 37: 21–33.

Kittay, E. F. 1999. *Love's Labor*. New York: Routledge.

Leathwood, C. 2013. "Re/Presenting Intellectual Subjectivity: Gender and Visual Imagery in the Field of Higher Education." *Gender and Education* 25 (2): 133–154.

Leathwood, C., and P. O'Connell. 2003. "'It's a Struggle': The Construction of the 'New Student' in Higher Education." *Journal of Education Policy* 18 (6): 597–615.

Lingard, B. 2014. "Policy as Numbers." In *Politics, Policies and Pedagogies in Education, the Selected Works of Bob Lingard*, 27–50. Abingdon: Routledge.

Lolich, L. 2011. "And the Market Created the Student to its Image and Likening: Neo-liberal Governmentality and its Effects on Higher Education in Ireland." *Irish Educational Studies* 30: 271–284.

Lolich, L., and K. Lynch. 2015. "The Affective Imaginary: Students as Affective Consumers of Risk." *Higher Education Research & Development* 35 (1): 17–30.

Loxley, A., A. Seery, and J. Walsh. 2014. *Higher Education in Ireland: Practices, Policies and Possibilities.* Basingtoke: Palgrave Macmillan.

Luttrell, W. 2013. "Children's Counter-Narratives of Care: Towards Educational Justice." *Children & Society* 27: 295–308.

Lynch, K. 2006. "Neo-liberalism and Marketisation: The Implications for Higher Education." *European Educational Research Journal* 5 (1): 1–17.

Lynch, K. 2010. "Carelessness: A Hidden Doxa of Higher Education." *Arts and Humanities in Higher Education* 9: 54–67.

Lynch, K. 2013a. "Why Love, Care and Solidarity are Political Matters: Affective Equality and Fraser's Model of Social Justice." In *Love: A Question for Feminism in the Twenty-first Century*, edited by Anna Jónadóttir and Ann Ferguson, 173–189. New York: Routledge.

Lynch, K. 2013b. "New Managerialism, Neoliberalism and Ranking." *Ethics in Science and Environmental Politics* 13 (2): 1–13.

Lynch, K., J. Baker, and M. Lyons. 2009. *Affective Equality.* Hampshire: Palgrave Macmillan.

Lynch, K., B. Grummell, and D. Devine. 2012. *New Managerialism in Education: Gender, Commercialisation and Carelesness.* Basingstoke: Palgrave.

Lynch, K., M. Lyons, and S. Cantillon. 2007. "Breaking Silence Educating Citizens'." *International Studies in Sociology of Education* 17 (1): 1–19.

Lyon, D., and M. Glucksmann. 2008. "Comparative Configurations of Care Work Across Europe." *Sociology* 42 (1): 101–108.

Mariskind, C. 2014. "Teachers' Care in Higher Education: Contesting Gendered Constructions." *Gender and Education* 26 (3): 306–320.

Masschelein, J., and M. Simons. 2002. "An Adequate Education in a Globalised World? A Note on Immunisation Against Being-Together." *Journal of Philosophy of Education* 36 (4): 589–608.

Massy, W., and R. Zemsky. 1994. "Faculty Discretionary Time: Departments and the 'Academic Ratchet'" *The Journal of Higher Education* 65 (1): 1–22.

McGovern, F., and D. Devine. 2016. "The Care Worlds of Migrant Children – Exploring Inter-Generational Dynamics of Love, Care and Solidarity Across Home and School." *Childhood* 23 (1): 37–52.

Moreau, M.-P., and C. Kerner. 2015. "Care in Academia: an Exploration of Student Parents' Experience." *British Journal of Sociology of Education* 36 (2): 215–233.

Morley, L. 2001. "Producing New Workers: Quality, Equality and Employability in Higher Education." *Quality in Higher Education* 7 (2): 131–138.

Morley, L. 2007. "The Gendered Implications of Quality Assurance and Audit." In *Challenges and Negotiations for Women in Higher Education*, edited by P. Cotterill, S. Jackson, and G. Letherby, 53–63. Dordrecht: Springer.

Naidoo, R., and I. Jamieson. 2005. "Empowering Participants or Corroding Learning? Towards A Research Agenda on the Impact of Student Consumerism in Higher Education." *Journal of Education Policy* 20 (3): 267–281.

Noddings, N. 2005. "Identifying and Responding to Needs in Education." *Cambridge Journal of Education* 35 (2): 147–159.

Nussbaum, M. C. 1995. "Emotions and Women's Capabilities." In *Women, Culture and Development: A Study of Human Capabilities*, edited by M. Nussbaum, and J. Glover, 360–395. Oxford: Oxford University Press.

O'Brien, M. 2007. "Mothers' Emotional Care Work in Education and its Moral Imperative." *Gender and Education* 19 (2): 159–177.

O'Brien, L. 2010. "Caring in the Ivory Tower." *Teaching in Higher Education* 15 (1): 109–115.

O'Connor, K. 2006. "'You Choose to Care': Teachers, Emotions and Professional Identity." *Teaching and Teacher Education* 24 (1): 117–126.

OECD. 2004. *Review of National Policies for Education in Ireland.* Paris: OECD.

OECD. 2006. *Higher Education in Ireland*. Paris: OECD.

OECD. 2013. "Education at a Glance 2013: OECD Indicators." Accessed March 15, 2014. doi:10.1787/eag-2013-en.

O'Sullivan, Denis. 2005. *Cultural Politics and Irish Education since the 1950s: Policy Paradigms and Power*. Dublin: Institute of Public Administration.

Ouellette, L., and J. Wilson. 2011. "Women's Work." *Cultural Studies* 25 (4): 548–565.

Peters, M. 2001. "National Education Policy Constructions of the 'Knowledge Economy: Towards a Critique." *Journal of Educational Enquiry* 2 (1): 1–22.

Peters, M. 2005. "The New Prudentialism in Education: Actuarial Rationality and the Entrepreneurial Self." *Educational Theory* 55 (2): 123–137.

Pryor, J., S. Hurtado, L. De Angelo, L. Palucki Blake, and S. Tran. 2010. *The American Freshman: National Norms Fall 2010*. Los Angeles, CA: Higher Education Research Institute, UCLA.

Reay, D., G. Crozier, and J. Clayton. 2009. "Strangers in Paradise' Working-Class Students in Elite Universities." *Sociology* 43 (6): 1103–1121.

Robert, S. 2014. "Extending Theorisations of the Global Teacher: Care Work, Gender, and Street-Level Policies." *British Journal of Sociology of Education* 37 (3): 445–464.

Saunders, D. 2007. "The Impact of Neoliberalism on College Students." *Journal of College & Character* 8 (5): 1940–1639.

Seddon, T., J. Ozga, and S. Levin. 2013. "Global Transitions and Teacher Professionalism." In *Educators, Professionalism and Politics: Global Transitions, National Spaces and Professional Projects*, edited by T. Seddon, and S. Levin, 3–24. London: Routledge.

Slaughter, S., and L. Leslie. 1997. *Academic Capitalism: Politics, Policies and the Entrepreneurial University*. Baltimore, MD: John Hopkins University Press.

Tronto, J. 1993. *Moral Boundaries: A Political Argument for an Ethic of Care*. New York: Routledge.

Tronto, Joan C. 2013. *Caring Democracy: Markets, Equality and Justice*. New York: New York University Press.

Walker, C., A. Gleaves, and J. Grey. 2006. "A Study of the Difficulties of Care and Support in New University Teachers' Work." *Teachers and Teaching: Theory and Practice* 12 (3): 347–363.

Index

Note: Entries in *italics* denote figures
Entries in **bold** denote tables

academia *see* higher education
academic self 58
accountability culture 2, 58, 118
address, mode of 74
affective labour: antipathy to rights of 10, 20, 22; and entrepreneurialism 123; in higher education 6, 118–19, 126; liberal misappraisal of 8–9, 17, 125; by students 127–8n7
affective relations: and economic security 123; in higher education 6, 115–16, 118–21, 123
AFL-CIO 16–17
Africa, colonial narratives of 68, 79
agency: in academia 48–52, 60–1; in new material feminist theory 38
agroecology 6, 100–1, 103–6, 108, 110–12
Andrews, Morris 19
Annoni settlement 105
arbitration legislation 9, 21–3, 24n13
arts-based research 52–3, 62
autoethnography 4, 48, 50–4, 62

bad teacher narratives 30
base nuclei 106, 108–9
bathrooms, gendered 92–5
Bentham, Jeremy 86
best practice 79, 118
bilingualism 58
binary gender 71–2, 74–7, 84–92, 94–6
biodiversity 103–4
biological gender 72–3, 86, 88, 90, 92–3
bodies, disciplining 87–8
Brazil, agrarian reform in 101, 105
Brown, Wendy 66
Brown women teaching assistants 4–5; autoethnography of 50–2, 61–2; introducing 53–5; othering of 48–9; student evaluations 55–8; support networks of 60–1; visibility of 58–9
bullying 90–1

capitalism, and neoliberalism 30
care, circles of 127n2

care consciousness 116
care imaginaries 115
care labour 3, 9–10, 15–17, 22–4, 110, 116, 118; *see also* affective labour
carelessness 118
care relations 116, 127n2; *see also* affective relations
caring, breadwinner model of 122–3
caring relationships 68–9, 75, 116
caring self 115–16
CCSS (Common Core State Standards) 29, 39–40, 44n2
CIRP (Cooperative Institutional Research Program) 119, 127n6
CLOC (Latin American Coordination of Rural Organisation) 106
collective action 8–10, 22
collective bargaining 18, 21
collective consciousness 50–1
collective identities 17, 22
collectivisation 102
commodity production, and neoliberalism 102, 104
common sense 85, 91, 94–5
common spaces 88, 93–4
competition 5–6, 62, 95, 102, 115–16, 118–19
condom usage 66–7
COOPTAR 102
corporatisation 5, 62
counter-hegemony 104, 107, 111
Creekview and Townsend Elementary Schools 28–9, 31–2, 35, 39, 44
cultural biases 57
curricular materials 11, 29, 32–3, 37, 39–44, 44n5
curriculum, gender-oriented 107

decision-making, and neoliberalism 2–3
dehumanisation 2
Democratic Party, Wisconsin 16
deprofessionalization 54, 59
dialogic power 22

INDEX

discipline: gender as 87, 90–1, 94, 96; and self-fashioning 43; and surveillance 5, 84, 86
discrimination, moments of 52
diversity 55, 61, 95–6

economic rationality 2, 69
economism 8–9
Educar *see* Instituto Educar
education: challenging gender discourse through 107; formal 106, 109; multicultural 96; neoliberal purpose of 43, 86–7; public funding for 42; *see also* higher education
education workers, and neoliberalism 1–3
effectiveness 66–7
embodiment 43, 50, 84–5, 92, 112
emotional ecologies 118–19
emotionality 52
empowerment: and gender 75–6, 78; and neoliberalism 43, 69; pedagogy of 107
English language 58, 71, 73, 77
enterprise of affect 121
entrepreneurialism 1–2, 42, 123
entrepreneurial self 115, 117, 121–3
ethics, in higher education 118
ethnographic research 70–1, 84, 88–9; *see also* autoethnography
expertise 77, 80, 119, 121

family: raising a 120, **122**, 123; structure 104–5
Fausto-Sterling, Anne 88
Feilbach, Don 18–19
femininities and masculinities 1–3, 72, 74, 78; *see also* gender roles
feminism: in agrarian struggle 106–7; and care 116; and gender 78; new material theory 28, 31, 37–8
food sovereignty 5, 103–4, 111
Foucault, Michel 36, 38, 75, 86
freedom, as regulation 70
Freire, Paolo 87, 101, 103

gender: articulating concept of 77–8; encounters with 7, 66–8, 70–1, 73–9; in ethnographic research 71; and HIV prevention 67–8; and schooling 86; in sexuality education 68–73, 79–80; *see also* binary gender
gender asymmetries 101, 107
gender awareness 106–7, 109, 111–12
gendered identities 66, 72–5, 78–9, 92
gendered self 78
gendered spaces 75, 92, 94
gender equality, and education 66, 73, 75–6, 100–1, 106, 111
gender inequalities 66
gender-neutral facilities 92, 95
gender non-conformity 90
gender-oriented pedagogy 6, 100–1, 107, 110–12
gender power 77

genderqueer 88
gender relations, transformation of 106–9
gender roles, contesting in education 67, 71–2, 74–6, 100, 108–10
globalisation 49, 115, 117, 126
Gollnick, Ed 15
good teaching, in neoliberalism 30–1, 37–40, 43, 44n5
governance: assemblages of 1; managerial 117; neoliberal modes of 38, 69
governmentality 70, 117
graduate students 49, 54, 58, 60
Gramsci, Antonio 85, 100–1, 104
groundBREAKERs 70–1, 77
GSA (gay-straight alliance) 88–9, 93–4

hallways, in high schools 88, 92–5
harassment 87, 90–1
HEA (Hortonville Education Association) 12–15, 18, 21
HECSU (Higher Education Careers Service Unit) 119, 127n6
helping others 120–1, **122**
heteronormativity: and binary gender 5, 84, 86–7, 89–92, 94–6; and neoliberalism 69, 85; and sexuality education 67–8, 73
higher education: care in 6, 115, 123–6; as caste system 48; as colonised space 50; neoliberal conception of 4–5, 48, 57, 60–2, 116–19; resistance within 118; social context of 49; women of colour in 48–51, 53–5, 61 (*also* Brown women teaching assistants)
high schools: gender and sexuality in 5, 86, 88–9, 91–2, 95; neoliberal 3, 84, 90; strike action in 13–14
hijab 51, 53, 56
HIV: educational responses to 68; prevention 5, 66–71, 73–5, 78–80
homophobia 76, 90–1, 95–6
Hortonville, Wisconsin 11–12; local control rhetoric in 19–20; teachers' strike 3–4, 9–10, 12–18, 20–1, 23–4
human capital 116, 126, 127n1

identities, production of 84, 89
igualada 56–7
illiteracy 101
ilobola 73, 80n2
immaterial labour 10, 17
indigenous knowledge systems 103
individualised resistance 126
individualism 2, 69, 84–5, 94–5, 108, 118, 123
inequality, structures of 84
Instituto Educar 5–6, 100–2, 112n1; and agroecology 103; and gender equity 107–10; women in 105–6
intellectual property 42
intelligibility: of gendered identities 78; grid of 38; lines of 75

INDEX

interdependencies 118, 126
interest arbitration 11, 21, 23, 24n13
intersectionality 96
intersex 88
intra-actions 37–40, 43–4
Ireland: higher education in 6, 115–17, 119–20, 125, 127nn3–5, 128n11; student attitudes in **120–2**
isiXhosa language 75, 77
ITA (International Teaching Assistants) 56; *see also* Brown women teaching assistants

Jornada de Luta Contra o Agronegócio 106

KBE (knowledge-based economy) 6, 115–17, 120, 122–4, 126, 126–7n1
knowing-through-being 38
knowledge: decolonising 51; emotionality as 52; technical 107
knowledge economy *see* KBE

labour: intellectual and manual 108; neoliberal analysis of 36–7; sexual division of 100–1, 104, 107–11 (*see also* gender roles); teaching assistants as 60
labour market 2, 120, 122
labour movement: legal strategies of 21–2; opportunism in 22–3; solidarity in 16–18; white supremacy within 19–20; *see also* teacher unions
land rights 105
Lawton, John 20
learners, ideal 116
lesson plans: buying and selling 29, 33, 35–42; for sexuality education 80
LGBTQ folk 84, 86, 88–91, 93–6; *see also* transgender
liberalism, and labour movement 8–9, 17, 20, 24
linguistic minorities 54, 58, 62
literacy 57, 86–7, 92, 94
local control 4, 19–20, 23, 24n9
locker rooms, gendered 92, 94–5
love4Life 5, 67, 70–3, 76–8

managerialism 117, 125
markets, neoliberalism creating 36, 42, 70
Marxism 107
masculinity, hegemonic 74
material actants 28, 31, 38, 43
materiality: embodied 37; stubborn 70
meaningful activities, creating 39
measurability 117–18
mentors 59
microaggressions 51, 54–5, 59, 89–91, 95–6
middle of things 71
Milwaukee, labour movement in 18–21, 23
minority women *see* women of colour
mística 107
monoculture 104, 106

moralization 70, 76
MST (Landless Workers' Movement) 5–6; education system of 100–1, 103–8, 110–11; gender relations in 106–7; resistance to neoliberalism 102–3
MTEA (Milwaukee Teachers Education Association) 9, 18–20, 24n9
Muelver, Ed 16

NEA (National Education Association) 12, 15
neoliberal discourses: of development 69; of education 40
neoliberalism: in Brazil 102; in education 2–4, 8; gendered nature of 10, 28–31, 43–4, 84–6, 92–4, 96; and globalisation 49, 75; inclusive 69; and international development 69; resisting 42, 102–3, 111; use of term 1, 85
neoliberal political rationality 66, 68–70, 73, 75–80
neoliberal subjectivity: in education 2; gendered nature of 28, 30–1, 35–6, 73; in higher education 59, 121, 126; and success 36–8, 40, 43
neoliberal university *see* higher education, neoliberal conception of
North Carolina 93

objectivity 50–1, 57, 61
Ocean-Hills Brownsville strikes 19
opportunism 4, 8, 11, 21–3
organic intellectuals 104
Other, and self 79
Othering 4, 48–9, 53, 61

panopticon 5, 86
parents, as students 125
passing 92
patriarchal culture 102, 107, 110
peasants 100–4, 106–8, 111, 112n6
pedagogical practices of definition 73–4, 78
pedagogy 3; alternating 103, 111; cooperative and collective 108, 112; critical and emancipatory 11, 76, 101, 107
Pedagogy of the Oppressed 106–7
peer educators 70
people of colour 61, 89–90, 96; *see also* women of colour
picket lines 13–14, 16, 18
Pinterest 4, 28, 31–2, *34*; teachers' use of 32–3, 35, 37–8, 40–3, 44n3
political rationality 5, 66–7, 69–71, 76, 79–80; *see also* neoliberal political rationality
positionality 50, 54, 89
positivist epistemologies 50–2
post-structuralism 37
post-welfare citizenship 126
power: analysis of 96; negotiation of 89; systems of 87; technology of 75, 78
privilege, gender in 87

INDEX

production metaphors 117
professional identities 52, 60
PRONERA 101, 105
pseudonyms 44, 77, 96n1
public sector, and neoliberalism 49
public-sector unions 3–4, 8–11, 21–3
public-sector workers: community support for 13, 15; right to strike 24n12; state protection of 23–4

qualitative research 50, 70

racial contracts 8–9, 17, 19, 23
rape 73–4, 77, 90–1
reflection 51
relationality 115, 120–1
re-nationalisation 80n1
research, dominant discourses around 50–1
resource sharing 34, 102
responsibility, in neoliberal discourse 69, 78–9
rights, labour movement appeals to 10, 16, 19–20, 23–4
right-to-work 11
Rural Women Workers' Movement 106

safe spaces 5, 56, 84, 86, 90–5
Saussure, Ferdinand de 87
schools: Foucault on 86; production of identity in 84; *see also* high schools
school supplies, teachers buying 40
self-awareness 78
self-reflection 51–2
self-regulation 36, 43, 69, 86
self-surveillance 5
sexuality education 5, 66–72, 77–80
silences 60, 76
smart economy *see* KBE
social identities, and gender 73–5, 78–80, 85
social imaginary 85, 91, 94–5
social justice, and higher education 49, 53
social justice unionism 17, 19–20
social media: and teaching 28, 35; visitors by gender *33*
social problems 97, 120
social reproduction 3, 69, 115
social semiotics 84, 87, 90
social studies 88–9
solidarity, with striking workers 4, 8, 15–18
South Africa 3, 5, 66–8, 70, 72–4, 80n1
space: gender division of 112; pedagogical use of 75
STEM subjects 117
student consumerism 119
student evaluations 51–2, 54–7, 59
students: care needs of 116, 120–1, 124–6; entrepreneurial 6, 115, 117–18, 123; paid work by 128n12

subjectivity: gendered production of 28, 30–1, 38, 42–4; in research 51; in South Africa 72; of students 117, 119; *see also* neoliberal subjectivity
surveillance 53, 84, 86, 91–2, 94, 96, 117
sympathy strikes 4, 9, 18, 20
systemic injustices 52–3

TAs (teaching assistants) 4, 48, 50–2, 55, 57, 60; *see also* Brown women teaching assistants
task cards 29, 39–41
teacher education 54
teacher quality, and neoliberalism 2–4; *see also* bad teacher narratives; good teaching
teacher subjectivity 43
teacher unions: in 1970s 3–4, 9–10; at Hortonville 12–15; and neoliberalism 8–9, 21–4; and social justice 19–20
teaching: care labour in 15–17, 24, 115, 118; feminization of 30 (*see also* women teachers); social media as resource for 43
TpT (Teachers Pay Teachers) 4, 28, 31, 33–5; and CCSS 29; lesson plans bought on *41*, 44n5; screenshots *34*; and subjectivity 37–9, 42–3; women teachers on 35–6, 39–42
transgender people 5, 84, 87–8, 92–3
transphobia 88, 90, 95–6

underserved communities 5, 53, 62
USAID (United States Agency for International Development) 80

Via Campesina 106, 112n6
Vigilante Association 14–15
violence, and heteronormativity 74, 85, 90–1, 94–6
visibility 2

WEAC (Wisconsin Educational Association Council) 15–23
white supremacy 19–20, 85
Wisconsin: labour movement in 10–11, 21–3; rural 3–4, 8–9 (*see also* Hortonville)
Wisnoski, Mike 12–13
women: as care workers 17; and condom usage 67; in Irish higher education 120; in MST 101–3, 111; as passive subjects 116; in peasant agriculture 104–7; in public sector unions 9–10
women of colour 48–50, 52–6, 58, 61–2
women's bodies 44, 74
women teachers 3; and neoliberalism 28, 30, 35, 38–40, 43–4; questionnaire for 47; *see also* academia
workers' rights 9
World Bank 69
Wynn, Laurie 14, 18–20